Australia

modern architectures in history

This international series examines the forms and consequences of modern architecture. Modernist visions and revisions are explored in their national context against a backdrop of aesthetic currents, economic developments, political trends and social movements. Written by experts in the architectures of the respective countries, the series provides a fresh, critical reassessment of Modernism's positive and negative effects, as well as the place of architectural design in twentieth-century history and culture.

Series editor: Vivian Constantinopoulos

Already published:

Australia
Harry Margalit

Brazil
Richard J. Williams

Britain
Alan Powers

Canada
Rhodri Windsor Liscombe and Michelangelo Sabatino

Finland
Roger Connah

France
Jean-Louis Cohen

Greece
Alexander Tzonis and Alcestis P. Rodi

India
Peter Scriver and Amit Strivastava

Italy
Diane Ghirardo

Russia
Richard Anderson

Turkey
Sibel Bozdoğan and Esra Akcan

USA
Gwendolyn Wright

Australia

modern architectures in history

Harry Margalit

REAKTION BOOKS

For Georgia, Sam, Max and Thea

Published by Reaktion Books Ltd
Unit 32, Waterside
44–48 Wharf Road
London N1 7UX, UK

www.reaktionbooks.co.uk

First published 2019

Printed and bound in India by Replika Press Pvt. Ltd

A catalogue record for this book is available from the British Library

ISBN 978 1 78914 124 5

Contents

"I can just see . . . some telegraph poles . . . colourful hoardings . . . comfortable bus shelters . . . and it will be as lovely as any older suburb."

Introduction

Any consideration of Australian history must contend with the profound influence of geography on the modern nation. It is not simply the age of the continent, with its smoothed mountains, nor the dryness of much of the interior, nor the seasonal heat. Rather it is the location, between Asia and Antarctica, that vexed the English-derived society created on its shores from 1788. While always latent in the nation's character, in 1966 Geoffrey Blainey named this phenomenon in a phrase that served as a title for his history of Australia: the tyranny of distance. Flung out by colonial imperative and opportunity to the antipodes, if anything Australian culture – and architecture in particular – attests to the power of cultural yearning.[1]

As a consequence, the Australia of today, objectively viewed, strikes even its own inhabitants as implausible. It has as Head of State a remote Queen, although this serves mainly as a confounding factor in its sentimental development. The Westminster system is, by its nature, based on compromise, and when the legal threads connecting a colonial project – as Australia was – to its English roots remain, the country comes to resemble the aftermath of a punch thrown on a sports field. So many hands holding so many collars and shirtsleeves that no one can move.

George Molnar, *Sydney Morning Herald* cartoon, 1964. Molnar, a Hungarian-born architect, arrived in Australia in 1939. He was a prolific cartoonist whose work spanned four decades, and satirized both popular and high culture. Like many Australian architects he lamented the tacky visual clutter that easily appended itself to urban developments in the 1950s and '60s.

This logjam of interests works against any radical shifts and is highly prized by immigrants from countries where radical shifts made them uncomfortable or worse. It lends an inertia to perceived acts of transformation leading to uncertainty, as evidenced in the defeat of the 1999 referendum on Australia becoming a republic.[2] Landlocked countries may struggle to keep their independence and their identity separate from their neighbours, but if Australia wished to become adrift it could do so with consummate ease. Staying connected to the rest of the world has been the challenge since settlement.

The issue of colonization has shaped society in myriad ways, and in its culture the incomplete native is the lot of those not aboriginal. This is not to say that allegiance is owed to anywhere else – indeed most Australians are profoundly attached to the country and the idea of the country. But its relative newness as a modern nation precludes any myths of origin for those in its population from Europe, Asia or Africa. Voyages are recorded and ships' logs available for tracing ancestry, and the tales they link to are often sobering. Save for missionaries and surfers, there were few instances of people coming here to fulfil a higher calling.

Out of this was shaped a country of deep pragmatism. Lineage counted for little, and even those states founded as penal colonies could transform the lives of convicts once their time had been served. Social mobility has been possible through luck, making money or acquiring land. The brutality that attended these in the early years has largely disappeared and there is a prevailing expectation that the vulnerable should not be exploited.

For a people often viewed as laconic, there has been a surprising vigour to Australian history. Partly this has to do with the size. Moving about has never been easy, and as recently as the 1950s a truck journey from Sydney to Perth required mechanical and camping skills.[3] The country is roughly the size of Brazil or the U.S., but with a fraction of their populations. Most cities are close to the shore, but rail and road links are primitive compared to the U.S. or Europe, because of the poor ratio of taxpayers to the distances involved. This is despite a population that per head is among the wealthiest in the world.

Recent inquiries have uncovered a history of institutional brutality towards indigenous people and immigrant children in the twentieth century, but Australians were, and are, prone to also acting with great decency. As in many immigrant countries, diverse cultures are permitted to thrive in parallel with the mainstream public realm. The basic compact is that life in most cases improves for immigrants, and this has been the reason for the Australian success in social integration. But credit must also be given to its legal structure, with its inherited reflex to value the individual to an uncommon degree.

In architecture, much of the country has been self-built. Large tracts constructed by owner builders in the 1950s solved a dearth of housing, and the modest houses on their treeless lots may look austere to contemporary eyes, but they enabled couples to move out of their parents' houses. They had space, and privacy, when these things mattered. But as a rule few of these houses had an architect involved.

This remains true today, with the vast majority of new detached houses being constructed from standard plans. This alone gives a class inflection to architecture, since so few people will actually deal with an architect for their house or apartment. Those that do will live in wealthier areas and may have complex legal restrictions to negotiate. Because of economies of scale, an architect-designed house will be at least twice the cost of a mass-produced one. There is currently a shift to apartment building in major cities, but again the average buyer will not deal with the architect.

Architecture in Australia, then, is a service restricted by class. It is labour-intensive and not essential to making buildings stand up and remain weatherproof. But it has always had the capacity, from the early decades of the colony, to assume a role of signification in proportion to the skill and education of the practitioner. In this its function has gone beyond material demands, but what and how it signifies has been taken, in this work, to be rooted in how different groups perceive and project their interests. This generally divides along social class, but in Australia there are sectarian interests at work too, as well as the tension between valuing the local, but looking for validation internationally.

Modern architecture was well aware of its class role, and its intentions included the utilitarian principle of bringing its benefits to as many people as possible. The advent of modern production methods aided this, and we understand tract housing, for example, as a modern phenomenon relying on mass production, but also subject to generic signification. Tract houses look the same because that is their economic logic. Modern architecture in Australia has had a particular struggle to embrace mass production, but also to polish its products and techniques into exemplars of symbolic potential. This latter process has produced what we might call the high architecture that is the product of professional architectural services and is celebrated through national architectural awards.

Those familiar with architectural history will recognize the influence of key historians in this book's approach. It is, in the final analysis, materialist. That is, it seeks, at bottom, to locate different buildings and architectural ideas in the lived circumstances of those designing them, as well as in how they were paid for and built. But the beauty of architecture is that it can be imbued with intent, often in subtle ways. Buildings, being social products, convey aspirations as fragments of a longed-for utopia, or states of repose, to paraphrase the great Italian architectural historian Manfredo Tafuri.[4] What that utopia is made of reveals details of its proponents and of their version of a collective aspiration.

Reading these fragments is an act of interpretation, built on imagination. Hence the benchmark that it be only plausible and not necessarily true. This degree of latitude is important to allow history writing, with its necessary imaginative leaps, to proceed. This is not to claim that all history is in the eye of the beholder, but rather to acknowledge that there is a beholder, and an eye. Personal history and taste will always come into play.

One of the more difficult challenges of writing a historical survey of architecture is to grasp the scale of the work at hand. A book this size makes no pretence to being comprehensive. For that one could do no better than Goad and Willis's *Encyclopedia of Australian Architecture*, which covers the topic with all its themes and players. It is also not a guide to Australian architecture for the interested tourist, because there are many fine buildings that have been omitted. It is, rather, an attempt to tell the story of architecture in the country as artefacts of various ideologies. It links buildings with context and aspiration, based on the view that these are indeed connected in fundamental, but mediated, ways.

One of the key shortcomings of materialist history, especially cultural history, was the tendency to see the arts as literal portrayals of how people lived their lives. Within this tradition the idea of ideology may have conveyed the opposite idea – that art sets out to obscure the real truth of people's subjugation – but this negation is equally literal in its own way. The best cultural histories grasp that the story is subject to imprecision, inversions, irony and all the tricks that play with our attempts to give history meaning and structure.

The major challenge to materialist history came through the re-assertion of the capacity of culture to signify – in other words that culture was not simply an extension of material existence, but that it had its own rules that linked to the material world in complex ways. This challenge, when articulated in the 1970s, did so through a rediscovery of the rules of language set out at the beginning of the twentieth century by de Saussure. It found the weak link in the materialist chain: the claim that culture is a reflex induced by productive forces. Re-asserting the primacy of language presented an alternate view, one which could not be simply reduced to ideas of culture as a mirror of reality. Instead it presented culture more as a movie, where the sets may be real but the product has to be understood as involving a script, a director and actors.

This challenge to history has a parallel in architecture itself. High modernism, from the period after the First World War, sought to grasp history by finding the aesthetic or design technique most consonant with the industrialization of building itself. The elimination of ornament, the adoption of repetitive components and the shaping of buildings to reflect their function all derive from a view of the role of architecture in leading, rather than following, historical trends. While this view only achieved wide acceptance in Australia in the 1950s, it is deeply influenced by a materialist logic that demanded that architecture be understood in relation to production – how things were made, distributed and consumed. Ornament was seen to obscure these things, for the purpose of social control by one class over another.

The irony that there may be pleasure in this obfuscation, even for its apparent victims, was absent in the earnest view that anything symbolically endowed was suspect. Hardline modernist architecture, where everything needed a purpose, splintered when this was pointed out. It was only with the slow acceptance that even the most utilitarian architecture, in some measure, symbolized its very utility, that the many beauties of high modernism could be appreciated as cultural history.

These observations are broad-brush and describe the international shift from modernism to post-modernism and back to a revived modernism that shapes so much contemporary work. These themes are visible in Australia as well, with timing and manifestations that are distinctive to the country and its regions. The aim of this book, then, is to try and shape a story of many threads but some cohesion out of buildings designed by architects since the Federation of Australia in 1901. The date is significant because it not only saw the modern nation take shape from a group of separate colonies, but it precedes the events of the First World War out of which so much nation-making arose.

The date of Federation is convenient, but it neither marks the advent of buildings that might be called modernist, nor of a society that suddenly achieved a modern form out of feudal antecedents. The country, since its colonization, had witnessed periods of rapid and widespread change, equal to or indeed greater than the comparable change we imagine is the hallmark of our age. From 1850 to 1880 the Australian non-indigenous population grew from 405,000 to 2,232,000: a fivefold increase in just thirty years.[5] Gold rushes drew opportunists and adventurers from across the globe, and the wealth unearthed spawned a new and opulent Melbourne, and its architectural manifestation, the Boom style. The imprint of land ownership was laid across a big continent, where even now large gold nuggets remain undiscovered just below the surface, because no one interested in them has chanced by.

If we take modernity to be that ceaseless change that attended these events, then the date of 1901 is in no way a starting point. Rather it seems an apt one because the act of Federation was the culmination, in Australia, of a growing awareness of the nation state as the primary historical vehicle for the age to come. In the same way modern architecture can be traced to any building that utilized industrially produced components, regardless of its appearance. The great exhibition palaces of Sydney (1879) and Melbourne (1880) would fit this definition of modern, as would many of the mass-produced articles presented as exhibits within them. The date of 1901 is not chosen to capture the earliest modern buildings, but rather as one where they assumed significance in a new political entity that superseded the interests of individual colonies. In their separate histories could be found penal colonies and ones founded by free settlers, as well as great movements of opportunists in search of gold or land. This in itself created a unique culture, influenced by international itinerants who travelled from California to Victoria, or from Yorkshire to Western Australia. As much as the Australian colonies owed their origins to the British Isles, they also felt a kinship with the optimism of the Canadian or American or South African frontiers.

The process of selecting buildings also required some firm framing. The book length could never allow all those buildings in the first rank of architecture, from Federation onwards, to be included, or it would read like a breathless catalogue of meagre descriptions. I have chosen buildings that are significant for telling the story of Australian architecture as I have come to see it over nearly three decades of research, and as long in practice. In consideration were small buildings of great influence, and large buildings that have few progeny. In sum these factors needed to be balanced, and I found myself excluding buildings and architects that I think are excellent, and including others that may not reflect my taste but are of undoubted significance. The main criteria were whether the building sat astride the main ideological currents of the time, and how valuable they were in delineating these. Put another way, they are not always the most accomplished products of the period considered, but rather those that best illustrate architectural works as cultural products embedded in everyday life. Having said that, every building included has a serious architectural intent in my view, carried through with skill and commitment. I have worked too long in architecture not to respect the sheer effort that goes into directing the construction of a building. Some commentators who have not experienced this imagine that architecture is a designer's will made manifest. The actual process is very far from this and involves cunning, humour, persistence and the ability to argue as if your life depended on it.

The book has been written with the interested lay reader in mind, as well as the architect and academic. I have tried to avoid jargon and to frame things in a vocabulary not confined to architectural history. This has involved some compromise, and some imprecision, since architectural history turns on subtle distinctions. Perhaps the most important of these is the issue of periodization: why buildings have family resemblances, and what those resemblances mean. These are the basic tools of the discipline, because they facilitate grouping buildings together by common attributes, and searching for the historical patterns or processes that might account for the commonality. The most familiar term to describe this is 'style', a term now in disfavour but one I have used because it is widely understood. I have also tried to show that there may be common attributes of intent by which buildings may be grouped, but which is not always reflected in shared forms or details.

Uncovering this intent is one of the trickier aspects of historical writing. One must undertake a reconstruction of what architects of the period were concerned about, and what they believed was historically necessary or relevant. What we might call issues of style are bound up in bigger concerns about how life ought to be lived, a difficult enough contemporary question, let alone one to be reconstructed for other periods with whatever patchy evidence is at hand. One of the pleasures of architectural history is that buildings of a period are complete and complex artefacts, and it is possible to read many things from them in detail when paired with some knowledge of social context. This is where imagination is necessary: to explain buildings by extrapolating from what evidence is at hand.

This book is offered as an overview that extends the work of previous Australian authors in the field. In survey terms the work of Max Freeland, at my own institution, the University of New South Wales, was more ambitious, but less thematically focused. Robin Boyd produced histories with a strong point of view, and more recently Jennifer Taylor undertook several comprehensive surveys that recorded the long period she observed as architect and historian. In recent years there has been an expansion of scholarship into Australian modernist practice at leading universities, notably the University of Queensland and the University of Melbourne.

In my own research I have charted the rising faith in rationalism as a practice over the twentieth century, and the many missteps that marked its advent. Part of the Australian story is also the reaction to rationalism, and the acknowledgement of those things poorly grasped in its ambit. While these themes have extensive literatures elsewhere, they are very much embedded in the main story of architecture in Australia over the period since 1901. They also appear in my writings on urban history, and they manifest in other facets of life.

At times this book also touches on ideas about cities. These are important to the story because they provide the matrix within which buildings are shaped: the rules that govern them and the policies that nudge them in this direction or that. Over the last century Australia has been politically cautious but technologically progressive, and this is reflected in how our cities are governed and how movements like modernism have been received. Within these inclinations I have periodized the buildings according to social and economic cadences. The first charts the period from Federation to 1929, the eve of the Great Depression. This period saw many of the critical early acts of national self-definition, and their architectural extensions. It also saw the emergence of metropolitan identities for the major cities, and the rise of heavy manufacturing.

Few countries suffered more from the Great Depression than Australia. Its effects, from the withdrawal of foreign capital to the shanty towns of the unemployed, scarred a generation and produced a severe dip in the birth rate. While it may have shaken faith in capitalism and fostered alternative political views, the uncertainties of the age were thrust aside by the

Second World War. This period, 1930–45, is the subject of the second chapter. The third takes up the story of the pre-war idealism that was held in abeyance during the war years, and was revived by the general enthusiasm for social reconstruction after 1945. This movement set up the remarkable flowering of architecture, particularly in the public realm, that continued until 1980.

The last two decades of the twentieth century were marked by the passing of modernist certainties and a retreat from the public realm. They form the subject of the penultimate chapter. The last is devoted to buildings in the new millennium, a period marked by private interests and the dominance of large institutions that are increasingly corporatized: universities, hospitals, investment funds.

Despite modern travel and communications, and the Internet, Australia's geographic location remains keenly felt. Even as American and English influences abound, together with a universal commitment to al fresco dining, the enduring issues of climatic appropriateness, cultural pathfinding and reconciliation with pre-colonial cultures demand attention. This last is particularly pressing, because it goes to the heart of the moral legitimacy of the state. The fragility of the country periodically claims our attention, its broad slow rivers draining an interior of intimidating vastness. Sometimes these things infiltrate the architectural consciousness, modifying the everyday desire to be culturally relevant at the same time as being stubbornly different. The physicality of the place, the prevalence of the visual, remain hallmarks of this country whose stitching together of history and place can still be discerned, and present us with a culture still evidently under construction.

chapter one

From Federation to Metropolis, 1901–29

Australia never sought modernity. It was embedded in the very institutions that attended English settlement from 1788, despite the evident cruelty of transportation to New South Wales as a criminal punishment. The status of convict may have had a lingering social stigma in the nineteenth century, but hardly circumscribed the material circumstances of the convict once they had served their sentence. Early colonial society in New South Wales was made up of a good proportion of ex-convicts, and even through their sentences they were at pains to maintain their identities as British subjects, with all the status that attached to this. No entrenched class position ensued from a sentence, and almost from the beginning it was observed, either in truth or in hope, that the Australian-born Europeans were distinct from their parents. In 1819 Commissioner J. T. Bigge, sent to Australia to assess the local administration just 31 years after settlement, remarked that: 'In their tempers they are quick and irascible but not vindictive . . . they neither inherit the vices nor the feelings of their parents.'[1]

This conviction that those born in Australia – the currency lads and lasses of the early nineteenth century – have qualities that redeem the failings of European origins, has persisted in the national self-image. This new identity drew on the hope of vast possibilities as the colony pursued self-definition, and encouraged a sense of separateness even as Australians affirmed their continuing sentimental and legal attachment to England. The point is important because the matter of immigration is so crucial in understanding the evolution of Australia as a political entity, as an idea and as an ongoing project.

The rapid colonization of the continent not only outran its convict origins, but it allowed the evolving society to traverse a number of social formations in rapid succession, each leaving a watermark on the law and on social structure. The initial frontier was too vast to be policed and the process of occupying the land for grazing proceeded with astonishing rapidity, with the prior aboriginal inhabitants displaced by usage, and in numerous cases by murder. The practice of de facto possession of land, or squatting, gave rise to a class of landholders, or more strictly leaseholders, who formed a proto-aristocracy within half a century. The short and crude history of their privilege, however, promoted a backlash and by the 1860s smaller parcels of land were made available for selection by homesteaders, to encourage farming and to counter the perceived monopoly on land held by the squatters. The safety valve of selection allowed the survival of the squatters and their vast stations: the wool they produced became Australia's staple export for decades, and the itinerant seasonal workers who moved from property to property came to play a major role in the image of the country as it emerged through both the organization of labour and its attendant mythology.

It is a curiosity of the country that the rural areas produced so many of the tropes of national identity in a country that was so largely urban and peopled by immigrants from the British Isles who came predominantly from cities. This is even more remarkable given the enormous influx of immigrants following the gold rushes of the 1850s, which saw the population of Victoria leap from 76,000 in 1850 to 540,000 ten years later. These were not pastoralists or farmers but opportunists seeking personal freedom working a small claim, with the chance of striking riches. By 1868 the settler population of Australia was 1,540,000, of whom more than 40 per cent were born in Britain and Ireland.[2] The proportion of the Australian population born overseas has fluctuated as immigration waxed and waned, but it has always been an indicator of the country's changing fortunes and the degree of attraction it holds for those from elsewhere wishing to make a new life.

The influx of people through the nineteenth century brought not only increasing specialization of intellect and craft, but political ideas to feed the notion of national unification of the continent's six self-governing colonies. The project reached fruition in 1901 with the establishment of the Commonwealth of Australia, which is the starting point for this history, but some consideration of the condition leading to the Federation of states is useful to sketch the tenor of the times. The political progress of the nineteenth century towards voting rights, self-government and land reform was driven, in part, by a desire to redress the brutality that attended the early colonial years. The rapidity with which this was achieved, and the liberal mood of the British parliament in fostering a colonial outpost with legal equality for its inhabitants, made for a widespread social idealism. The lateness of Federation benefited its proponents, since Britain had opposed slavery for half a century by then, and the American Civil War provided a harsh lesson in the consequences of legal subjugation. Also fresh in the political mind was the British North America Act of 1867, which established the federation of Canada as a modern state.

The driving sentiment in Australian politics of the late nineteenth century was the winning of personal freedoms, perhaps a heady consequence of the social mobility that Australia afforded to immigrants from class-bound Britain and Ireland. The conditions for voting were not hard to meet from 1850, and within a decade the vast majority of Australian men could elect parliamentarians. This included Aboriginal men, although few understandably showed interest.[3] By the 1890s political idealism included ideas of how society might be organized in the collective interest, balanced with the signal Australian individualism. In the popular press the rural worker or contractor became the carrier of national values: not men of property but captains of their souls, they fought for their collective right to sell their labour as they saw fit, and to move from property to property with a contempt for the political posturing of their employers, descendants of the early squatters.

Sporting high literacy rates, and shaped by the satirical cunning of publications like the *Bulletin*, these men formed the backbone of the growing labour movement. By 1890 they had formally organized and the following year adopted a menacing presence in inland towns in Queensland as they held out for the right to bargain collectively. In part this was a response to harder times, as the export price for Australian wool began to drop, and the squeeze on profitability set pastoralists against the organized labour of the shearers. The consequence was defeat for the shearer's union and disillusionment. These defeats on the economic front fostered a contrary impulse to utopianism and fed the eclectic beliefs that flourished in the 1890s. The most influential work from among the writers circulating – Marx, Ruskin, William Morris, Stanley Jevons – was Edward Bellamy's *Looking Backward* (1888), a novel set in Boston that portrays an imagined future for America where the perceived ills of late nineteenth-century society have been addressed through socialism.[4] Mirroring the United States, Bellamy Clubs arose across Australia to discuss the novel and to translate its vision into political action.

Serialized in the publication *The Worker* in 1890, the novel's most ardent convert was the journal's editor and founder, William Lane. For Lane the novel sketched out a society that embodied ideals of abstinence from drink and a voluntary communism. Indeed Lane's vision assumed a hold on him so strong that it was not for compromising, and he is best remembered for organizing a group of 238 settlers to move to Paraguay, and there to create a community called New Australia, free from the practical restrictions he saw in the political landscape of eastern Australia. The project folded under Lane's singular and dictatorial hand, and by 1899 he was back in Sydney, although a number of his followers remained in South America.

The setbacks for labour in the 1890s were temporary as it reorganized itself into parties to contest parliamentary elections, with growing success in the new century. More devastating to the country was the advent of severe drought in the mid-1890s, which compounded the sense that the long period of growth and promise from the 1850s was ending. The lure of Australia as a place where fortunes might be realized, and social status transformed, all but evaporated through the last decade of the nineteenth century. Immigration became a trickle: between 1891 and 1906 only 8,000 newcomers arrived.[5] In the end Federation of the colonies of Australia in 1901 had an air of pragmatism about it, rather than the fervent idealism that had fed earlier discussions of its form and intentions.

In an intellectual climate marked by a desire to entrench personal freedom, both as a progressive impulse and a practical choice in employment and movement, it is not surprising that nostalgia for a self-sufficient pre-capitalist past took hold. These values were discerned in the writings of William Morris and John Ruskin and found ready acceptance in Australia as it sought to entrench a political compromise between capital and labour, terms that were in common usage by the 1890s. Craft was valued even as it was under threat, and in the person of the selector arose the image of a humble but free yeomanry living an alternative life to that of the city. In a similar way the figure of the shearer embodied free labour, selling his skills on his own terms, his dignity intact despite his lack of property.

A National Character in Architecture

The translation of these sentiments into architecture, or at least attempts to articulate a consistent position, found voice in the decades before Federation and in its early years. The generation of architects that steered the profession through the last decade of the nineteenth century held many English-born and trained immigrants. Prominent among these were Robert Haddon, who arrived in Melbourne in 1889, and Walter Liberty Vernon and John Sulman, who made their way to Sydney in 1883 and 1885, respectively.[6] Sulman, in particular, had become engaged in the question of national style, an elusive and often contradictory quest that nonetheless became part of the cultural speculations that attended the debate on how the various colonies of Australia, and perhaps New Zealand, might be federated into a single political entity.

Within two years of arriving in Australia, and despite difficulties in establishing himself in practice, Sulman published a series of articles in the *Australasian Builder and Contractor's News* arguing his view of a relevant Australian style. The quickness of the settling of his convictions is telling: they follow less than two years of local travel and practice, but Sulman had by then also founded a Palladian Club with some of Sydney's leading practitioners, including fellow Englishman Vernon.[7]

Sulman, like many of his generation, had travelled extensively in Italy and recounted how his early enthusiasm for the Gothic Revival and for the English Queen Anne Revival had waned, with neither in his opinion exhibiting the strength or flexibility needed for contemporary building. He sets out the determinants of a logical Australian expression: bright sun necessitating shade, occasional heavy rain, the high cost of labour and the crude building materials locally produced.[8] Sulman's key point, though, is his inversion of the English association of vernacular craft with the Gothic Revival. Both of these traditions had been fostered as alternatives to Neo-classicism, the veneration of the architecture of ancient Greece and Rome. In Sulman's eyes this opposition disappears in Australia, where the climatic conditions are so akin to Italy as to invoke that nation's ancient journey from vernacular to classical architecture. In short, a robust classicism could be to Australia what a rude medievalism might be to England – an authentic expression of climate and culture.

In attempting to carve out a position that showed some integrity, Sulman was compelled to draw on views that had been influential in reviving the English vernacular. His position on Victorian cast iron, a staple of Australian building in the late nineteenth century, owes much to Ruskin's abhorrence of the material, which was derided succinctly in Aphorism 15 of his *Seven Lamps of Architecture*: 'Cast-iron ornamentation barbarous.'[9] In Aphorism 10 Ruskin also passes judgement on the use of iron structurally, where he condemns its use to bear weight or displace wooden beams.[10]

Sulman's argument for using Italy as a source for architectural styles that evolved from vernacular to higher forms of refinement was not the only persuasive one. The inventive work of H. H. Richardson in the eastern United States had elicited broad appeal for its perceived stylistic independence, a position forcefully expressed in Sydney by American immigrant architect John Horbury Hunt after his arrival in 1863. Thus the Shingle Style also found a place in Australian architecture prior to Federation and helped supplant Victorian tastes by the turn of the century.[11]

While these positions influenced architectural practice, for many firms the question of style was more a matter of selection than moral imperative. Architects could work across a number of modes, and a large office like the New South Wales Government Architect's Branch (GAB) under Walter Liberty Vernon's direction from 1890 to 1911 could range in expression from an academic classicism to a syncopated and asymmetrical Arts and Crafts. However one element was consistently embraced across all schools of thought: the verandah, regarded as a climatic necessity and a versatile device in building composition. John Bede Barlow, who practised with

Richard Williams, Olevanus, Sydney, 1903–11.

Hunt, proclaimed its relevance to New South Wales in 1903: 'The necessity for verandahs and balconies in this semi-tropical climate of ours . . . is slowly but surely evolving a house in this State which may be claimed to be almost distinctly Australian.'[12] Hadden echoed these sentiments, as did Sydney architect and educator James Nangle, who wrote in 1900 that 'the verandah is an essential in Australian domestic architecture on account of the climate which renders shade to rooms necessary. It is moreover a feature which, if well designed and well constructed, adds much to the appearance of the house.'[13]

Federation Architecture

The watershed year of 1901, which commenced with the proclamation of the Commonwealth of Australia as a single nation, also saw the death of Queen Victoria and the passing of the era that bore her name. There had been architecture synonymous with her rule, but in Australia it had become associated with grasping commerce, shoddy construction and facile mass-produced ornamentation. The houses that emerged in the first decade of Federation were stylistically diverse, but united in their adherence to Ruskin-influenced notions that eschewed ironwork, favoured solidity and incorporated increasingly elaborate brickwork for polychromatic effect. The invention of the cavity brick wall in the 1890s, which separated the two brick skins of the exterior with a 50mm air gap, meant that the porous nature of brick no longer transmitted moisture to the building interior. Prior to this stucco had been applied to facades for waterproofing, but the cavity wall allowed bricks to be used to their full visual potential.[14]

The image of the Federation House has continued to exert a hold on the Australian imagination, although the period it refers to only spanned the years from Federation to the start of the First World War. It is encapsulated in developments like the Appian Way in the Sydney suburb of Burwood, which comprised 36 houses set about a curved roadway, with matching fencing and gardens. Designed and built by Richard Williams for industrialist George J. Hoskins to rent to model tenants, the houses show the variety of versions that could flow from a single designer. Number 4 Appian Way, 'Alba Longa', displays the banded brickwork, terracotta tiled roof and the picturesque roof forms that marked the most popular form, with much of the timberwork picked out in white. Number 6, 'Olevanus', has a prominent steeply shingled roof with numerous ridges and valleys, punctuated by sculptural corbelled chimneys. While the painted timberwork is common to both, details differ markedly and testify to the eclectic origins of these two houses. Both sport prominent verandahs and use the deep shading as an effective contrast to those surfaces of brick that appear in full sun.

The houses of the Appian Way give the impression of some playfulness in the way each is considered as an exercise in creating a work of stylistic consistency from a different antecedent. The Queen Anne Revival, much altered from its English roots, is evident. So too is the Shingle Style. Particularly prominent are the curved forms of turn-of-the-century European Art Nouveau, which invoked the rhythms of natural forms against the primary geometries of classicism.

But it is the Arts and Crafts movement, with its valorization of labour, that found a particular resonance among Australian designers around the time of Federation. Its popularity owed much to Ruskin's writings, which were read for their political idealism as well as their architectural exhortations. Despite the downturn of the 1890s, when the promise of Australia as a place to transform lives had shattered, the country still clung to its aspirations as a working-man's paradise. The houses of the Appian Way may have seemed inventive but not compelling models for Australian living, but the pairing of Arts and Crafts with a vision of a fulfilled and free artisanal culture should not be underestimated. Its most complete demonstration was the work of the mercurial Australian-born Harold Desbrowe-Annear, Melbourne's most inventive domestic architect of the period. He had signalled his leanings in a 1900 lecture in which he had recommended Ruskin's *Elements of Drawing* and *The Seven Lamps of Architecture* as the architect's 'most constant companions containing the essential ethics of his art'.[15] His design for three houses at Eaglemont for his in-laws, the Chadwick family, provided the opportunity to test his ideas in an artistically minded community. Now subsumed by some of Melbourne's most desirable suburbs, the group presents a collective view of Desbrowe-Annear's proposition for peri-urban living. The most striking, the Chadwick House (1903), shows a mix of influences that all affirm a period notion of integrity. The deep verandahs shade the half-timbered walls of the house, and are framed with lattice screens that, in sections, form the balustrading. The curved elements of the framing evoke the decorative flourishes of Guimard or Horta, while the verandahs establish the climatic credentials of the now century-old device in Australia, and the half-timbered walls retain the nostalgic Englishness of Pugin. The interiors are consistent with this, more village than country estate, and modest in their evocation of homeliness. The house is perhaps most remarkable for its knowing demonstration of the symbolic content of these elements. That Desbrowe-Annear could unify them testifies to the spirit of invention fostered by the larger project of Federation itself.

The Arts and Crafts practitioners also undertook the dissemination of the movement's ideals and techniques. Local periodicals established in the 1890s illustrated its tenets, and Desbrowe-Annear established the T-Square Club at the Melbourne Working Man's College in 1900 to foster its aims across architecture and associated craft.[16] The prevalence of Arts and Crafts influence can be seen across the whole range of buildings associated with the Federation era. Harriet Edquist sees in the Australian movement the precursors to a later modernism to follow: indeed she speculates that

> if we positioned the Arts and Crafts movement as the central tradition of turn-of-the-century Australian architecture, and 'federation' as the speculative and ultimately unproductive tail-end of the 1880s Queen Anne and English domestic revivals, we get a very different story, one that helps explain the development of early modernism.[17]

While this perhaps elides many tendencies into one overarching theme, it does draw attention to the potency of the movement in early twentieth-century Australia. For the English-trained architects who arrived in the 1880s, Arts and Crafts presented a third way between the academic classical tradition, seen by the mid-nineteenth century as stifling in its

Harold Desbrowe-Annear, Chadwick House, Melbourne, 1903.

adherence to precedent, and the Gothic Revival, which by the 1860s had lost its potency as a critical counterpoint to classicism and had itself become encumbered by a desire to be historically accurate. The Arts and Crafts circumvented the academicism of both these tendencies by seeking out vernacular precedents, shaped by the Ruskinian view that materials ought to be used with due regard to their nature. In 1901 this movement was still excavating English and American examples perceived as vernacular, or in some sense free of the academies, for their flexibility in how parts could be borrowed and put together.

In domestic architecture Desbrowe-Annear's counterpart in Sydney was George Sydney Jones. Jones had both Arts and Crafts sympathies and a nativist inclination to introduce Australian motifs in stained glass. His most striking tendency, though, was his use of flat roofs to circumvent the complex pitched forms necessary to cover the asymmetrical and attenuated plans of the period. Of the three houses he built in 1908–9, the house and surgery 'Lorne' for his brother-in-law was the most elaborate. The flat roof emphasizes the primary volumes of the house, which is surmounted by a small shading projection at the upper storey, below the balustrade wall enclosing the usable flat roof. A contemporary account describes the house as being 'of the Moorish style', referring to what appeared to be a rooftop garden.[18] The introduction of the flat roof by Jones shows two prevailing tendencies: the ease with which influences from various parts of the world, especially those considered to be climatically similar, were absorbed, and the impulse towards simplified forms that the veneration of vernacular styles encouraged.

The Federation period also highlights an enduring theme in twentieth-century Australia, with the divergence of concerns between domestic, commercial and public buildings. The rise of the suburb brought with it the aspiration that the home should be unlike the realm of work, and the domestic house becomes a vessel for architecture intent on pursuing ideals of authenticity in form and in life. Home was where the true individual, defined by sentiment rather than commercial arrangements, could find repose. In contrast, in the city proper the rapid installation of electric trams created a network radiating from the core, giving rise to vast shopping emporia at the intersection of tram routes. Occupying whole city blocks, department stores like Anthony Hordern and Sons' New Palace Emporium in Sydney (Albert Bond and Isaiah Wellings, 1901–5) presented the challenge of clothing these enormous spaces with some architectural skill. As products of commerce, they were beyond any attempts at authenticity,

George Sydney Jones, Barncleuth, Sydney, 1909.

Albert Bond and Isaiah Wellings, Anthony Hordern and Sons (New Palace Emporium), Sydney, 1901–5.

and certainly too vast for the application of the craft or planning tenets prevailing in houses of the period. Instead they fell back on the Victorian models that had arisen to deal with the scale and materials of industrialized building. Clothed in a loose amalgam of pilasters, pediments and large fanlights, the articulation of the facade rarely transcends the simple expedient of rendering the surface visually acceptable to eyes accustomed to ornamentation. The building type here has outrun a profession not yet comfortable with the challenges thrown up by contemporary engineering and commerce.

The government works of the period present a more complex set of architectural issues. Walter Liberty Vernon had steered the Government Architect's Branch (GAB) in New South Wales from 1890, and the new century brought problems of scale and taste equal to those in commercial building. Vernon's exposure to Arts and Crafts, and the Gothic Revival, has been well documented. His inclination, judging by earlier works, was towards those traditions as they were codified in the years of his training and early practice in England.[19] The large public works that appeared

NSW Government Architect's Branch under Walter Liberty Vernon, Central Railway Station, northern facade to Belmore Park, Sydney, 1904–8.

under his hand in Sydney in the first decade of Federation were, perhaps atypically, conventionally classical. These include Sydney's Central Railway Station (1908), the long-awaited completion of the Art Gallery of New South Wales, and the Mitchell Wing of the State Library of New South Wales. In the years before Federation Vernon had become interested in early colonial buildings, partly due to their early adaptations to climate and partly for their potential as a workable vernacular of sorts. In New South Wales these buildings were modelled on the English Georgian, a simple symmetrical style that was often adorned with a verandah locally. Among the finest works to emanate from the GAB showing this influence is the Wagga Wagga Courthouse (1902), one among many built for country towns during Vernon's tenure. The complex of buildings is distinctive for its colonnaded court, a device that gives visual depth to the building and creates a shaded, internal space that mitigates the heat for those entering, leaving or waiting. The attached tower, with Venetian accents, marks the civic importance of the building, while the interior courtroom shows the influence of the coffered ceilings of key colonial Georgian buildings like St Matthew's, Windsor, by Francis Greenway (1822). Taken together, these devices mark a divergence from issues of style to those of climate and precedent. The building is spatially more open, more permeable to breezes, than its predecessors. It also shows a drift to simplicity. The ornate curves emanating from European work are suppressed, and the carpentry of the colonnade is soberly orthogonal in its geometry. The building entry presents a symmetrical face, unlike the picturesque asymmetry of much of the Arts and Crafts tradition.

In Sydney's public buildings designed by the GAB the scale was much greater, and the device Vernon used was that of the 'temple front' based on Neoclassical rules, which made up the civic or street facade masking a more modern complex of spaces behind. In the Mitchell Wing of the State Library, opened in 1910, the sequence of spaces proceeds from the Neoclassical portico, through an entry vestibule, to the voluminous reading room with its arcing glazed roof surmounting one of the city's finest public interiors. The structure of the roof is Victorian in its ambition and elegance, using contemporary materials and engineering. That it needed to be married to a Neoclassical facade indicates the depth of

J. W. Fawcett and H.P.C. Ashworth of Victorian Railways, Flinders Street Station, Melbourne, 1901–11.

feeling for the civic credentials of that style. Similar sentiments attend the building of the great urban train stations – Sydney's Central Railway Station (1904–8, also under Vernon's direction), and Melbourne's Flinders Street (1901–11) by J. W. Fawcett and H.P.C. Ashworth. Both rely on elaborate public facades drawing heavily upon academic convention to screen the engineering behind.

The extent of urban construction in the first decade of the twentieth century testifies to the dynamic economies of the cities as the nation rebounded from depression and drought. If we seek stylistic modernism, as it has come to be understood, then there is little evidence of a move to technological sophistication manifest as building form, or an impulse to radically simplify facades and eliminate ornament. But the great city buildings show the challenges of adapting the prevailing mode of working to the spaces of modernity: the railway terminus, the emporium, the exhibition building.

Thus we see, by 1910, different tendencies at work in the domestic, commercial and public spheres. Rising labour costs across the board forced a reconsideration of ornament as a matter of practicality for all buildings, but inevitably the act of Federation gave rise to questions of national identity. Leadership in style implied leadership in thought, and the prominent role architecture played in the claim of urban business interests to shape the new nation saw a new earnestness take hold. The dearth of immigrants from 1890 onwards made for an increasing proportion of native-born Australians, and the large influx of English architects in the 1880s had no counterpart in the new century. Instead a climatic rationalism emerged, as the Englishness of Australian building diminished with the declining experience of England itself. In 1894 about 29 per cent of Australians were born overseas, overwhelmingly in Britain and Ireland. By 1914 this had declined to about 17 per cent, and it continued to drop to its lowest point of 10 per cent in 1944. The significance of this can be imagined: links to Europe became attenuated, and a land previously regarded as exotic became the unremarkable backdrop for everyday life.

The Design of Canberra

Yet before the issues of climate and light as determinants of architecture took hold, one more chapter of architectural self-definition needed to be written for the new nation. It involved the building of a new capital at Canberra. The decision to site the capital at a remote location was a consequence of the vote on Federation itself. In the 1898 referendum on the proposal to federate the colonies, New South Wales voters failed to reach the required number to assent to the bill. Concessions were made to entice that colony towards greater support, and in the following year a second referendum succeeded. One of the altered conditions was to place the national capital in New South Wales, provided it was more than 160 kilometres (100 mi.) from Sydney. After extensive survey and some persistent lobbying, the site for present-day Canberra was chosen.

A kit of survey documents, models and photographs was prepared to inform competitors in an international design competition, but opposition to its organization saw professional bodies including the Royal Institute of British Architects refusing to take part. Their objection was to political interference in the process, since the Australian Minister for Home Affairs, King O'Malley, reserved the right to make a sole determination despite his lack of training. O'Malley remains one of the most colourful of early federal politicians, and he could not but dominate the events he set in train. Probably born in Kansas, despite his claim to come from Quebec, he had some success selling insurance in the American Midwest, and he also founded a church of his own invention before arriving in Melbourne in 1888. Resorting again to selling insurance, by 1896 he was established in Adelaide where he stood for, and was elected to, the local parliament. In 1901 he stood for the new Federal Parliament in Tasmania and was again elected. With strong views on most issues, his stewardship of the competition for Canberra was heavy-handed, erratic and prone to conflicts.

Entries were due on 31 January 1912. An advisory board of three had been appointed to assess the entries, but they split 2–1 in the judging, with the majority recommending the design of Walter Burley Griffin. Griffin was a native of Chicago and had worked alongside, and for, Wright. Together with his wife, the gifted architect and illustrator Marion Mahoney, Griffin moved to Australia in 1914. Sensing that his work needed defending, he had made a prior trip to reassert the virtues of his design in the face of a local derivative plan, prepared by government officials in the aftermath of the competition. Despite his title of Federal Capital Director of Design and Construction, a post he held for seven years, Griffin never entirely succeeded in implementing his plan.

Griffin's competition plan had a seductive quality deriving from its geometric purity, which he artfully integrated with the topography and a proposed new lake, as well as from the beautiful set of fifteen drawings prepared with Marion Mahoney. While the development of the city proceeded in phases over the next century, with each phase marked by new fashions and planning strategies, the central components of the plan eventually reached some fruition. The Griffins were committed in their social idealism, Marion having been active in a liberal Unitarian congregation for the two decades prior to arriving in Australia. Strongly influenced by

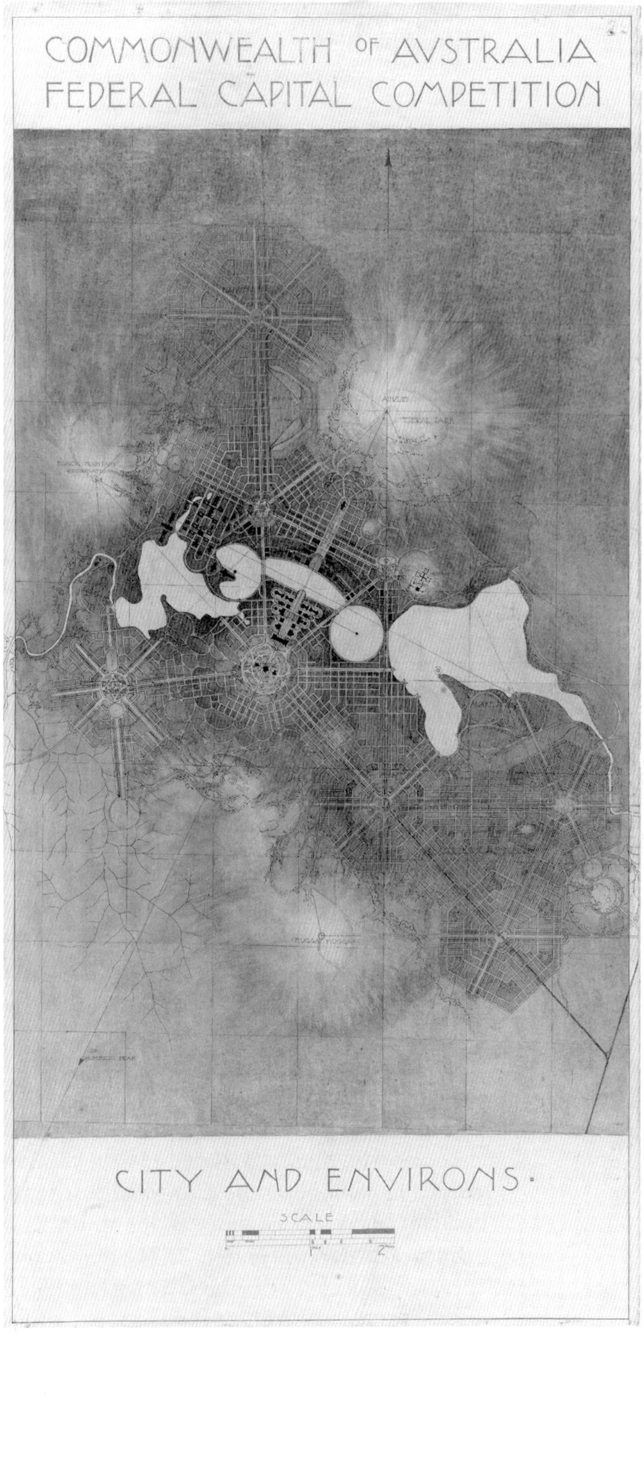

Walter Burley Griffin with Marion Mahoney Griffin, Canberra: City and Environs (competition entry), 1912.

Ralph Waldo Emerson's Transcendentalism, which diffused the Divine among both broad creation and humanity, Marion remained a lifelong seeker after spiritual succour. Griffin, too, came from a liberal theological background, his home church being Congregationalist in form, and decentralized in spirit. Both were profound believers in democracy as both a manner of governance and a spiritual ideal. As James Weirick, historian of Australian landscapes, has noted, for the Griffins their Canberra plan was an ideal made manifest: 'At the time they planned Canberra, both Walter and Marion were political idealists, American progressives imbued with a Jeffersonian commitment to freedom and democracy.'[20] Weirick also notes that Griffin was a supporter of Henry George, who advocated for a single tax on land value as a means to social reform. George had a large following of Single Taxers in Australia, due to the perceived progressive nature of his tax: it was largely levied on the wealthy and it captured some of the increase in land value brought about by urban development. Through this cause Griffin had formed a view of Australia as a nation in the 'vanguard of political progress'.

In the geometric purity of the Griffins' initial plan can be read their aspiration to a purity of political form. The plan titled 'City and Environs' is heavily rendered in watercolour, gouache and gold oil paint. The hills of Mugga Mugga, Mount Ainslie and Black Mountain, which define the city centre, are sunburst splashes, with the city layout and foreshores rendered darker to throw the artificial lake, which divides the city, into sharp relief. The plan is a series of concentric constellations, a multi-centred city with seven nodes initially evident. The geometry of the radiating street patterns is either six- or eight-sided, with the patterns reconciled through portions of regular street grids enmeshed in the ripples from the centres. While the plan itself devolved into zones by function, forming a recreation group and a government group, the dominant image of the plan is of a skilled reconciliation of the tenets of Ebenezer Howard's Garden City layout with the constraints of geography, using rectilinear rather than arced or curved elements. The orderliness of this initial approach was visually distinctive: the introduction of more curved roads around the Capitol in Griffin's revised plan of 1913 has diminished the power of the original vision.

The transcendent aspects of the original plan can be discerned in the sections and aerial views that accompanied it. The centrepiece of the government group of buildings was to be the Capitol, surmounted by a building of stepped ascending form, which served as a symbolic focus of national assembly and Australian culture. The Houses of Parliament (upper and lower, as in Westminster) were located below the Capitol, at the apex of the governing triangle. The alignment of building form towards the

Capitol is a straightforward configuration of the perceived importance of the arms of political power, but the similarity of the proposed Capitol Building to the Burmese temples illustrated in James Fergusson's *History of Indian and Eastern Architecture* has been well observed, since the book was part of the Griffins' library.[21] This reference was, in part, acknowledgement of the reality of Australia's location in the East, but it was also an expression of an ur-architecture, culturally diffuse but drawing on exotic models as an act of cultural conciliation. These sentiments were not new: they had been prefigured in the embrace of comparative religion that inspired James Vila Blake, the minister in Marion Mahoney's childhood Church of All Souls, who had declared that 'the religious nature is not created by any institution, nor depends on a form, nor is bound to a doctrine. In its divine activity it neither awaits nor permits an authoritative book. It is itself the source of all forms and creeds.'[22]

The view of the Griffins that democracy in Australia was unique, advanced and had the capacity to create something new and just, in a location that demanded the symbolic melding of building archetypes, was fated from the outset to flounder on the reality of competing interests that motivated the Canberra project. Within months of the winning scheme being declared, an alternate plan was produced by the Departmental Board of the young Federal government, which shouldered aside Griffin's. It was considerably more modest and peppered with the practical considerations that constituted their view of planning. It assumed that the city needed compact beginnings and retained Griffin's nodes only as specific institutions: Capitol, mint, orphanage, university. There is the heavy hand of pragmatic engineering in the road and railway layout, but its supporters were powerful enough to force Griffin to respond with a revised plan that incorporated some of its elements. This game continued for some years after Griffin's move to Australia, leading him to write in some frustration to Prime Minister Hughes in 1920: 'Had my time and energies not been frittered away meeting manufactured difficulties and obstruction, the essential guiding plans ensuring efficiency, harmony, and particularly, economy, would have been in existence long ere this.'[23]

It is moot whether this could have been achieved. The plan Griffin produced in 1918 was indeed adopted as the guiding one for Canberra and was gazetted in 1925. Geometrically it is very different from the original, with both curved and faceted geometries generated by the multiple nodes. Much of it is still in evidence, but the story of Canberra's plan as pure intention corrupted by bureaucratic ineptitude and spite has lingered in Australia. The plan of Canberra was perhaps the last flourishing of visionary idealism that attended Federation: soon the exigencies of war, and the testing of imperial loyalty, became more pressing issues.

The outbreak of hostilities in 1914, the year of the Griffins' arrival in Australia, did not end their plans to continue in private practice. Setting up office in Melbourne, they cultivated friendships and clients in parallel to the work on Canberra. Probably through their Georgist connections, and helped no doubt by their non-sectarian outlook, they secured the commission to design a new Catholic college at the University of Melbourne, Newman College. King O'Malley, who had overseen the original Canberra competition, was also known in the labourite and Catholic circles that were to steer the fate of the college, and he remained well-disposed towards the Griffins. Originally proposed as a symmetrical building of two L-shaped cloisters, with a library at one corner and a

Walter Burley Griffin, revised plan for Canberra, 1913.

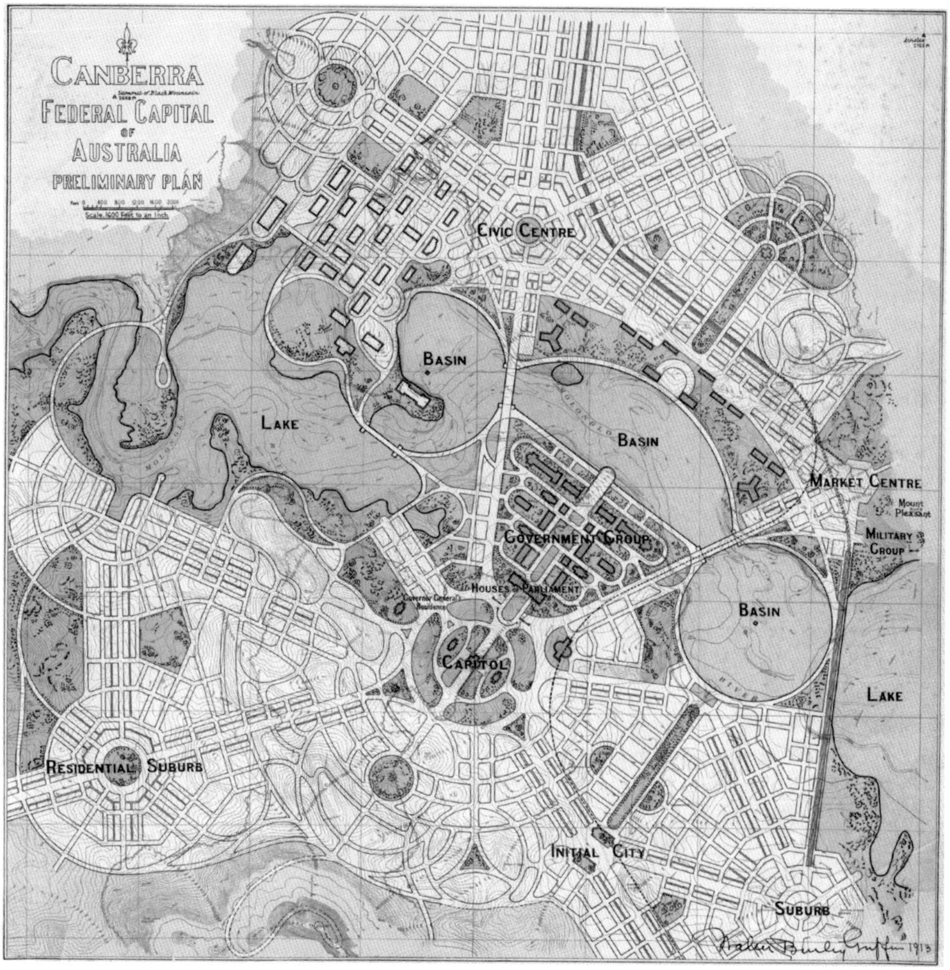

Walter Burley Griffin with Marion Mahoney Griffin in association with A. A. Fritsch, Newman College, Melbourne, 1915–18.

dining hall at the other, only one wing was built to the couple's design. It provides a comprehensive vision of their architecture: deeply shaded, massive and with a heavy debt to the Gothic. The association carried the design, since the Gothic Revival had sought to recapture not only the modulated half-light and symbolic richness of the High Gothic, but the apparent cultural authenticity of a pre-Reformation Britain. In this the Griffins also rode on the association that the style had with ecclesiastical architecture in the nineteenth century. But in working out their architectural symbolism the Griffins moved beyond an academic revival of Gothic to a new and inventive set of architectonic details, the fantastical form of which echoes their contemporary Gaudí, working half a world away.

While in Melbourne the Griffins designed buildings for an eclectic range of clients that included successful immigrants from Ukraine and Greece, and prominent Australian members of the Chinese Nationalist Party, followers of Sun Yat-sen. They also formed a circle with Roy Lippincott, who had married Griffin's sister and moved to Sydney in 1914, and Melbourne two years later. The largest work they undertook was the Capitol Theatre, completed in 1924. Structurally ambitious and spatially magnificent, the theatre's stepped ceiling used a complex and highly decorative set of plaster elements to diffuse the beams of myriad hidden lights. While some theatres used concealed and pinpoint lighting to evoke the night sky, the Griffins conjured up a crystalline interior that imagined subterranean spaces as rendered by a geometrically inclined deity. This combination was both a Deutscher Werkbund trope and a feature in many early modernist visions, but it is doubtful if it appears in more compelling form anywhere.

A Transcendent Nationalism

The period of the genesis of Canberra also saw the retirement of a generation of English-trained architects who had been so influential before Federation in both governmental and private practice. These included W. L. Vernon, James Peddle, George Oakeshott, John Sulman and J. T. Hobbs. Others of this generation continued in practice into the new century, but the taste for elaborate houses declined as a growing suburban

Walter Burley Griffin with Marion Mahoney Griffin in association with Peck & Kemter, ceiling in Capitol Theatre, Melbourne, 1921–4.

middle class sought models reflecting their own thrift. The American West Coast was experiencing a parallel rapid urbanization, and the California bungalow held more modest aspirations than the Australian reworking of the Queen Anne style that has subsequently become synonymous with Federation. Yet neither style was vested with a sense of historical appropriateness, a failing recognized by Sydney architect William Hardy Wilson.

Wilson, Sydney born, had been articled to the firm of Kent & Budden. Typical of his generation, his in-office training was supplemented with night classes at the Sydney Technical College. An avid painter and illustrator, Wilson left Australia in 1905 to study at the Architectural Association in London and to travel with his future practice partner, Stacey Neave. The classicist tenets of the American colonial revival appealed to Wilson in their evocation of an ideal architecture based on proportion rather than ornament or elaborations of form. This accorded well with his experience of Australia's colonial architecture, typified in the works of Francis Greenway, an early exponent of colonial Georgian who arrived in Sydney as a convicted forger in 1814. In 1924 Wilson published his drawings of significant surviving colonial-era buildings as *Old Colonial Architecture in New South Wales and Tasmania*. It is a volume that evokes an idyllic

Francis Greenway, Hyde Park Barracks, Sydney, 1817–19.

William Hardy Wilson, Eryldene, Sydney, 1913.

period characterized by purity of form as a consequence of both isolation and modest colonial means. Setting aside the well-documented venality of the earlier period, Wilson instead sought out the components of what he considered the long-standing appeal of the Georgian period.[24]

The elements of this fascination are still visible. Greenway's ensemble of the Hyde Park Barracks (1819) and St James's Church, facing each other across Macquarie Street in Sydney, remain exemplars of refined Georgian composition. Wilson illustrated his version in his seminal design for the 1913 house 'Eryldene' for the academic E. G. Waterhouse. Located in Sydney's northern suburbs well before they became easily accessible by the opening of the Harbour Bridge in 1932, the house acquired additional outbuildings and pavilions by the firm of Wilson, Neave & Berry over the following two decades. The modesty of the house belies the importance it acquired in Australian architecture. Set back from the street and approached via a paved path, the house has a marked simplicity when compared to the elaborate Federation houses of the area. Single storey, its roofline is a simple shingled hipped roof free of gables or projections. The main house presents a symmetrical facade to the street, with a prominent verandah and summer sleeping alcoves. There is no hint of the amalgamation of influences that sustained other contemporary houses, or of the sinuous decorative details pointing to familiarity with European *fin de siècle* naturalism. The Georgian model Wilson used evokes an austere version of American colonial work, if anything. But most influential was the confident proclamation of an architecture of restraint, paring away the excesses of the Federation period, which Wilson saw as indicative of a confused identity. For the English-born architects who preceded him, stylistic experimentation may have seemed intriguing, perhaps even important. For the native Wilson it was an issue of existential gravity. Obsessed with finding a historically resonant national identity, not one cobbled together from an amalgam of stylistic fashions, his models became those styles that he identified with the earliest risings of great civilizations. It was not a utilitarian logic, based on climate. It was reductive, but in pursuit of an essence that defined identity in transcendent, not pragmatic, terms. Indeed in his fondness for small architectural follies, of which there are several in the grounds of 'Eryldene', we see his belief in an essential uselessness as part of design, a restating of the Kantian idea of aesthetic judgement grounded in 'purposiveness without a purpose'.[25]

The early years of Wilson's career were the most fruitful, since he felt compelled to move at regular intervals. His travels in China in 1921 left a profound influence and he came to regard the fusion of Eastern and Western cultural identity as desirable, if not inevitable, at least in Australia. Part of this was based on simple geographic expedient, but part was an expression of his desire to uncover historical essences, which found beauty in a generic classical ideal that he discerned in both ancient Greece and pre-modern China and Japan. It rested on distillation rather than elaboration in his view, a tenet he applied increasingly to matters of social organization. The release of *Old Colonial Architecture in New South Wales and Tasmania* saw him feted as a proponent of revivalism on his return to Sydney from Europe, and the work of Wilson Neave & Berry became admired for its valorization of local precedents and its simple yet effective use of light, shade and proportion. Yet there was more at stake. Wilson had become absorbed in matters of national destiny, and the age of nationalism was uncovering and reinventing ideals of aesthetic unity in how it imagined its citizens would appear. In this project the eclectic, occasionally magnificent, buildings of the late Victorian age held little allure since they were so clearly transplants. The same was, of course, true of Sydney's early Georgian, but this latter style was free of the taint of mercantile success and opportunism that characterized the Victorians. It seemed purer and closer to the Grecian ideal that was infusing notions of the Australian type in both building and citizen.

The drive to aesthetic consistency seems a particular reflex of nationalism. As Enzo Traverso has observed, empires by definition are resigned to differences among subjects.[26] The idea of aesthetic or racial consistency is an affectation adopted by nations, and it has dogged many countries aside from Australia. Wilson's specific views were atypical, given his idealization of Chinese, Japanese and Indian cultures as he saw them through his anti-modern lens. The early tendency in Australian political life was to maintain racial homogeneity for a number of reasons. After Federation cane farmers were given four years to repatriate indentured labourers brought from the South Pacific to exclude any stain of slavery. Immigration to Australia was effectively confined to native English speakers through the use of a dictation test to determine eligibility to enter the country. The motivation here, at least as expressed by Prime Minister Deakin, was to exclude Chinese and Japanese immigrants because they seemed inured to the hardships they faced, and accepted conditions of work that were intolerable to Australian unions.[27]

Wilson seemed unconcerned by these objections. His view was bereft of class as a distinguishing characteristic, unlike Deakin. He saw only the corrupting effects of modern life, its awkwardness in creating things of value on the run, and the desirability of bringing together the distilled nobility of contemplative artistic traditions grounded in agrarian ways of life. In 1927 Wilson designed a small tea house for the gardens of 'Eryldene', in which he demonstrated his vision of a fusion of East and West. He describes it, in his characteristic third-person telling, as 'in the northern Tang style' with straight columns surmounted by Greek Doric capitals: 'It was all that he could show of his study in China and in Greece. To adventure forth in quest of a new style was beyond the imagination of his people.'[28]

In 1919 Wilson contributed to the volume *Domestic Architecture in Australia*, published as a special edition of the journal *Art in Australia*. An unremarkable book in appearance, its influence was to be surprisingly persistent, and its appeal broad and compelling. Wilson vetted the selection of buildings and images, so the book bears the imprint of his judgement, but the other contributors are equally noteworthy. Desbrowe-Annear made the Victorian selection and supplied a short opinion piece; Walter Bagot represented South Australia, and Robin Dods, Queensland. The book was given some academic standing through the essay by Professor Leslie Wilkinson titled 'Domestic Architecture'. The noteworthy aspect of the book in the development of a national architectural outlook lies in the authors, save for Wilkinson, all being born in Australia or New Zealand. But Wilkinson had been comprehensively seduced by his experience of Italy: one could argue that he was already lost to English traditions.

Newly arrived in Sydney, Wilkinson had been appointed to the Chair of Architecture at the University of Sydney in 1918. His talent for sketching and measured drawings had enabled him to rise from solid middle-class origins to prize-winning student at the Royal Academy, but like a number of his contemporaries, concerns about his health and the lure of the opportunity to transcend class restrictions led him to Australia. He was eminently suited to the role. His extensive travels and sketching in Southern Europe had left him with a fascination and feel for the massing and light of Mediterranean structures, and the poor conditions at his boarding school soured his native loyalties, despite his military enlistment in the First World War. From his arrival Wilkinson advocated for the adoption of architectural models other than those inherited from the Federation period, as he makes explicit in his essay when he asks 'is it certain that it is wise to attempt to follow Northern methods of building under conditions so dissimilar? Geography suggests that the shores of the Mediterranean may be richer in suggestion, or the Californian coast manner so largely derived therefrom.'[29] A similar point is made by Bagot: 'Racial traditions may make our English Georgian more readily assimilable; but climate points the way to the Mediterranean as our closest parallel – and climate is the dominating factor.'[30]

The prevailing view in the essays is that the simplicity of the colonial Georgian architecture of New South Wales and Tasmania could happily blend with Mediterranean materials and precedents, as long as they both conformed to a new modesty brought about by the growing expense of servants. The issue was clearly current: Dods even suggests that houses arranged in clusters of a dozen could share domestic staff in a bid to retain the advantages of their expertise and their hands, adding ruefully that 'two or three cooks at salaries comparable to those now paid to University professors and with commensurate skill and training, could appear like prima donnas on alternate nights'.[31]

Dods, by 1913, had established a reputation as a leading domestic architect in Brisbane, but he subsequently moved to Sydney. Brought together with the other authors through a commitment to a studied simplicity, his Queensland houses had demonstrated both the subtle prevailing admiration for American architects like Charles A. Platt, and the potential for verandahs to evoke colonnaded classicism and contrasts of light and shade. The Littledike House of 1902 shows the recurve verandah screen frame that Dods popularized, a geometrically simple framing beam that eschews the free-forms of the European *Jugendstil* framework. This geometry, together with the repetitive forms that Dods used in his verandah framing generally, invoke classical tastes more than the free forms of Arts and Crafts. While Dods had worked in more ornate modes, his inclination was towards simplifying house forms in line with the work of Wilson. The Littledike House is simply prefiguring this reductive drift, which would appear after the excesses of the Federation styles faded from fashion. His Sydney residence, 'Fenton' (1920), has dispensed with a front verandah and is more an exercise in the simple updated Georgian that Wilson espoused. Indeed its appearance is of a shuttered villa of austere modesty, with an entry marked by a simple recess with flanking Doric columns. As a contemporary account notes, it evokes in its simplicity houses of both Northern and Southern Europe, and its modest tenor 'has all the best features of a modern home, which make for convenience without any meretricious ornament'.[32]

In 1919 Wilkinson was yet to make his distinctive contribution to the debate in the form of his own architecture. So it was Wilson's polemical account of the design and building of his own house, 'Purulia', that was most widely quoted. In it Wilson records his delight in the discomfort his neighbours felt on seeing this small, rectangular house emerge, in contrast to their 'multangular villas'. Yet his garden wins them over, with its lack of formality and the way it shades into the surrounding bush. Seductively photographed by the prolific Harold Cazneaux, who also recorded the earlier 'Eryldene', the ensemble of house and garden illustrate an idyll of its times. The house has many similarities with the contemporaneous 'Fenton' by Dods, with shuttered windows set in textured, painted walls. The composition, as in 'Eryldene', is symmetrical and follows the colonial Georgian in studied simplicity. Surmounted by a simple pitched roof, again shingled, it is Wilson's personal comment on the age. The provocation lies not only in the simple domestic arrangements that underlies its planning, and its servant-less accommodation. It also shows the curious reverse-engineering of style that attended the transition from colonies to nation. In England the revivals of English vernacular in the late nineteenth century had attempted to retrace the idea of folk traditions feeding into higher forms of architecture. In Australia Wilson and his co-authors were attempting the opposite: the distillation of a historically resonant vernacular from a suite of imported styles.

Curiously, there is no mention in *Domestic Architecture in Australia* of the First World War, despite Wilkinson's service and the profound effect the war had on Australian society. On the one hand the country's participation can be seen as an extended effort at self-definition, fighting as part of the British Army. But the casualties were horrendous, if distant, and the imperious manner of British officers occasionally rankled the ANZAC troops from Australia and New Zealand, who were all volunteers. Wilson's partner Stacey Neave was one of those who volunteered and on his return he gave some stability to the firm, which suffered from Wilson's restlessness. However the lessons of the war were more veiled and were tied in with the sentiment that the whole world had changed in many ways, from the availability of maids to the imperatives of national leadership.

Both of these were evident in *Domestic Architecture*, although the latter must be sought in diffuse arguments that recur in the book. It appears in Dods's contention that 'The standards of architecture are made and maintained by the cultured minority . . . The public must learn to defer to the architect, and the architect must endeavour to be worthy of this deference.'[33] Desbrowe-Annear describes it thus: 'The dwellers in good houses well designed would then show that elastic ease of aristocratic well-being which should be the true heritage of all good Australians.'[34] And in Wilkinson's words, 'The value of simplicity has been urged and, were examples needed, there stand in all the older settlements and in Macquarie Street, Sydney, airy, roomy comfortable houses, full of dignity and tasteful charm.'[35]

This apparent consistency in outlook portrayed a history that had generally favoured primary production. The concerns of the architects writing in *Domestic Architecture* arose in a country heavily skewed towards mining, pastoralism and farming. The perfecting of refrigeration in the 1890s opened up British markets to Australian produce, a momentous event since meat and dairy products could be exported rather than having to be consumed locally, as only wool could previously survive sea journeys unpreserved. This spurred farming to diversify into herds and crops geared to English tables, and by Federation the products of mines, forests and farms made up the vast bulk of exports. In 1927–8 agricultural produce accounted for 83 per cent of exports, with wool alone comprising almost half the total value of goods sent abroad.[36] The country's reliance on trade can be gleaned from the proportion of two-way trade as a percentage of GDP. At Federation it was over 40 per cent, and even through the Depression years it averaged nearly 30 per cent. By comparison America's imports and exports in the 1930s averaged less than 10 per cent of GDP.[37]

In this context it is easy to see why the references in architecture continuously return to rural ideals. It was not simply a case of where money was to be made. Wealthy urban businessmen bought country properties in the 1920s because, in the words of economic historian Edward Shann: 'In the land hunger of successful Australians social ambition plays a part, as well as economic calculation; for socially "the hewers of wood and the drawers of water" . . . are respected as the most typical Australians and respect themselves in proportion as they remain independent of state subsidies.'[38]

It is curious that this ambition endured even as Australian cities, especially Sydney and Melbourne, grew to significant size and provided comprehensively urban experiences. The census of 1921 shows a metropolitan population of 900,000 in New South Wales, and 767,000 in Victoria, making up between 40 and 50 per cent of the total state population. The rest were divided between small towns and rural properties, which held about a third of the state's inhabitants. A picture thus emerges, despite popular images to the contrary, of an urban majority in all states except Tasmania. In occupation, too, primary producers on the land ceased to be a majority of workers for the first time, having been displaced by those in industry. Despite its poor performance in exports, small-scale industry had become the backbone of Australian domestic production by 1921, in a country largely urbanized.

In most respects this was a modern economy, with a small number of employers, three-quarters of breadwinners working for wages or salary, and a developed urban infrastructure with extensive tram networks and electricity and gas reticulation. Yet within this we find leading architects, all city-dwelling, extolling the virtues of a lifestyle and corresponding building styles that hanker for a lost simplicity. This is not unusual: indeed the measure of a country's modernity can often be gauged by the strength of its concomitant anti-modernity. The Arts and Crafts movement is one such example, and its adoption in Australia was for the same antagonistic tenets that it held towards progress in both Britain and the United States. The suburban house, too, rested on a view of the suburb as the antithesis of work or business, where the male breadwinner could find relief from the stresses and sparring of wills found in commercial life.

In short, the purpose of *Domestic Architecture in Australia* was to submit a bid for the leadership of Australian architecture by recognizing the aspirations of the bourgeoisie, a class marked by the alliance of its urban and rural constituents, cloaked in an inherited fondness for the trappings of a distant landed gentry. Farming or running cattle or sheep spoke of the nobility of primary production, coupled with the fortitude of a frontier colonial project that was well over by the 1920s. The business of the towns and cities, the buying and selling, had always been regarded with distrust by a rentier class, and this pejorative view of the city coloured the Australian outlook. Yet the claim of Wilson and his fellow authors was stunningly successful on the dynamic field of local cultural identity as it evolved within cities.

Of the book's authors, Desbrowe-Annear was perhaps the most eclectic, and his output most varied in style and reference. While the Chadwick House continues to define the turn-of-the-century Arts and Crafts Federation house, two of his works from the war years demonstrate his interest in the virtues of simplicity. 'Inglesby' (1915) and 'Broceliande' (1916) appeared to be proto-modern in their cubic massing and lack of adornment, but as his biographer Harriet Edquist has pointed out, the provenance for these houses was more likely Irving Gill's work in California of the same period,

First volume of *The Home* (February 1920), showing a new domestic ideal with Hardy Wilson's Eryldene as backdrop.

which attempted a reworking of Spanish Mission buildings through an Arts and Crafts sensibility. The result appears modern not only in formal terms, although Desbrowe-Annear returned to historicist styles in the 1920s with little apparent angst: in a more significant way it is modern in meeting changed social patterns. The overwhelming majority of Melbourne people who listed their occupation in the 1921 census as 'domestic' were women, but between 1911 and 1921 the actual number dropped despite

Victoria adding almost 20 per cent to its population.[39] In New South Wales the trend was less evident, but the decline of domestic servants and its portent of greater self-reliance in middle-class households was a clear sign of things to come. Of 'Inglesby', Desbrowe-Annear noted that the profusion of built-in furniture 'is without doubt more sanitary, leads to easier cleansing and makes the upkeep very much less than in an ordinary house'.[40]

Taken together with Dods's vision of houses sharing domestic servants, and Wilson's description of 'Purulia' as having 'the plan of a maidless flat', it seems that the speculation on the future that these architects had in common was prescient. They were not overly concerned with the passing of domestic servants. Indeed, Wilson tied it into the general tendency towards political equality:

Harold Desbrowe-Annear, Broceliande (also known as Troon), Melbourne, 1916.

> A study of the history of the kitchen in New South Wales from 1800 to the present day throws a clear light on the progress of

> humanity towards equality . . . Briefly told, the kitchen began its advance from beneath a detached roof at the rear of the house. First, it entered a wing facing a courtyard; then it slowly moved along the wing side by side with the struggle for political freedom. By the time all men were equal at the poll, the kitchen was separated from the parlour only by a narrow servery.[41]

There is no sense of nostalgia for the earlier arrangements. Instead Wilson imagines a future where the repose of the landed gentry is combined with the individualism of householders free of the obligations attaching to servants. In other words it is an aesthetic ideal that welcomes the freedom of modern men and women to be independent of social expectations, while immersing themselves in the texture of everyday life of the enlightened squatter.

This looking forwards and backwards, so much part of the post-Edwardian shock administered by the First World War and its aftermath, drew the attention of the generation maturing in the 1920s. Leslie Wilkinson could hardly have chosen more fertile ground for his Mediterranean-inspired reveries. As he took the helm of the new course at the University of Sydney, the native-born students who enrolled took advantage of full-time study in an intellectual setting to formulate a very different view from the office-trained architects of the previous generation. They were free to consider architecture as shaped by exigency and aspirations, as opposed to the practical art that formed the basis of articled instruction.

This is not to say that previous generations in Australia had been loose in their ideological framing of their work. Clearly this was not true for Hardy Wilson, or for Dods, but they were unusual in their quest for consistency. For most architects the sentimental associations that attached to various styles, complex as they might be, were historically constituted. As professionals they were the medium, through their understanding of the conventions of each style, by which the various conventions were reproduced, and perhaps recombined. With the advent of university education, the process was reversed: cosmologies, ideologically constituted, could be transformed into architecture.

Wilkinson fostered this process with his academic understanding of the elements of architecture. His students, in the early 1920s, could gain a classical education as well as a technical one in the Bachelor of Architecture. The course was unique at the time of founding: the University of Melbourne followed with its own Bachelor degree in 1927. Wilkinson, as the first professor in the field in Australia, set about demonstrating his preferences in his own house in 1923. Named for the colonial architect Francis Greenway, author of the buildings so admired by Wilson, 'Greenway' showed a development of local taste that eschewed the verandah, long a staple of Australian domestic building. Instead Wilkinson proposed two-storey buildings, carefully oriented, as being more apt for Australian conditions, since the verandah made the control of light into the interior difficult. Like Wilson, Wilkinson judged his window sizes astutely, so the interiors received both direct shafts of sun as well as reflected or diffused light. He added shutters for versatility and texture, and colonnaded wings or loggias to provide areas of undercroft. Supplemented with pergolas and profuse native planting, 'Greenway' and its successors quickly established a benchmark for ensembles of house and garden that made clear reference to colonial Georgian, Italian and English precedents, but in a manner that evoked just the right level of class aspiration. The house itself is never

Leslie Wilkinson, Greenway, Sydney, 1923.

Waterhouse & Lake, Ailsa, rear view at completion, Sydney.

dominant, but forms part of a walled precinct with added wings and free-standing arches and pillars in the garden. The result was finely balanced and its charm freed it from the polemical frugality of Wilson's earlier Purulia. Located in Sydney's Eastern Suburbs, with filtered views to the harbour, Greenway created a continuing demand for Wilkinson's designs among professionals and business owners of the area.

The bid for national architectural leadership could have come from other quarters. In Sydney's desirable suburbs Waterhouse and Lake had built a number of steep-pitch roofed houses that were cohesively massed in the American-sourced Shingle Style, as opposed to the additive roof forms of the Queen Anne-derived Federation style. Though much admired, their perceived opulence may have negated their wide appeal for a democratic age. The style had been championed by Horbury Hunt in the late nineteenth century, but its American roots also diminished its credentials in an age of rising nationalism. The California bungalow, too, was a form with great currency, and many superb versions were built in Sydney and Melbourne. Alexander Stewart Jolly produced a variant in Sydney that emphasized rough-hewn timbers, notably shown in the house 'Belvedere' in Cremorne. The climatic relevance of the style was not lost on Australians, who regarded California as a historical parallel in its quest for an appropriate architecture. In Footscray, Melbourne, Schreiber & Jörgensen designed 'Pebbles', a studied version of a California bungalow true to the work of Greene and Greene. Despite proving popular in Australia, the style ultimately lacked the historical resonance championed by Wilson, Bagot and Dods.

Rural Ideals, Urban Realities

The issue of cultural identity, especially as portrayed in the arts, proved to be persistently slippery. The cities, despite their constant growth and adoption of modern infrastructure, struggled to aestheticize their form and lived experience. The dystopian visions of an industrial proletariat subjugated and restive, such as haunted Europe, found little purchase in a country where organized labour not only bargained for better wages and conditions but could be elected to govern. Despite the rise in numbers of Australian industrial workers, the country had yet to industrialize at scale by Federation. Steel was largely imported until the opening of new steelworks in Newcastle in 1915. All large plant was imported, as were the components for the country's power stations. Thus the economy was enmeshed in international trade through its primary exports of minerals and farm products, and its imports of plant and machinery. Protectionism was a dominant political issue: whether to charge tariffs on imports to

Schreiber & Jörgensen, Pebbles, Melbourne, 1920.

keep local production, with its high wages, competitive, or to allow free trade and drive down the cost of living through cheap imports. Indeed in the election for the first national parliament the two main parties were distinguished by their opposing views on the matter.

With the consolidation of pastoral holdings, the number of rural workers began to fall from 1910. The trade of the pastoral contractor, shearer or stockman was ever more distant from the average city worker and dweller. The numerical weight in architecture was with city buildings, in both ambition and value, even as the architectural profession lauded an ideal evident in but a handful of structures, and hardly engaged with Australian cities as they were. In this context the Griffins, ever watchful for architectural opportunities, sought to turn their hands to creating utopian communities. After a visit to America in late 1924, they returned not to Melbourne but to Sydney, to live in a model community they designed and founded at Castlecrag, overlooking the reaches of Middle Harbour. Disillusioned with the self-interested politics he had been subjected to in his Canberra work, Griffin and his wife sought a new start despite having recently completed the Capitol Theatre to wide acclaim. In anticipation of this move, the Greater Sydney Development Association had been formed in 1920 with Griffin at the helm, with the intention of buying and developing a new suburb. The present suburb of Castlecrag is a portion of the original 263 hectares purchased, and its street layout and topography were planned as the antithesis of the gridded suburbs appearing elsewhere. The first lots were sold in late 1921, with modest houses appearing in the following year.[42]

It is a challenging site, dropping steeply to the water, and accessed through one feeder road. Here the Griffins carved secondary roads through the local sandstone, which appears as remnant projections and features. It was intended as an alternative community in outlook as well as in form, and they drew around them a coterie of nonconformists and the spiritually inclined. They designed and built fifteen houses consistent with their overall vision for the project, as well as approving designs by others. Many of the early houses are modest, marked by heavy stonework inset with geometrically ornate windows. The crystalline iconography of the Capitol Theatre is continued in more muted form, as a broad symbol for the rational structure inherent in nature as a manifestation of the divine. This belief took an unconventional turn in 1926, when the Griffins began their association with the Theosophical Society. Founded in New York in 1875, but subsequently headquartered in India, the Society in Australia was reinvigorated in 1926 by the arrival of George Sydney Arundale. The group served as a way for the Griffins to meet a genteel clientele also at odds with contemporary Australia, but it was too hierarchical for their tastes and by 1929 they had become interested in anthroposophy as espoused by Rudolf Steiner. While these affiliations are hard to trace in their built work –indeed it has been argued that they largely continued on a path set in train by Sullivan and Wright – they are symptomatic of the gap between the expectations the Griffins held when entering the Canberra competition and the sometimes-venal reality of the Australia they encountered in the early decades of the twentieth century.[43]

The urban experience of the time was bound up with reformers who aimed to improve living conditions through planning, broadly understood. Speculative building was producing shoddy semi-detached houses, and the growing numbers of the urban poor were seen as an embarrassment, at best, to nationalist unity. The European and American movements advocating planning in advance of speculative development were known through the study tours of Robert Irvine of the University of Sydney in 1912, and

Walter Burley Griffin, Cheong House, Sydney, 1924.

the Melbourne architect J. C. Morell three years later.[44] When the Town Planning Association of New South Wales was formed at a public meeting in 1913, there were noted architects, politicians and administrators present, as well as the developer Richard Stanton, later responsible for some of Sydney's most ambitious and stylistically cohesive suburbs. Also present were Florence and George Taylor, publishers of *Building* magazine, which zealously chronicled the building industry for nearly half a century.[45] George died in 1928, but Florence continued writing and publishing into the 1950s.

Florence Taylor had served her articles and completed the architecture course at the Sydney Technical College in 1904. Unsuccessful in her bid to become a member of the New South Wales Institute of Architects, she turned to publishing as an outlet for her interest in the building industry in all its facets. With no family loyalty to either pastoralists or urban money, she had a natural inclination to value personal endeavour and freedom above all else. The Taylors travelled extensively and were particularly taken by the energy and industry of New York. They were active in the town planning movement as part of a general enthusiasm for city development, generally following City Beautiful ideals. Initially supportive of the Griffins, the couples soon fell out, with the Taylors finding the Griffins' transcendent idealism far removed from their own pragmatic, conservative views on politics and the working class. The Taylors espoused a form of paternalistic development, advocating for the poor to be rehoused in suburbs where the Victorian city's unpredictable mix of density and poverty could be denatured through sun, air, stronger family relations and an ethic of self-improvement.

What the Taylors had in common with Wilkinson and Wilson was an abhorrence of the ideas that rode on the news of the Russian Revolution. While workers had been organizing in Australia since the 1860s, the notion of a complete overthrow of existing institutions was anathema to a society where labour fought for greater personal and economic freedom. The existence of an urban proletariat with no options but violent revolution seemed exotic, and it was argued that it could be warded off locally through the orderly improvement of working-class life. When the term 'Bolshevistic' is used in *Domestic Architecture*, it is taken to mean anarchistic and without internal coherence. The Taylors, however, understood more clearly its implications, and the threat it implied produced more than one piece of wild invective, and plenty of planning proposals.[46]

Their travels fed their predilections in favour of capital, which they made explicit, as well as for futuristic schemes that would cater to the growing urban populations in Australia. They had a keen feel for progress as expressed in figures, and their championing of engineering as the key to urban development is in marked contrast to the debate over stylistic appropriateness that occupied many of their contemporaries. In 1924 they published proposals for an elevated rapid transport system designed by engineer R. C. Lafferty, following on his similar ideas to relieve traffic congestion in his home city of New York. While this earlier scheme was given serious consideration, in Sydney his ideas gained little traction despite the pages devoted to them by the Taylors. But their anticipation of the fate of the scheme is already clear in their view that the aldermen of Sydney were more interested in personal rivalries than the future of the city, coupled with a failure to grasp 'the courage and foresight of the schemes put forward by private enterprise, which can always be relied upon to cope with every situation, if allowed to do so'.[47]

The picture that emerges from *Building* magazine stands in sharp contrast to that presented by leading architects. The Taylors were representative of another stance, one that was pro-development, with the logistical problems of Australian cities superseding those of identity. Their inclinations were revivalist, but imbued with advanced engineering. This was a distinctly urban view, based on the evident and dramatic development of Sydney and Melbourne to the mid-1920s. Even the war had not dented this growth, since trans-Pacific shipping and trade continued away from the European and Middle Eastern theatre of war. The dynamic is instructive here: the Taylors proved astute in their interpretation of the direction the new nation was taking. In reading its aspirations as symbolically framed, they took exception to visions that upset the status quo. As in other dynamics evident in Australian architecture of the 1920s – the quest for simplicity in the face of unprecedented change, the varied reception afforded the Griffins, and the formulation of a historically constituted identity – their stance was to reappear through the twentieth century.

City buildings also exhibited this technical progress sheathed in tradition and would continue to do so for at least a decade. The Commonwealth Bank in Sydney opened in 1916, with an ornate banking chamber spanned by a two-way beam system, supported on Ionic columns. The bank had been founded by an Act of government in 1911, to provide banking services in competition to the private institutions. The swastika symbols that decorated the floors had not yet attained their menace (they were understood as 'Grecian'), but as a bank of the people it could not be distinguished from the classicist aspirations of its competitors.[48] Dominating Sydney's financial precinct of Martin Place, the building drew large crowds to its opening in the midst of war. Its division into four sections through varying degrees of surface ornament and rustication hides one of Sydney's earliest complete steel building frames. The bank presented an image of conservative stability

CATHEDRAL
· ARCADE ·
Police

at street level through ornate polished stone facings and classical details. The upper floors become progressively less ornate, but the large surmounting cornice reinforces the solidity laid down at entry level. The architect, John Kirkpatrick, was responsible for all the bank's buildings in its initial years. He was also, not coincidentally, the cousin of its first governor, Denison Miller.[49]

The 1920s saw little change in the conservative nature of commercial architecture. In 1926 the Harry Norris-designed Nicholas Building opened on Melbourne's Swanston Street. A Classical Revival building with a seductive retail arcade at ground level and offices above, its distinctly trabeated form still hewed to the conventions of the previous century. The building is noteworthy for its facing in terracotta, in order to keep its appearance fresh as a commercial imperative. Norris was very productive and he worked across a number of styles, but his commercial acuity recognized the value of prevailing conventions in attracting custom. The same was noted of the 1929 design for the Commonwealth Bank in Brisbane, designed to 'inspire their clients and the public at large with confidence in the stability and dignity of their operations'.[50] The treatment of the bank followed a reductive interpretation of Neoclassical conventions, and the architects of the Commonwealth Department of Works and Railways were commended on their restraint. The plea for an architecture that favoured careful proportions over exuberant details seemed, by 1930, to be gaining adherents.

Nonetheless the examples cited above were all undertaken with due regard to convention and the wider association of classicism with commercial stability to the lay observer. Alternative approaches were known through publications and travel, but they had not yet been accepted in the commercial realm. Indeed even the conservative *Building* broached the issue of the advent of European modernism, and in 1928 Florence Taylor editorialized extensively on 'Modern Architectural Development: Tradition or Vision'.[51] While admiring the American propensity to build higher and bigger, she saw this as an extension of that country's capacity to marshal large sums of capital in the continuing dance of progress and capital circulation and accumulation, for 'in no part of the world do we find such freedom from fetters as in this modern country [America] . . . where difficulties are welcomed as problems to master, and not accepted helplessly as retardations to progress'. Le Corbusier is mentioned for his polemic *Towards a New Architecture*, but the judgement is not sympathetic, with the 'ultra-modern' homes designed by European modernists described as frightful, since they dispense with homeliness and the astute selection of historic styles that signifies good taste. Related terms – futurism, cubism, modernistic art – are described as 'esoteric commonplaces'.

Harry Norris, Nicholas Building: interior arcade, 1925–6.

With a sharp eye for ideology, Taylor observes that 'the doctrine of the Socialist is observed clearly enough through the eccentric veneer of Modernist design, which claims to ignore art as a luxury, and beauty as an accessory of the old regime'.[52]

Thus towards the close of the 1920s there is little resistance to progress per se, understandable in a country acutely aware of its geographic remoteness from markets as they were in 1900, and one in which labour had been valued for its relative scarcity. For architects like Wilson this trend could be met through a simplicity in living, and his outlook would sooner embrace an Australia where Chinese and Indian traditions and structures could dominate, rather than one despoiled by the grasp of mercantile capital, let alone industrialization. For the Griffins Australia remained an ideal, its transcendental possibilities resting on its early move to political equality, but undercut by the crudeness of its political institutions. For Florence Taylor the future of the country lay in the embrace of growth and technical invention, but the symbolic necessity of remaining true to English roots precluded either the carving out of new hybrid styles or the adoption of exotic ones. The issue of climatic suitability, in this view, hardly mattered in a vision where domestic convenience would be met mechanically.

In this the Griffins, Wilson and the Taylors represent three parallel streams that have been constants in modern Australian design, in varying proportions. Each is founded on a paradox, which the overarching project of nationhood distorted. The first stream, typified by Wilson, is that of the nativist, a position that emerged surprisingly early and shows the quick remaking of English social conventions within a generation of colonial founding. As it matured it viewed the experience of Australia as unremarkable, but its paradox lay in seeking validation of the local through news and comparisons from beyond its borders. The second stream is that of the globalist, in modern terms, whose loyalty is to the most advanced experiences available, regardless of provenance. This had its roots in the concept of Empire, where loyalties have a transnational character, and it seeks validation in good sense. It was broadly the outlook of the Taylors. The paradox here is that this imperial vision must be realized locally, a source of some frustration.

The third stream is that of the immigrant or outsider, like the Griffins. This view continually sees Australia afresh, adding its interpretation at the same time as it accepts the limited appeal of this material to the historical flow it attempts to join. This stream has added enormous interest to the country, but its products serve as a repository of possibilities, rather than viable broad alternatives. Put another way, the immigrant view is of interest if it represents something unique, or a deeply informed architecture, but its assimilation into the dominant strands of architectural thinking depend on what resonance it has to their particular aspiration. The immigrant practises, unsurprisingly, at the pleasure of prevailing interests. How the balance of these forces played out in the 1930s reflected both declining immigrant numbers and a new confidence in a generation for whom Australia was a domicile and not an adjunct of empire.

chapter two

Harsh Lessons and their Effects, 1930–45

> The architects' suggestion is only a palliative: the only way to deal with any incurable disease is not to treat it, though some attention may be necessary, but to prevent its occurrence altogether. This, in the case of slum dwellers, can be accomplished by the Government passing an Act of Parliament to prevent the criminally intent, the habitual drunkard, the mentally deficient and the diseased element in our community from propagating their kind by sterilisation, for this is the element that creates our slum and underworld areas.[1]

There is much to dislike in the pronouncements made by architects and their fellow professionals in the interwar period. The concept of nation, with its striving for a homogeneous identity clothed in physical ideals, produced its own absurdities. Once again it was Hardy Wilson who gave voice to these tendencies, his admiration for the pre-modern artworks of the East offset by his obsession with the role of Jews in contemporary society. His ideas are more complex than simple prejudice will allow, but his proposed creation of an Eastern Jewish Republic of New Guinea underlines the tactic of unity through exclusion. The issue arose not only in relation to race: the respected John Sulman was seduced by the arguments of eugenics, in a prejudice born as much of class as of culture. His call in 1921 for the segregation and control of the mentally unfit, as identified by experts awake to the subtle social camouflage of the high-class moron, finds resonance in his planning proposals that advocate for a population derived from the fittest individuals as concomitant to the tenets of the City Beautiful movement.[2] Folded within these views was the long-running distrust of Irish nationalist sympathies from the early days of the colonies, manifest as an occasional suspicion of Catholic motives by the Anglican establishment.

The issues were sharpened by the decline in the 1920s of the economic base that had sustained Australia since the late nineteenth century. Its death knell was the advent of the Depression in 1929, which revealed how exposed the country was to the withdrawal of foreign capital in an economic downturn. The roots of the new industrial era had been laid down some years before. The Broken Hill Proprietary Company, or BHP, had commenced mining in western New South Wales in 1885. It expanded

C. Bruce Dellit, ANZAC Memorial set within Hyde Park, Sydney, 1929–34.

into steelmaking in 1915, opening large-scale steelworks in Newcastle. Emblematic of a new phase of Australian capital development and accumulation, it commenced operations with a workforce of 1,450, but struggled for a decade to become profitable. By 1935 it had absorbed its main rival, Australian Iron and Steel, whose works were situated at Port Kembla near Wollongong.[3] The general manager at BHP from 1921 was Essington Lewis, a key figure in the development of Australian industry who subsequently directed the manufacture of munitions and aircraft nationwide in the Second World War. Conservative, anti-union and a rationalist in organizing production, he represented the forces of manufacturing modernity that diversified the Australian economy, and ushered in a new identity that was urban-based and conducive to the class consciousness fostered by modern industrialism.[4]

BHP was not the only large vehicle of this transformation. The Melbourne group Collins House mined, refined and worked zinc and copper, and later dominated paper production. It became another example of a large Australian enterprise as a joint venture with foreign capital, rather than an overseas arm of a British-domiciled company. The interwar period also saw the rise of local car manufacturing to avoid import tariffs, with Ford and General Motors both having large Australian plants by 1930. In their wake came a slew of smaller suppliers of tyres and car parts, in parallel with glass, drug and paper manufacturing. With the expansion of electricity generation, the city slowly began to match the countryside in economic importance and as the locus of national self-conception.

War Memorials and Architectural Self-image

The First World War also played its part in forming the idea of modern Australia. As a British Dominion, the country followed Britain into conflict with Germany and the Ottoman Empire in 1914. Initial enthusiasm for the war was dampened by the losses suffered by Australian troops in the larger campaigns of Gallipoli and the Western Front: nonetheless by the war's end more than 416,000 Australians had enlisted. Of these 60,000 died, and 156,000 were wounded or captured. Thus at least half of the Australian Imperial Force were either buried in Europe or the Middle East, or returned home bearing some scars from the conflict. The effects of the war were not often appreciated on repatriation, and cases of quiet despair among those who had served were common. The conversion of the horror of the war into part of nationalist mythology would take some years, and 25 April became a public holiday, ANZAC Day, 'state by state between 1923 and 1926'.[5]

The wartime losses in France had been a harsh way to lend a sombre gravity to the idea of nationhood, but they had been partly offset by the remarkable success enjoyed by Australian troops and their commanders, notably John Monash, in the last months of the war. Following the formal declaration of ANZAC Day, the desire to memorialize the war as the defining episode of identity forged through sacrifice gained traction, with each city creating its own shrine to the martial tradition that emerged. The iconography, secular in intent, became markedly pagan, drawing from classical ideals in both building form and racial sentiment. In Sydney this caused some resentment, soon directed at C. Bruce Dellit's design for the memorial to the fallen of the Australian Imperial Force. Won by competition in 1929, the ANZAC Memorial, named for the combined Australian and New Zealand Army Corps, illustrates the difficulty of settling on a single architectural expression that embodies collective values in memorializing such seminal events.

The stories of these monuments – each city and town proposed one – embody key sentiments pertaining not only to the war itself, but to its aftermath and its symbolic incorporation into public life. The push to memorialize both the dead and the living Australians who had played their part in the war began even before the war concluded, with the correspondent and historian Charles Bean agitating for an Australian War Museum in 1917. Bean would play a major role in the building of the Canberra War Memorial, but each city would memorialize events in its own way, and in its own time. Often this process proved fractious and lengthy, with buildings taking years to reach fruition.

The stumbling blocks to memorialization included differing views of how the dead should be remembered and honoured, how the returned servicemen and women should be aided, and where the funds should come from. The Sydney memorial was preceded by a simple cenotaph in Martin Place, the street abutting the central Post Office, which served as Sydney's symbolic heart and had become the scene of commemorative rallies. But the modesty of the cenotaph could not reflect the immensity of the war experience, and social activist and returned services supporter Dr Mary Booth urged for the provision of a worthy monument that was symbolic, rather than one that served as headquarters for the Returned Services League. Aware that Melbourne was embarking on its own shrine of remembrance – the religious term weighed heavily on the genesis of both buildings – the trustees of the ANZAC Memorial decided on a site in Sydney's central Hyde Park. Its formal axis already boasted a new fountain commissioned from a bequest by J. F. Archibald, former editor of *The Bulletin*, intended to symbolize the bonds between Australia and France.

The unveiling of the Martin Place cenotaph had exposed deep resentment towards the Labor premier of New South Wales Jack Lang, whose own stance (and that of his party) had been generally pacifist and against conscription during the war. This had ensured that the Australian forces abroad had consisted of volunteers, but there persisted a feeling that this was an abrogation of imperial obligations and that it had made things harder than they should have been.[6] By 1929 even Lang was in favour of the new Memorial, to be paid for from donations raised between 1916 and 1919. The competition was open to British subjects in Australia, as well as natives abroad, and was assessed by Leslie Wilkinson, Professor in Architecture at Sydney University, and his fellow academic Alfred Hook. E. J. Payne represented the funding bodies. In the judging Wilkinson inclined towards the circle of columns supporting an entablature proposed by John D. Moore, but he was outvoted in favour of C. Bruce Dellit's entry. This design has been lauded as an early and adept example of Australian Art Deco, following on the seminal 1925 exhibition in Paris that popularized both the term and its stylistic components. In the ANZAC Memorial, however, Dellit argued that classical precedents would detract from the contemplation of the recent events if they were remembered through evoking ancient Greece and Rome, a radical view in 1930 given the pervasiveness of classical references in memorials of the late nineteenth century.[7]

When built, Dellit's ANZAC Memorial owed much of its power to the incorporation, from the outset, of sculptures executed in the workshop of Rayner Hoff. The English-born Hoff had moved to Sydney in 1923 and had already proved his ability to execute memorial works through his sculptures for the South Australian National War Memorial in Adelaide (1931), working with the architect Louis Laybourne Smith. The sentiment against classical forms had produced, in short time, two tendencies that are part of modern architecture in the broadest sense: an incorporation of machine motifs and a valorization of the primitive. The former can be seen in the stylized representations provided by Hoff, who had seen service in France from 1915 and retained strong anti-war feelings. In the Sydney Memorial numerous bas-relief scenes adorn the interior and exterior, as well as sixteen seated and four standing figures arranged around the exterior. Within the building the centrepiece consists of a group in bronze composed of a soldier, naked in death, lying on a shield supported by three women. Missing from the original conception are two groups to the east and west of the building, titled 'Victory after Sacrifice' and 'Crucifixion of Civilization'. Photographs of the initial plaster models for these sculptures appeared in local newspapers. 'Crucifixion of Civilization' drew sharp criticism for its appropriation of Christian iconography, as the crucified figure representing Adolescent Peace was female and naked, dying atop figures broken in battle.[8] The objection exposed the schism between Catholic and Protestant clergy in Sydney, with Dr Michael Sheehan stating that the memorial was 'intended only for Protestants' and he would boycott the laying of the foundation stone.[9] The trustees responded by eliminating both groups of sculptures in an attempt to restore the memorial to a position of non-sectarian significance, aided by objections to the works by Protestant clergy as well. While the realism of these sculptures may have stoked negative sentiments, the angular and massive figures of fliers, soldiers, sailors and nurses reveal the infusion of a mechanized angularity, evident also in the English Vorticist movement of the war years.

The building itself is a complementary ground for the art. The stepped roof and the massive pilasters are pointedly generic in their evocation of monumentality, while the interior uses the dome to create a central, sombre focus. This searching for historically resonant forms that were not allied to prevailing revivals, either classical or Gothic, is a key development in Australia from about 1930 and would play out over the following decade.

School of Rayner Hoff, ANZAC Memorial sculptures of serving men and women, Sydney, 1929–34.

It indicates an awareness of events overseas and the specific reception they received in the Antipodes: the resemblance of Dellit's design to Goodhue's fourth-placed entry for the design of the Liberty Memorial in Kansas City has not gone unnoticed.[10] The 1921 American competition also resulted in the well-known building designed by Harold Van Buren Magonigle, whose ambition and break with classicizing models received extensive praise when completed in 1926.

The swiftness of this shift in sentiment in Australia can be discerned in the design chosen for the Melbourne Shrine of Remembrance, which opened some two weeks before the Sydney Memorial. Perhaps as a final gesture to Melbourne's impending displacement as the seat of national government, the Shrine of Remembrance is a more imposing affair than any other monument to the war nationally, although the Canberra one is larger. Its competition was held in 1923, and the chair of the assessment panel was Sir John Monash, whose national popularity as a wartime leader remained unique. The architects, Phillip Hudson and James Wardrop, were returned servicemen, and the whole process was shepherded by Monash using his influence and his assertion that the 'Australian Army Corps was the most formidable instrument of war that any war has produced'.[11] Monash's tendency to aggrandize notwithstanding, the sentiment has some basis in fact. His clear-eyed biographer Geoffrey Serle writes that from August to September 1918 the Australian Imperial Force under Monash, acting as spearhead for the British Army, yielded a series of victories 'unsurpassed in the annals of the British army'.[12] These events served as a more comforting source of national mythology, redeeming the disaster of the invasion by British and ANZAC forces at Gallipoli in 1915.

The design for the Shrine of Remembrance was predominantly classical, surmounted by a distinctive pyramidal roof, and its placement as an extension of the axis of St Kilda Road gives it a prominence in Melbourne's visual lexicon that is greater than its Sydney counterpart. While both buildings terminate an axial view, the Sydney one is restricted to the formal setting of Hyde Park. The Melbourne Shrine also sits atop a large stepped base, and the rising approach to the Shrine plays out over several hundred metres. Set in the gardens of Melbourne's cultural precinct south of the Yarra River, its forecourt serves as the focus for thousands of attendees on ANZAC Day. While its central hall is small and focused to the heavens, its large base has been converted to a crypt museum. Perhaps more than its Sydney counterpart it shows the effort expended by the architects to create a sacred space from secular precedents, not quite shorn of their pre-Christian overtones.

Monash died in 1931, three years before the dedication, but his influence remains in the support he garnered for the project, and his collaboration

Phillip Hudson and James Wardrop, Shrine of Remembrance, Melbourne, 1927–34.

in writing the inscription. Despite the building design generating less criticism than in Sydney, its opening was even more fractious. Catholics, Protestants and the leftist All-Australia Congress Against War all had their respective ceremonies, and there were those who still asserted that the money would be better spent supporting war widows and their kin.[13]

By contrast, the Brisbane Shrine of Remembrance was more modest and had stricter classical roots. Designed by Buchanan & Cowper, it was based on the Tholos at Epidauros, comprising a circle of columns supporting an engraved entablature. A Lamp of Remembrance was included at its centre, inspired by Stafford Buchanan's earlier visit to the Tomb of the Unknown Soldier in Brussels. The overt classicism of the design proved no impediment to its adoption in Brisbane, despite the rejection of a similar scheme in the Sydney competition in favour of Dellit's more diffuse symbolism.

The monument that took the longest to reach fruition was the Australian War Memorial in Canberra, which originated in the lobbying of Charles

Bean. The war correspondent's commitment to the project persisted to its dedication in 1941. The competition for the building called for a memorial, museum and secular shrine with a Hall of Memory. The requirement to have all the names of the dead inscribed in the building proved difficult, since it required a vast Hall of Memory, and the final design has the names extending into cloisters flanking a central court. The building is the work of two designers who were asked to amalgamate the best aspects of their respective competition entries. Public works architect John Crust had proposed the cloisters, while Emil Sodersten, a contemporary of Dellit's, had exhibited a better grasp of the conventions of memorial architecture as they developed in the 1920s and '30s. Again the reference was to the American memorial in Kansas City, and in his competition design Sodersten incorporated the towering shaft of the newly built Magonigle scheme in Kansas City. The collaboration with Crust deleted the shaft, but retained the cloisters and emerged with a compact Hall of Memory, its ambience (as in Sydney and Melbourne) intended to be that of a secular chapel. When opened in 1941 the building was still incomplete, the Hall simply a shell and the names of the dead yet to be inscribed in the cloisters. Only the lower galleries functioned as intended, filled with exhibits and memorabilia to convey the experiences of men and women on active service.

Buchanan & Cowper, Shrine of Remembrance, Brisbane, 1930.

John Crust and Emil Sodersten, Australian War Memorial, Canberra, 1927–41. Looking towards the Hall of Memory, with flanking cloisters holding the Roll of Honour of Australians killed on active duty.

These memorials were key in thrusting the symbolic function of architecture into the public purview, particularly in how they generated non-sectarian, indeed pagan, sacred spaces and iconography. This was the essence of the strong reaction by Catholic clergy to the proposed sculptures in Sydney and the attempts to hold separate dedications. The fractures in Australian identity were still keen, with Irish sectarian sympathies and a distrust of English imperial motives present in the Catholic community. In Melbourne the popularity of Monash, a secular Jew, helped diffuse these sentiments, but the claims on the significance of the war dead remained divisive.

Shifts in Commercial and City Buildings

The importance of Art Deco in Australia has been played down in favour of the later, polemical, modernisms that emerged. However its rise and popularity holds more significance than has been credited.[14] There was never any doubt about its derivative or synthetic nature, as opposed to the arguments of historical resonance accorded the Georgian revival by Hardy Wilson, but the popularity of Deco across all emotional registers, from the frivolous to the sacred, bears comment. It is testimony to the widespread experience of change in the texture of everyday life in the 1920s and '30s, one extensive enough that a new mode of architecture followed rather than led broader aesthetic tastes. While the motifs of Deco – its references to non-Christian societies, combined with machine-derived forms – were fed by popular images of industrial production and archaeological discoveries, the simple desire to replace the ornate classical facades of city buildings with something more up-to-date played its role. The use of an academic knowledge of the orders of classical architecture to indicate social distinction was in decline, and the city centres showed that capital itself, increasingly unsentimental, was open to newer forms of representation.

The banks continued to lean to the classical, but through building large trabeated structures that slowly came to terms with the physical scale of new city buildings. In Sydney several large banks were completed before the onset of the Depression in 1929, notably the Commercial Banking Company on George Street at the intersection with Martin Place (Kent & Massie, 1925), and the imposing Commonwealth Savings Bank fronting Martin Place itself, as the thoroughfare emerged as Sydney's financial heart (Ross & Rowe, 1928). The former shows the effort made to clothe steel-framed structures in the garb of the Renaissance palazzo, with polished stone facings at ground level, and engaged Ionic columns giving way to sandstone cladding at the upper levels.

The Commonwealth Savings Bank, by contrast, is tripartite composition writ large, its overscaled Ionic columns on a granite base surmounted by an entablature reiterating the credentials of the classical orders as ciphers of stability. It eschews the palazzo model of urban buildings and adopts instead the credentials of the temple for its most public facade. Yet its monumentality through overscaling is unusual among city buildings of the time, since the demands of building on urban sites of uneven dimensions encouraged looser compositions and cladding designs that sacrificed less of the usable floor area to deep facade modelling.

The establishment of university courses in architecture through this period did not, of themselves, usher in an era of progressive sentiments. At the University of Sydney Wilkinson reiterated the advantages of a traditional education and his hand in competition judging was conservative, though not dogmatic. In Melbourne the Atelier established in 1919 served to enhance students' architectural designs after they had completed their articles, but by 1929 it had formalized this process in awarding a diploma, as well as disseminating ideas in contemporary design following director Leighton Irwin's travels in Europe. These changes did provide a small number of architects the opportunity to view design as a form of intellectual leadership. While this had always been an aspect of professional life, it assumed greater significance when allied to the philosophical ambitions of the universities.

These effects were not fully evident for some years, but when Bruce Dellit in 1934 earnestly asked, 'Why then should not the men of modernity, already enriched by the masterpieces of creative thought of past ages, go to work in a healthy way in sympathy with scientific progress . . . and by the aid of modern science reach beyond our present dreams to artistic creations as yet undreamt of', he was simply voicing an inevitability.[15] The shift to modern architecture is as significant in Australia as anywhere else, but the impression of the radical superseding of an ailing tradition by a fresh approach is overly simplistic. There was, in Australia, little avant-gardism in the political sense. Modern design, architecture included, was seen as modish, its practice championed by an upper-middle-class intelligentsia with little enthusiasm for radical reform. This reflected English practice as well, which viewed events in Europe with some alarm and discerned, quite

Ross & Rowe, Commonwealth Savings Bank: facade to Martin Place, Sydney, 1928.

THE COMMERCIAL BANKING COMPANY OF SYDNEY LIMITED
BURBERRY
Sydney CBD

accurately, the degree to which seminal European modernists like Mies van der Rohe had allied themselves with revolutionary sentiments, if not movements. In David Dean's pithy summary of the English scene, 'emancipated in sober truth from what ordinary people thought of as homely and comfy, modern man saw himself keen-eyed, progressive, a natural leader'.[16]

The period from 1925 to 1935 also reveals some of the dilemmas that had dogged the interpretation of Australian architecture of the period. Once architecture self-consciously assumed a historical role in national leadership, the balancing act commenced whereby avant-garde practices were subsumed into a movement to advance the country technically, while also ameliorating working-class conditions to ward off radical political proposals. Political ideas circulated easily – in a country with strong labour movements of many hues, on any Sunday morning in its large cities one could hear a soapbox orator call for revolution.

Nonetheless, on the eve of the Great Depression there was considerable optimism in the Australian building industry, typified by the new mixed-use city buildings that were designed in the period, though not always completed. Two representative examples are the Grace Bros building commanding a large corner site in downtown Sydney (D. T. Morrow & Gordon, 1930), and the Manchester Unity Building on Melbourne's prominent intersection of Swanston and Collins Streets, designed by Marcus Barlow and completed in 1932. The buildings were designed in the Gothic Revival style, a reworking of the revival of the nineteenth century but applied to large commercial structures. The irony of a style initially vaunted for its integrity and spiritual resonance being adopted for rentable retail and office space went unremarked, and was met with some enthusiasm by critics keen to see the revival styles undergo one further round of validation. The models for the Grace Building were openly acknowledged, its debt to Cass Gilbert's 1912 Woolworth Building in New York, and the winning entry for the 1922 *Chicago Tribune* competition by Raymond Hood and John Mead Howells being duly noted.[17] Both buildings have corners featuring stepped and buttressed towers, a Gothic conceit that nonetheless solves the problem of giving a strong identity to structures that are composed of heavily fluted repetitive bays. The Melbourne example is the more elegant in proportion and retains a seductive decorated arcade, but despite their success as distinctive and popular urban landmarks the style flowered only briefly. These buildings missed the appeal of Art Deco and lacked the exoticism that was attached to Egyptianate or Pre-Columbian architectural details and massing.

Kent & Massie, Commercial Banking Company, Sydney, 1920–25.

The onset of the Depression saw new building volumes fall dramatically across Australia. The two sectors that weathered the downturn best were retail, which enjoyed continuing cash flow through staple goods and

D. T. Morrow & Gordon, Grace Building, Sydney, 1930.

Opposite: Marcus Barlow, Manchester Unity, Melbourne, 1929–32.

KEEP
LEFT

clothing, and the life insurance sector. Harry Norris's work for the retailer Coles in Melbourne spanned the 1920s and '30s and revealed the eclectic tastes that the era embraced. Norris travelled at regular intervals to absorb trends in international design, and like many of his generation he drew inspiration from events in the United States. The highly malleable tenets of Deco appealed to Norris, and the progression of his work from Spanish Colonial-themed, as in the slender and romanticized Majorca House (1928) in central Melbourne, through the decoratively arched and fluted G. J. Coles store of similar date, to the more distinctly modernist influence in his later work is a reminder that not all architects of the time aspired to stylistic integrity. Indeed in the early 1930s the sheer diversity of work is bound only by its supersession of nineteenth-century revivalisms.

This soft modernism was led not by a polemical commitment, but by the continuing desire to remain relevant and informed in the outpost of European modernity that was Australia. The American experience provided the clues as to how this might happen aesthetically, but the awareness of European political developments continued to exert a pull on a country that had enthusiastically participated in a largely European conflict from 1914 to 1918. In many respects the American experience, with its periodic labour shortages, its progressive agriculture and its origins as a settler-colonial project, was a more apt reference, but imperial ties to Britain still made London the first port of call for a generation of architects coming of age in the 1930s. Travel was critical for overcoming cultural isolation, as well as for making the comparison between the Old World and the New that affirmed for many Australians the promise of their national enterprise, despite its conservative tendencies.

The major difference between Australia and the United States in the interwar years was the great migrations that America was absorbing at a time when they had almost ceased to the Antipodes. With few immigrants the proportion of native-born Australians steadily increased, and as a consequence their parallel British identity required continual reaffirmation. By 1930 we also see the curious phenomenon of Dominion architects becoming champions of modernism in England, as part of the process of professional wanderings. Significant names include the Canadian Wells Coates, Australians Raymond McGrath and Henry Pynor, and Amyas Connell and Basil Ward from New Zealand. Many others spent time in leading British practices and returned to Australia to play major roles. However in the early 1930s their influence in their home countries was still some years away, and developments in architecture proceeded in a more piecemeal fashion as the country sought to stay abreast of international trends in the symbolism adopted for both public and private commissions. This eclectic approach can be discerned in the works through that decade of the memorial architects Dellit and Sodersten, as well as in the buildings designed by Harry Norris's practice.

After his success in the ANZAC Memorial competition in Sydney, Dellit continued to pursue a version of Deco that sought in its many sources new symbols of expanding modernity. The medium for this was travel, still the domain of the wealthy but increasingly portraying the exotic as counterpoint to the quotidian, as popularized in the Sydney magazine *Home*.[18] Air travel had not only made exotic places accessible, it exposed travellers to refuelling stops on long flights. For Australia, a European heritage was not sufficient to inform its antipodean identity. While the symbols of indigenous culture were limited and not potent enough to graft onto this European legacy, there was some attempt to incorporate local fauna and flora into architectural sculpture. This had been undertaken at least since the 1860s, but was revived in the 1920s as the search for primitive and exotic references took in the local, ironically, as worthy material. The 1930 building for the British Medical Association in Sydney, won through competition by Fowell & McConnel, is representative of this trend. It is a heavily decorated building, its facade testament to the skill of local tile manufacturer Wunderlich, who created the terracotta faience cladding, as well as the seated figures of knights bracing shields that sit atop truncated pilasters at the upper floors. Also present are gargoyles, koalas and Moorish-inspired latticework. The medieval references continue into the interior, with its domed octagon and timber-coffered ceiling to the entrance hall. In general its stylistic details lie comfortably within a received English mythology, with Australian fauna added to mark a new chapter in the story of England.

The execution of the facade goes beyond the prevailing standard in buildings of the day. The Wunderlich firm showed great enthusiasm for their work and for the incorporation of decoration into contemporary buildings. For the most part Australian architects, including Dellit, had absorbed the motifs and tendencies of the Deco style via publications and second-hand accounts. But there had been two significant visitors to the original Exposition Internationale des Arts Décoratifs et Industriels Modernes in Paris in 1925. The first was Leslie Wilkinson, who left without enthusiasm for its tenets, and the second was Ernest Wunderlich, one of the proprietors of the firm of the same name. Wunderlich was very taken with the exhibits and on his return the firm commenced manufacturing a range of architectural finishes and cladding, whose availability and quality inspired numerous facades around the country before the Second World War.[19]

Nonetheless the British Medical Association, like the Gothic-inspired city buildings of similar date, was the swansong of the conventional

revivalism that had emanated from Britain in the Victorian period, when the relative claims of the Gothic and the classical were debated with a vigour that masked their inevitable decline. Thus, despite his training under Wilkinson, Dellit could wholeheartedly pursue his version of the Deco tropes – the soaring central arch as both window and vaulted space, and impressive artwork and metal craft imbued with themes of hope. His 1931 Kyle House, fronting one of Sydney's small irregular squares, has a spatially powerful entry via an unenclosed archway surmounting two flanking staircases. It is unique in the city as a commercial loggia, downplaying the building's interior to create an adjunct space, deep and cool, to the triangular refuge of Macquarie Place. Dellit's third contribution to the city came some years later. Built for the Bank of New South Wales, Delfin House (1940) reprises the arched theme, but with a composite insert of bronze doors, filigree fanlights and a granite bas-relief titled 'Sunrise over the Pacific'. It is an exercise in antipodean optimism, its themes in both symbols and architectural details showing his faith in the ability of Deco, with its eclectic sources and combinations, to represent modern Australia coming to terms with its geographic isolation.

Emil Sodersten also found his voice through the window of invention opened by the many historical sources deemed plausible, if not suitable, for interwar buildings. His most impressive work opened in 1936, an office building for City Mutual Life. Like Dellit he championed decorative work and sculpture, but the most striking aspect of the building is the folded fan-like wall treatment to both principal street elevations. This enriches the interior, allowing views along the street, as well as injecting dynamic light and surface into the intersection it fronts. The building corner is chamfered, with inset vertical windows rising above a stone entry into which are set sculptures in bronze executed by Rayner Hoff.

The City Mutual Life building was one of several major office blocks, all tall by the standards of the day, designed and built for the life insurance industry. In an era of little government support for families whose breadwinners died or became incapacitated, the life insurance policy served as social self-insurance. Sold by travelling salesmen, the policies were both insurance and subscription saving schemes, and the income stream they generated for the underwriting companies remained almost untouched through the Great Depression.[20] These in turn created three of Sydney's most significant interwar buildings: Sodersten's City Mutual Life, the ACA Building for the Australasian Catholic Assurance Company (Hennessy, Hennessy & Co., 1936) and the MLC Building for the Mutual Life and Citizens' Assurance Company, completed in 1938. The ACA Building was an amalgam of contemporary modelling and details, from the neo-Gothic to the commercial Egyptianate, but of particular interest was the speed of

Fowell & McConnel, British Medical Association House with decorative tiling, Sydney, 1929–30.

C. Bruce Dellit, Delfin House, Sydney, 1938–40.

construction. After five weeks of excavation, the actual structure was built in 36 weeks, the result of Depression-era labour conditions and new plant and equipment.[21] The architect, Jack Hennessy, had visited the Chicago World's Fair in 1933 and the theatricality of the exhibition buildings, with their vertical shafts and pilasters and profuse, mechanically inspired details, left their mark. The exhibition also featured a reconstruction of a Mayan temple and a Seminole village, both conceived partly as anthropology, but largely as entertainment. The ACA Building has a matching counterpart in Melbourne, by the same architect in association with R. Morton Taylor.

The last of these, the MLC Building fronting Martin Place, was the work of the Melbourne firm of Bates, Smart & McCutcheon. Won through a competition held in 1936, the design was praised by the assessors for the authors' avoidance of 'any set period or style', as well as any exaggerated version of the modern.[22] The firm had recently completed a slender department store in Melbourne for Buckley & Nunn, its decorated facade of terracotta with steel windows displaying the toothed zig-zag pattern characteristic of the era. The firm's design for the MLC Building showed an

C. Bruce Dellit, Kyle House entry, Sydney, 1931.

ability to move easily from one decorative system to another. What is significant is not that their mode was eclectic, but rather that they paid attention to the internal consistency that was the hallmark of the better buildings of the interwar period. For the MLC they chose an Egyptianate style, which had enjoyed some currency with the discovery of Tutankhamen's tomb by Howard Carter in 1922. However, the roots of the Egyptian revival go back further, to Napoleon's conquest of Egypt in 1798, and an academic version can be found in the work of the English architect Herbert Baker at the turn of the twentieth century.

The significance of the MLC Building lies in the restraint it shows, indicative that the designer took the view that the Egyptian references were of more significance than fairs, such as the Chicago one of 1933, granted to the reconstructions they built. It follows the sentiments expressed by Sydney architect Kenneth H. McConnel in 1928, when he remarked that

> the modernists are getting back to something that is actually pre-Renaissance, and in a way pre-classic. Nothing was ever finer than the Egyptian sculptured lions and sphinxes; their secret was that they were conventionalised until every non-essential was cut out. Similarly much modern ornament seems to take its inspiration from early Christian work, which owes its beauty to its extreme simplicity. Some of the natural features sculptured by the early Christians are scarcely recognisable as such, and I like to think that this was more by design than by chance.[23]

McConnel articulates the impulse to a stylized primitivism that paralleled events in the visual arts, and the subsequent decade shows his prescience. In its consistency the MLC Building marks a high point of this movement, and the fact that its Egyptian references could be opaque to the assessors of the competition shows how far their sensibilities had been coarsened by the more lurid examples of Deco. These could be found in many building types, none more so than the plethora of cinemas that were being built across the country. Films and trams made a natural pairing in the interwar city, with the former providing escapist spectacles that drew on the tendency of the age to be seduced by almost anything new, and the latter making mass transit available late into the night and at weekends.

The Capitol Theatre by the Griffins had set a particularly high standard for theatre design, but the growth of films as recreation saw the construction of a number of seductive theatres in the late 1920s and '30s. The earlier theatres, such as the State Theatre in Melbourne (Bohringer, Taylor & Johnson, 1928), were elaborate exercises in eclectic romanticism, but the

Emil Sodersten, City Mutual Life Building, Sydney, 1934–6.

Bates, Smart & McCutcheon, front desk, MLC Building, Sydney, 1936–8.

Deco-inspired cinemas of the 1930s, like the Astor in St Kilda (R. Morton Taylor, 1936) or the elaborate Orpheum in Sydney (G. N. Kenworthy, 1935), present a more abstract version of visual opulence. Compared to many of their predecessors they too show the shift from direct reproduction of exotic elements to a more stylized scheme of patterning, with decorative motifs cast in shallow relief. Geometric sunbursts, curlicues, crystalline forms and chevrons dominate, as evident in the interior of the Orpheum. Popular taste embraced this shift to abstract ornamentation, well before it was supplanted by a reductive and sober view of decoration. Theatres also brought Deco to smaller cities and towns: Adelaide gained the Piccadilly (Evans, Bruer & Hall with Guy Crick, 1940), and Perth the Como and the Astor in 1938, both the work of Baxter-Cox & Leighton.

For all the success these buildings had as landmarks, they were not regarded as serious models for architectural aspirations. It was not that the style was inimical to idealism, but rather that their function as entertainment venues, along with a large number of suburban pubs, placed them squarely within popular taste. Any ideological references were muted, the better to foster escapism. This was not the case with commercial buildings of the period. These were often replete with sculpture, particularly bas-reliefs, that conveyed visions of Australia as bountiful, that dignified work and that welcomed material advancement and industrial power. That many of these were executed in the 1930s is a reminder of the subtlety of the ideological reflex – in a time of economic depression, visions of abundance constantly make their appearance. If anything this indicates the

Evans, Bruer & Hall with Guy Crick, Piccadilly Cinema, Adelaide, 1940.

Bohringer, Taylor & Johnson, State Theatre interior, Melbourne, 1928.

struggle to articulate Australian modernity as it assumed a new incarnation, that of an industrializing urban nation that retained a strong agricultural and mining base.

Articulating the Tenor of the Age

For architects this crystallizing identity was overlaid with news from Europe and America. The New World retained its draw because of its parallels with Australia, and especially its fostering of popular culture that appeared both novel and unthreatening. The attitude was summed up by Sir Hugh Denison on his return after serving as Australian commissioner to the United States:

> New York and the other big centres of America are seeking a tradition. They have wealth and everything wealth can buy, but they cannot buy tradition and they cannot buy a soul. The question we ask is, will their great acquisition of wealth prevent this being acquired by them?[24]

Conversely, the imperial ties with England exerted a countervailing force, and the rise of university courses in architecture created a situation where professional ideals were formed in parallel with training, rather than as a subsequent shaping of skills gained in the workplace. This process altered the practice of architecture in fundamental ways and it drew on the politics of Europe to feed those professional ideals. Through the 1930s travelling scholars, funded by the professional institutes, had their impressions published in professional journals, along with photographs of the buildings they visited. In some of these they found an affirmation of their particular taste, and in others the embodiment of class and nationalist politics.

In their assessment of architectural trends of the period, Australian architects were inclined to adopt the English approach of waiting to see the results of European innovations before adopting them. The equivocating that followed can be seen in numerous professional articles that accepted or welcomed change, but cautioned against too radical a turn. Modern architecture, a term in common use by the 1920s, was also framed as handmaiden to social and economic progress. Leighton Irwin, director of the influential Melbourne University Atelier of Architecture, assessed the situation thus in 1930:

> Mass production possesses the possibility of doing much good, as is evident in the case of the Ford car; and in connection with this development, standardisation must be adopted as a matter of economy . . .
>
> Everything tends towards simplification and massing . . . The establishment of great hospitals gives evidence of the extraordinary attention that is being paid to the health of people . . . and other buildings connected with the education and the general uplifting of the population are being established in such numbers, as well as on such a scale, as is unprecedented.[25]

Publications of the reports from travelling scholars were accompanied by photographs, so there was wide dissemination of new buildings in European countries. Germany was particularly well represented, with Australian architects touring until the eve of the Second World War. However the most popularly cited, with much admiration, was Willem Marinus Dudok's Hilversum Town Hall (1931), which deftly captured the balance sought by Australians between modern expression and a picturesque massing compatible with the asymmetrical techniques of Arts and Crafts composition.[26] The association was strengthened by the strong mullion pattern of the windows, and the result was a powerful pull on architects who held Voysey, and later Mackintosh, in deep affection.

Collectively these illustrations, and the first-hand visits, fed into the Australian profession as tropes to be worked and reworked. The commercial sphere provided opportunities for experimentation, since it was concerned with appearing broadly current in its merchandise and methods. Harry Norris, designing for the Coles group, showed how easy it was to adopt key elements of European modernism like the continuous horizontal window, and its illusion of floating spandrel panels. Having designed the house 'Burnam Beeches' for pharmaceutical maker Alfred N. Nichols in the early 1930s, Norris had some experience in composing a building with a horizontal emphasis that evoked streamlining. The house, in the early Yarra Ranges beyond eastern Melbourne, is eclectic in its fusion of decoration with large industrial windows, but Norris's subsequent work was among the most deft of the interwar period. His 1934 city building for Coles in Sydney (with H. E. Budden & Mackey) was seminal in its use of horizontal windows to the Castlereagh Street frontage, but retains the vertical implied tower that distinguishes the subsequent work both of Norris and of Budden & Mackey. This compositional device is used to give the building a distinctive identity, preventing it being subsumed into the undifferentiated street wall. The treatment held broad appeal, and even *Building* editorialized that the facades 'possess all the advantages which functionalist architecture claims'.[27]

The same device can be seen in Norris's best-known work, the striking Mitchell House on the corner of Lonsdale and Elizabeth Streets, Melbourne (1936). Here Norris adopts continuous horizontal windows, but the primary frontage has a vertical Deco-influenced engaged stair tower surmounted by the building name in the then-fashionable Gill Sans typeface. Contemporary accounts commend the building for the flood of natural light admitted by the large windows, whose uninterrupted line results from setting the steel stanchions some distance back from the building face.[28] Astonishingly the construction time was a mere five months. As in the Sydney Coles building, without this tower the building would be less prominent as a commercial entity. This convention is repeated in the major work of Norris's Sydney collaborators, H. E. Budden & Mackey. Opened two years after the Coles Building, their Railway House contained the offices of the New South Wales Railway Department. Still striking in its colour and workmanship, the building drew comment for its use of day labour payment as opposed to a fixed contract sum, as well as for the meticulous attention paid to detail and quality of construction.[29] In this it is testimony to the prestige of the Railway Department as integral to the economy of the state of New South Wales. It not only transported wheat and primary products from the country to Sydney for export, but was responsible for the Sydney suburban rail and tram

Harry Norris, Burnham Beeches, Sherbrooke (Victoria), 1930–33.

MITCHELL
HOUSE
MITCHELL HOUSE
277 Melbourne Computer Centre

H. E. Budden & Mackey, Railway House, Sydney, 1934–6.

network, as well as owning and operating two of the city's largest power stations at Ultimo and White Bay.

For Budden & Mackey Railway House was an opportunity to build for a client with enormous resources. The building sits atop Wynyard railway station, part of the suburban network that was expanded and buried under the city to service commuters. The station opened in 1932, fed by the rail links crossing Sydney Harbour on the newly finished Harbour Bridge. Railway House is faced in glazed terracotta tiles and mouldings,

Harry Norris, Mitchell House, Melbourne, 1936.

with bronze entry doors and windows meticulously manufactured and installed. The facade design was again pitched at popular taste, being described as 'colourful without being vulgar'.[30] Horizontal windows are also used to evoke the then widely accepted streamlined style, which had demonstrated the commercial advantage of large windows in saving on lighting costs. The ubiquitous Deco tower element is almost absent, its trace marked in vertical mouldings that barely interrupt the emphasis lent by the continuous spandrels.

This period of architecture, at its best, demonstrates a parallel version of the Bauhaus aspiration towards seamless craft. It derives from similar roots, though less integrated into a view of progress as imperative. For Australian architects of the 1930s industrial advancement was an opportunity to put into practice all those lessons of their early articled years, with its emphasis on architecturally designed buildings as crafted objects distinct from the shoddy construction of the speculative builder. They sought, to paraphrase Tafuri, not a utopia of form, but a utopia of craft.[31] To see these buildings up close is to appreciate the close direction given to the builder, and the joy taken in the logic of durability.

Concurrent with the construction of these buildings ran the travels of Australian graduates through Europe and their experiences in working in leading firms in England and the United States. Although well established as part of professional development (Budden, Mackey and Norris were all experienced travellers, for instance), the travelling scholars of the late 1920s and '30s found themselves subject to different forces. Architecture in Europe was enmeshed in questions beyond style and representation, and its function as ideology was under examination. For Australians travelling overseas this shift was particularly fascinating, since the simpler but related view of style as a reflex of nationalism was a familiar one in the first decades of nationhood. Framed in world-historical terms, in 1917 George Sydney Jones could assert that architecture 'being national in its essence, exercises an influence over and impresses upon everyone . . . the dignity and the ennobling power of beauty'.[32] The argument was made in favour of civic art, understood as both architecture and town planning, as a factor in the national life and was not unusual in the period. What changed for the Australians abroad was the transnational emphasis emerging in the interwar period.

It is easy enough to portray a quest for a national style as a motive for developments in the 1920s and '30s. Indeed it is explicit in many writings, either as an ideal as expressed by Jones, or as an affectation, in the view of Florence Taylor, that precludes rational thinking about fitness for purpose. How this then translates into architecture is not always as one would expect, since Jones has been marked as a progressive despite his spiritual views on national identity, and Taylor's scorn for the work of Le Corbusier is based not on his intentions, which she finds convincing, but on his aesthetics. In Taylor's view, the persistence of style is a rational necessity for architecture as an adjunct to taste, and she accuses Le Corbusier of not following his own advice.[33] These observations point to the dual quests of the period's architecture, sought in nationalist aspiration as well as in disciplinary cohesion.

The nationalist search, so evident in the formative years after the First World War, is by definition a product of a view that seeks a measure of concordance between national character, however it might be defined, and its plastic expression. This view, expressed in the writings of Hardy Wilson and Robin Dods, following on sentiments laid out by George Sydney Jones, slowly turned into a quest honoured as much in the breach as in the observance. Indeed Florence Taylor had remarked in 1928 that the quest had an unexamined air about it, with little regard to the validity of its object:

> Architects, artists, and designers in general have long awaited the development of a style of architecture typical of and peculiar to Australia. Why this should appear to be of such importance is not quite clear, since any style of structure which performs its utilitarian function in a beautiful and comfortable manner should be enough to satisfy our demands.[34]

Nonetheless the search would prove to be remarkably persistent over coming decades, as it captured political and social alignments that dissolved and transformed at the very moment of their fixing in brick, stone and steel.

The Politics of Emerging Modernism

It is a truism that in commercial architecture international trends are closely followed, as part of the constant search for a competitive advantage. Domestic architecture has always been a better yardstick of national aspiration in Australia, as it is more responsive to specific sites and notions of how life locally is best lived. Harry Norris may have built more challenging buildings, but Hardy Wilson had the more enduring influence with his modest oeuvre. The real significance of the 1930s, though, was the introduction of a new type of practice, that of an architecture that signalled its allegiance to the working class within Australia as part of a worldwide movement. When the term 'International Style' is used in the period, it signals not only its appropriateness across borders, but its internationalist politics.

The idea of architecture addressing working-class concerns was not new and had been articulated as a bulwark against political agitation from the period of the First World War.[35] What was new were reports of the European experience where architecture had indeed found a form and a politics encompassing this ideal. When this confluence was first publicized it was rejected as too radical for Australia, where employers were historically responsive to the demands of labour, which was generally in short supply. However travelling scholars sent back images of new planning and housing schemes from Europe, framed as part of an inevitable shift towards the needs of workers as a matter of logic rather than sentiment. This corresponded with the growing influence of Marxist ideas within the British academies, typified by the Cambridge University Club and the growth of Marxist-oriented societies at the University of Oxford. Of the travelling scholars, Frank G. Costello, later city architect for Brisbane, was among the best correspondents in conveying this trend.

Costello was awarded a travel scholarship, to experience buildings and cities abroad, in 1928, but his reports and proposals continued for a decade. One of his early summaries deals with the question of 'Town Planning and its Effect on the Liberty of the Individual'. While not overtly political, the piece argues for the curtailing of the expectation that individuals need look only after their own interests in order to effect a social good. This position, derived from Adam Smith but then, as now, associated with a libertarian outlook, is held up against the achievements of Hampstead Garden Suburb, the seminal development located in northwest London: 'A comparison of these, and such like examples, with the majority of developments by unrestricted individuals, leaves no doubt in the mind that wise restriction of individual liberty in the matter of Town Development is not only good, but is essential to the well being of the community.'[36]

While not overtly radical, these sentiments mark a shift whereby architecture is placed within the tenets of a nascent planning outlook, one that values the common good as a matter of collective endeavour. Indeed Costello is much taken with the planning of Rome under Mussolini, and his proposed planning scheme for Sydney rests on Geddes's popular exhortation to 'survey before plan', as Abercrombie did for London in 1943.[37] What is significant is that buildings are seen as elements in a rationally constructed urban and social matrix, with appeals to common sense running alongside appeals to political savviness.

Other travelling scholars of the period saw different opportunities and crucibles of idealism. A small group worked in Russia in the 1930s and brought back reports of something promising but disorganized. Henry Pynor, writing of his experiences in 1932–3 as an architectural consultant, gives a vivid summary of Russian daily life:

> Everything is fluid and in the process of change. Things are and they are not, and because they are not, they are. Expediency stalks in the guise of dialectical materialism. There is a continual riot of improvement and rationalization.[38]

Pynor also witnessed the turn in Russia away from a commitment to modernism towards a dull classicism, as a prelude to the triumph of the doctrine of art for the masses as dictated by Socialist Realism. Thoughtful and occasionally wry, Pynor worked in the United States and with Burnet Tait & Lorne in London, before returning to Sydney and eventually taking leadership of the Sydney Technical College architecture programme.

Perhaps most significant, in retrospect, was the emergence in Sydney and Melbourne of distinctive approaches to the issue of modernity, and its inflection in local architectural modernisms. While interwar architecture in Sydney and Melbourne, and in other state capitals, was dominated by commercial buildings designed in modes that drew on eclectic precedents, polemically modern buildings were rare. They were unsuited to the determining factor in the commercial world: finding a position between the new, accepted and widely embraced as part of modern life, and the restriction of not going too far. In commercial terms this medium was delineated by the work of Norris, Sodersten and others working in what would loosely be called Deco or the Moderne style. As an ideological representation of Australian finance and industry these buildings were rounded out by the engaging sculptures that surmounted their entries and adorned their facades, their intimations of abundant produce and honest toil portraying a popular vision of Australian interwar modernity.

At the level of domestic architecture, there was more experimentation if the client was amenable. Sydney architect John Brogan, for example, worked across several historical styles and found modernism of formal interest as one among many possibilities. With a client determined to innovate, he could shift to working in a contemporary idiom. Brogan's design for industrialist and idealist William Crowle's 1936 collection of terraced apartments, named 'Wyldefel Gardens', diverged sharply from his largely historicist work, and the complex is noteworthy both for its adept modernist expression and for its shared gardens and sports facilities. These shared facilities fostered a desire for sociability among residents in other modernist developments. Only partially extant now, the building shows that a travelled and unusually adventurous client could instigate a project that displayed a unity of social and formal ambition against the inclination of the architect, and that there were enough images and experiences of European models available locally to produce a work of some sophistication.

Others who had travelled and imbibed the language of a *sächlichkeit* modernism grounded in objectivity, and the rationalist vision across all walks of life that it conjured up, produced similar work but with greater commitment. In Victoria the firm comprising Geoffrey Mewton and Roy Grounds designed houses that remain markers of the advent of modernism in Australia. After completing their articles locally, Mewton and Grounds were among the early attendees at the University of Melbourne Architectural Atelier, followed by a period abroad where Mewton worked for Adams Holden & Pearson in London and Van Alen in New York. The Atelier, which offered advanced instruction in architectural design at what today would be called post-graduate level, played a key role in developing a sophisticated discussion around issues of the day for both university

John Brogan, Wyldefel Gardens, Sydney, 1935–6.

graduates and those who had completed their articles. From 1930 onwards, under Leighton Irwin, it fostered a set of principles conducive to modernist design.[39]

On his return to Melbourne, Mewton collaborated with Grounds on some of the earliest examples of flat-roofed, asymmetrically composed houses and flats in the country. The Stooke House in Brighton (1934) was among the earliest designs, and it presents a series of intersecting white cubes in brickwork, with horizontally struck jointing. A large steel corner window looks out to the street, but the programme of the house identifies it as firmly middle-class despite the austerity of its finishes. It is a single-bedroom dwelling, with living areas, separate kitchen and den, and the pinwheel composition of three wings around a core owes much to Suprematist painting. It is informed in its composition and references, but as a suburban dwelling it shows little programmatic critique or standing as a social model. This was broached in the later compact apartments designed by Mewton and Grounds around St Kilda on the Melbourne bayside. Two, 'Bellaire' and 'Woy Woy', were completed in 1936. 'Woy Woy' is a work of great confidence given its modest programme as compact flats. The exterior treatment is reductive in the extreme, with no superfluous detail save for raised lettering and date of construction. 'Bellaire' has a similar treatment, but in brick. Both are harbingers of a social modernity as well: the flat designed for the single person, unattached and free to enjoy the period between early dependence and later family life.

The advent of a more learned, European-inspired modernism in Melbourne had been presaged by a remarkably consistent interpretation of Dudok's public-minded take on cubist monumentality. The popularity of the Hilversum Town Hall among travelling Australian architects has already been noted, but the MacRobertson Girls' High School in South Melbourne adapted the Dutch schema to the English-derived techniques of the local building industry. Completed in 1934 to the design of Seabrook & Fildes, it quickly became acknowledged as a piece of seminal design. The composition retains enough elements to create visual interest, with horizontal white window hoods and cappings set against horizontally struck coursing in the cream brickwork. The windows are tied together as grouped elements, increasing the visual integrity of the primary masses of brick that make up the complex. At its construction it struck a careful balance between following familiar building conventions, and referencing contemporary European buildings to intimate a progressive approach to education. The firm continued to employ similar massing, materials and detailing in a series of fire stations for the Metropolitan Fire Brigade in subsequent years, confirming the relevance of the style for public works. The references were learned at first hand: Seabrook had worked in London for Burnet

Mewton & Grounds, Woy Woy flats, Melbourne, 1935–6.

Tait & Lorne, designers of the decorative pylons at either end of the Sydney Harbour Bridge. In all likelihood he had also visited Dudok's major works in Hilversum in the same period.

Indeed schools were often the means by which seminal modernist works appeared in the public purview, many displaying similar loyalty to Dudok. In Tasmania S.W.T. Blythe designed a number of schools for the Public Works Department, including the New Town High School in Hobart in 1936, that bear the imprint of his earlier travels. In Adelaide this took longer to come to fruition: Adelaide Boys' High School (now Adelaide High School) is of the same ilk, but the 1940 design by Sydney architects Edward Fitzgerald and John Brogan was only completed in 1951.

Travel abroad also presented the opportunity for dominion architects to become vectors of modernism in their own right. The Australian architects working at Burnet Tait & Lorne from 1933 onwards are credited with a role in turning the firm to modernism in the early 1930s.[40] Along with Raymond McGrath, a graduate of the University of Sydney's new architecture programme who established himself as an influential London modernist, they illustrate the curious situation of Australians playing key roles in English architecture before they did the same in Australia, if indeed they returned at all. These travellers were all Australian-born, and Seabrook, Grounds, Mewton and Bayne had attended the University of Melbourne Architecture Atelier under Leighton Irwin. This seminal group were responsible for many of the earliest modernist buildings in Melbourne, and their fates were linked in establishing an independent modernist culture in the city that has persisted through several generations.

The partnership between Mewton and Grounds dissolved in 1939, with Grounds continuing to design compact, urbane flats marked by his fascination with the potential of circulation areas as gathering spaces, and a fondness for primary geometries. 'Moonbria' Flats in Toorak shows all these attributes and is surmounted by a circular glazed tower holding the lift motor room that presages later projects with circular geometries. The enlarged circulation areas hold two significant ambitions: the first, to elevate movement as part of a dynamic conception of buildings in the modernist mode, as distinct from the static compositions favoured by the Beaux Arts tradition; and the second to create common spaces for residents to socialize. Given the compactness of these early modern apartments, the generous size of the circulation areas is idealist in the extreme, and shows an enthusiasm for the aspects of international modernism that encouraged chance meetings and interactions. It follows on the example of 'Cairo' flats, created in 1936 in the Melbourne inner suburb of Fitzroy by Best Overend. Tasmanian born, Overend had spent a productive couple of years in London from 1931 working for leading modernists, including expatriate Australian Raymond McGrath, and Canadian Wells Coates. During this period he, like Mewton and Grounds, became familiar with the idea of a minimum flat for singles or young couples, allowing them to live independent city lives without the amenities needed for nuclear family living. In the 'Cairo' flats, Overend arranged the units to face a

Seabrook & Fildes, model of MacRobertson Girls' High School, Melbourne, 1933–4.

generous garden. In keeping with the idea of encouraging communality, he also created a roof terrace accessible to all inhabitants, and the complex contained a small shop, a shared dining room and two shared laundries.[41]

Apartments, in the late 1930s, became a key building type in the development of an enduring modernist tradition in Australia. While there had been a flowering of Deco buildings with inventive glazing schemes throughout the decade, these affectations almost ceased with the onset of the Second World War. That there had been architectural developments at all over the period is remarkable, given the effect of the Depression on the volume of construction. From a high of £16.44 million worth of building in Sydney in 1929, the figure collapsed to £1.28 million in 1931, and had only recovered to £14.06 million in 1938.[42] Similar patterns prevailed across all states. However the acceptance of flats as an important building type filling a niche in the housing market, especially for young couples, led to a small boom in the pre-war years that carried through into the early 1940s. This was particularly pronounced in Melbourne, which had both a coterie of local practitioners with overseas exposure and a key immigrant with skill in the field.

German by birth, Frederick Romberg had studied at the Eidgenössische Technische Hochschule in Zurich and at the outbreak of war in 1939

Edward B. Fitzgerald and John K. Brogan, Adelaide High School, 1940–51.

Roy Grounds, Moonbria flats, Melbourne, 1941.

he was working for Stephenson & Turner in Melbourne. He moved on to private practice with Mary Turner Shaw, and in the early 1940s they designed two distinctive blocks of flats again comprising compact dwellings: 'Glenunga' flats of 1941, and 'Newburn' flats completed a year later. The buildings are learned in their references, with Glenunga incorporating influences from Aalto, particularly the Villa Mairea, in its angled windows and juxtaposed brickwork and stone walling. Newburn is an exercise in optimism, an amalgam of modernist forms and motifs that owes something to the breezy Zurich apartments of the Roth cousins working with Marcel Breuer, as well as the expressionist device of vertically repetitive rounded balconies popularized by Erich Mendelsohn. Never a strict purist, Romberg brought to Melbourne a well-honed sense of the sculptural possibilities inherent in the new objectivity that had gained traction in Germany and its neighbours before the dead hand of Nazism intervened.

It is worth reiterating the prevalence of flats in early modernism in Australia. This is the modernism that was firmly aligned with the rationalist tradition, as opposed to exercises in exotic motifs or streamlining. Despite their functional mode of design, these buildings secured an aesthetic that proved useful for reconfiguring many programmes and functions of everyday life. This is evident in Romberg's work both with Shaw and after: it exhibits a playfulness with form and expression that subverts any purely utilitarian claims for its origins. By the late 1930s this was well understood, even by locally trained architects. The news from Europe was constant and well observed as far as architecture was concerned, and the imperative that architecture should assume a political stance was also growing.

A case in point was the collaboration between Malcolm Moir and Heather Sutherland, two graduates from the University of Sydney in the 1920s who moved to Canberra. The city was developing slowly in rough accordance with the revised Griffin Plan, and in 1927 the Federal parliament relocated from Melbourne to a new provisional building in Canberra, thus cementing the status of the new capital and making the transfer of administrative services inevitable. Despite never having left Australia, Moir's own house of 1935 is a prescient piece of reductive design. Moir and Sutherland married in 1936 and in subsequent years they designed a collection of modest but stylistically unified houses utilizing brick with steel windows that continued the theme of Moir's earlier

Taylor, Soilleux & Overend, Cairo flats, Melbourne, 1935–6.

Romberg & Shaw, Newburn flats, Melbourne, 1939–42.

Romberg & Shaw, Glenunga flats, Melbourne, 1940–41.

work. They were not alone in Canberra. Public works architects Edwin Henderson and Cuthbert Whitley were working in a similar idiom, and the precinct for the Forrest Fire Station and associated housing has an affinity with the work of Moir and Sutherland in its proportions and window placement. The sobriety of the brick and timber windows stands in contrast to more exuberant examples of modernism elsewhere in the country, but the Canberra buildings added to the acceptance of a restrained architecture, with functionalist underpinnings, for subsequent buildings in the capital.

Indeed by the late 1930s a number of architects across the country had demonstrated the suitability of the style, and its attendant logic, for new building types. In Sydney the six-level car service centre built for the Hastings Deering Ford dealership (1938) showed the pull a strong functional brief could exert on even those suspicious of the modernist ethos. The building, conceived around ascending and descending car ramps, presented novel challenges to the builder in the setting out and pouring of the graded and radiused concrete ramps and flooring. The continuous horizontal windows around the free-standing structure were seen as a fitting expression of commercial architecture, allied to the idea of efficiency.[43] The architect was Samuel Lipson, Leeds-born and Glasgow-trained. Arriving

Malcolm Moir (with additions by Moir & Sutherland), Moir House, Canberra, 1935–7.

in Sydney in the mid-1920s, he worked alongside Edwin Henderson at the Commonwealth Works Department before striking out on his own, and then in partnership with Peter Kaad. Its counterpart in expression, if not function, was the factory in the wooded valley town of Warburton, near Melbourne, designed for the Sanitarium Health Food Company by E. F. Billson. The company was an initiative of the Seventh Day Adventist Church, and the building embodied a view that the modern workplace should be naturally lit and progressively rational in its layout. The cream brick finish merged the building's modernist European antecedents with the perceived virtues of masonry construction, virtues that ranged from durability to the warm tones that undercut the radical denaturing of surface evoked by fully rendered modern structures. The adjoining 1935 building, also by Billson, for the Signs Publishing Company is an even finer ensemble of modernist elements. Again devoted to an Adventist enterprise, its asymmetrically placed glass-brick stairwell enclosure and entry brick arch deftly counter the horizontal bands of windows and glazed bricks. Sitting on the banks of the upper Yarra, these two buildings present a startling testament to the occasional penetration of a refined modernism into rural communities.

While the Atelier in Melbourne had given some imprimatur to modernist designs, and immigrants like Romberg and Lipson had brought their own well-formed ideas to buildings of the 1930s, in general architecture in Sydney maintained its stance of treading gently with popular taste. The position expounded by Wilson, that the colonial Georgian represented a compelling ideal, had taken firm root and Leslie Wilkinson's alignment with this position, leavened by his fondness for the buildings of the Mediterranean, simply magnified this. It was a view that found resonance in Perth on the other side of the country. Always conscious of its isolation from the Eastern states, Western Australian architecture had struck its own path along naturalistic lines, as local practitioners argued that its true Mediterranean climate, with winter rainfall, made it particularly suitable for reproducing the architecture of that region. Wilkinson nudged this along when he drafted the conditions for the 1927 competition for the ceremonial core of the University of Western Australia, known as the Hackett Memorial Buildings. He subsequently joined the judging panel and the winning entry hewed close to his request for something sympathetic to 'a climate and setting which may be best described as Mediterranean'.[44] It was submitted by Conrad Sayce with Rodney Alsop, who had established the University of Melbourne Atelier in 1918. The complex and its centrepiece,

E. H. Henderson and Cuthbert Whitley, Forrest Fire Station and residences, Canberra, 1939.

E. F. Billson, Signs Publishing Company, Warburton (Victoria), 1936–7.

Winthrop Hall, reveal the hold that revivalism still held over the public imagination in the late 1920s. It is an exercise in academic Italianate architecture, carefully calibrated to extract maximum visual contrast from Perth's sharp daylight. Strongly textured, and with free-standing arched walkways creating linking cloisters, the design for the Hackett Buildings presented a strong model for a regional revival style (Alsop called it 'Renaissance') that left its mark on a maturing generation of architects.[45] Among these was Marshall Clifton, who completed his training in the Public Works Department in 1929 and soon left for his overseas tour. Exposed to the same influences as his travelling countrymen and women, including a period in Russia, he drew different conclusions. Travels through Spain left a profound impression on him and he developed a fondness for its simple rural dwellings. In the 'Day House' of 1939 this inspired the building blocks for what is a substantial family home. The house presents as a collection of rural-scaled rectangles, with pitched roofs, arranged at right angles to create the impression of a village cluster or the principal buildings of a hacienda.

Lipson & Kaad, Hastings Deering motor dealership, Sydney, 1938.

OFFICE

By contrast, Clifton's direct contemporary Sydney Ancher completed his training through night classes at the Sydney Technical College. Well aware in later life that this had given him different ambitions from the university-educated architects under Wilkinson, Ancher won a travelling scholarship in 1929 that allowed him to make his own assessment of developments in Europe. On his return in 1936, with a declared commitment to the leading European modernists, Ancher tried to set out his conclusions in the thesis required by the scholarship. Titled 'The Evolution of Modern Architecture', it reads as a plea for the adoption of a scientific method, free of emotion, in the pursuit of a modern or contemporary culture. The schism between the work of the 1930s and that yet to come is clearly delineated when Ancher writes that it was 'a calamity for the world when American Architects seized on the *arts décoratifs* motifs of the Paris Exhibition of 1925, with the belief they had found modern architecture'. On the contrary, he writes, they 'gave to the world a most deplorable heritage of bastard architecture'.[46]

These passages illustrate the extent of Ancher's desire to forge an architecture consistent with new building materials and his parallel belief in the rational, against what he saw as the dishonesty of a culture trying to hide

Alsop & Sayce, Winthrop Hall & Hackett Memorial Buildings, The University of Western Australia, Perth, 1927–31.

Sydney Ancher (Prevost & Ancher), Prevost House, Sydney, 1937.

profound changes occurring beneath its surface. He also disowned his early design with James Prevost for the latter's own 1937 house in Bellevue Hill, its glass blocks and curved forms seemingly indulgent against the austerity of his subsequent work.[47]

The most visible shift in architecture in the late 1930s, though, was the rise in state-sponsored building. The number of hospitals constructed was remarkable, most being the work of a handful of offices working in modes that expressed the science-based practices they housed. The uptake of modernism in this area was swift, with models like Aalto's Paimio sanatorium quickly absorbed into the Australian context. The most

NO
LEFT
TURN

successful practitioner, Arthur Stephenson, visited 64 hospitals in an intense three-month tour of the United States. Stephenson hailed from within Melbourne's elite, due to church connections rather than money, and had worked in the building industry before war service led him to the Architectural Association in London. There he met Donald Turner and instructor Percy Meldrum, both Australians and subsequent partners in the firms of Stephenson & Meldrum and, after 1937, Stephenson & Turner. The firm was predicated on a rational, indeed progressive, approach to its work and organization. Stephenson established the principle of the architect charging fees to the client alone, instead of to both client and builder. This created clear loyalties to the client and allowed the firm to advocate more vigorously for cost and quality control. An office photograph from 1932 also shows two women architects among sixteen, an unusual proportion for the time. These were Mary Turner Shaw, later in brief partnership with Frederick Romberg, and Ellison Harvie, a major figure in the firm through four decades from the 1920s onwards.[48]

Their first venture in modern hospital design came in 1934 with the Mercy Hospital in East Melbourne. It adds a set of continuous balconies to a building with Victorian window proportions, but the incorporation of sun and light as sanitary aids became a hallmark of subsequent works. The smooth exterior of the United Dental Hospital (1940), next to Sydney's Central Station, is an exception: nonetheless its circular glazed stair at the apex of the triangular site and the horizontal windows set into an unadorned wall plane signalled the very public advent of this austerely functional building type in the city. The scale of work multiplied quickly. After completing the King George v Memorial Wing at Sydney's Royal Prince Alfred Hospital (1941), a more playful building with some Expressionist and Aalto-inspired curves, the war years saw Stephenson and Turner undertake the Royal Melbourne Hospital (1942) and Yaralla Military Hospital on the upper reaches of Sydney Harbour. Both of these are substantial commissions, distinguished by a sense of order nested in repetition, and the careful delineation of vertical circulation – the stairs and lifts – and the wings they service. The aesthetic has retreated from the uncompromising United Dental Hospital, softened by the horizontal painted balustrade walls of the balconies and the use of brick for the main building envelope.

Of the other firms that garnered some of this huge investment in health, the most noteworthy was that of Leighton Irwin. Severe and demanding, he ran his practice in parallel to his teaching in the Atelier. Irwin designed a number of hospitals in Victoria and New South Wales, typified by Prince Henry's Hospital in St Kilda, Melbourne, now demolished. The boom in hospital building through the 1930s also cemented the dominance of the

Stephenson & Meldrum, United Dental Hospital, Sydney, 1936–8.

Stephenson & Meldrum (from 1938 Stephenson & Turner) in association with William A. M. Blackett, Royal Melbourne Hospital, 1936–41.

Melbourne-domiciled firms in designing these models for the developing nation state, undertaking a concerted programme for Australian health nationally. This was given direct impetus by state legislation such as the 1929 Public Hospitals Act in New South Wales, which for the first time established government control over standards in hospitals. This sector saw the last flourishing of building work before the economic efforts of the Second World War were directed almost exclusively towards the armed services and prosecution of the war effort.

Regional Differences on the Eve of War

To the observer of architecture, the generational shifts in Australian architecture were assuming clearer form on the eve of these events. By 1939 the differences between practice in Sydney and in Melbourne had crystallized into streams marked by a differing attitude to history and divergent taste. The southern city showed a composite face, albeit one that incubated a cultural difference. Home to both BHP and Collins House, stalwarts of Australian capital, it also boasted an urban culture that allowed a Catholic establishment to gain substantial influence, developments fictionalized in Frank Hardy's 1950 novel *Power Without Glory*. This was overlaid with a maturing Labor movement across the country, but one that drew on class enmities reflecting the politics of the Protestant Ascendancy. A small but influential Jewish minority within the city added a further register to the tenor of Victorian politics and social structure, and contributed to the patrician class that took up residence on the eastern periphery of the city. Collectively this more charged atmosphere was conducive to a nascent modernism infused with polemical intent, aided by institutions like the University of Melbourne Atelier, which served as nursery, in deed if not intent, for a generation of modernist architects.

Sydney retained its commitment to what Bernard Smith has called the Georgian Rule of Taste, the valorizing of early colonial architecture as an antidote to turn-of-the-century eclectic experiments in style.[49] As Hardy Wilson became isolated for his erratic and ultra-nationalistic pronouncements, his early sentiments on architecture were carried forward by Leslie Wilkinson and conveyed through the University of Sydney course. Sydney's committed modernists were more likely to come through the Sydney Technical College or from outside the city. Locally derived arguments for modernism needed to be framed within the sentiments of Georgian good taste, a tendency evident in Raymond McGrath's publications abroad, but rooted in his Sydney training, and in the later work of Sydney Ancher. This is also evident in the work of Morton Herman, who graduated from the university in 1930. After the obligatory overseas travel, he returned to Sydney to undertake the earliest rehousing scheme in the city in Erskineville (1938). While his interest in rehousing, or 'slum clearance' as it was termed, was cultivated in the English political environment of the 1930s, he also continued Wilson's work in documenting Sydney's early colonial buildings that were still extant.

The 1930s have the distinction of having produced the first clearly modernist buildings in Australia. These were typified in the work of Grounds, Mewton and Ancher, and are characterized by the absence of ornament and a severity of expression that distinguished them from the earlier Art Deco and its variants. While Deco appeared as modern because it superseded the copies of ancient Greek and Roman details that appeared in such profusion in commercial work to 1930, this displacement simply mirrored the broader shift in popular interest opened up by archaeology and travel. Many civilizations, it appeared, had risen and disappeared, leaving traces that intimated that the European experience was neither unique nor destined to endure. In a national image still forming, these seemed potent historical lessons.

What Art Deco did achieve in the early 1930s was to open a space for conjecture about styles and their historical resonances that had been missing under the conventions of the nineteenth-century academic revivals. It was a role played by Arts and Crafts some decades earlier, in regard to the question of what constituted an authentic architectural expression for building materials and local climate. At the turn of the century, before the advent of the steel frame and the modernizing of the building industry, a debate around craft could be sustained, but by 1935 these terms were outmoded. What becomes clear by 1935 is the penetration of a profound materialism into everyday life. The gradual erosion of the cosmologies of the nineteenth century and the displacement of the sentimentality that still underpinned Victorian life were almost complete by this time. When we read a radical opposition to sentiment in the buildings that claim to be modern, we simply see the most thoughtful members of a profession seeking to catch up with a view already pervading political and middle-class life.

The almost universal experience of travel among influential architects in the interwar years clearly played a role in these events. Travelling architects found that the language of architecture allowed them to feel a kinship with European counterparts that drew from the conventions of architecture as a discipline. This constituted a horizontal loyalty across national boundaries. In the vertical sense the return of these travellers allowed a local variant of modernism to be developed as part of a nationalist identity that worked through local circumstance. Thus the act of travel and return mirrored the dual loyalties of a bonded ruling class, its image validated abroad, its means cultivated at home. These impulses mark the axes along which the rules of local taste were formulated, with regional variation. This local story, as much prescriptive as narrative, forms the core of pre- and post-Second World War architectural identity in Australia. Immigrant architects are effectively formed outside of this, but this does not imply exclusion. Indeed their work was often well received and valued, in an act of internal self-validation. Names like Lipson, Buhrich, Oser and Fooks, born and educated in Europe and adept at their craft, featured occasionally in publications and have been the subject of recent scholarship.[50] For the most

Morton Herman and William Richardson, Erskineville Housing Scheme, Sydney, 1938.

part, though, they practised quietly among sympathetic clients, rarely achieving the influence of fellow immigrant Frederick Romberg. But the dominant architectural story in the decades between 1920 and 1940 is of a native-born generation finding their way as cultural contenders.

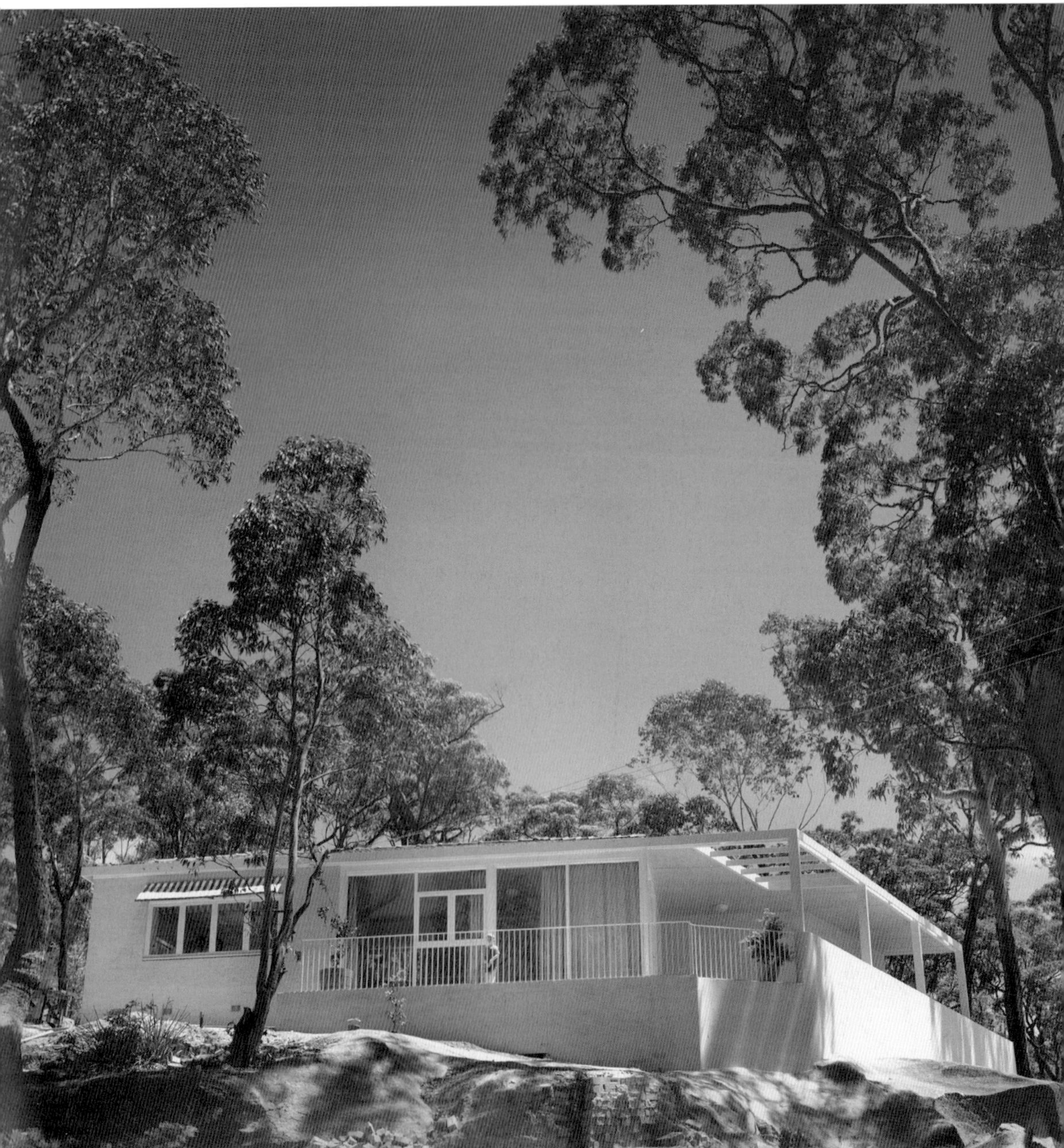

chapter three

Post-war Optimism: Everyone Becomes a Modernist, 1946–61

The virtual cessation of building through the period of the Second World War in Australia was a result of the nation shifting onto a war footing, with a tightly controlled economy and all aspects of production geared to the war effort. Proximity to the Pacific Theatre of action made Australia a natural base for American soldiers, and they fostered occasional resentment at their intrusion into everyday life, as well as exposure to American values and aspirations. These would become more influential as the post-war effort of nation building unfolded, driven as it was by a desire to emulate American consumption and a long-held view, derived from English roots, that the state had a role to play in ensuring social fairness.

Australia had entered the war with an acute sense of social frustration engendered by the long Depression, and by the paucity of building that culminated in a housing shortage that hampered the formation of new families and households. The fertility rate, or lifetime number of children per woman, had shown a steady decline from Federation, when it stood at about four. At the depths of the Depression this had almost halved, but a slight increase in childbearing rates from the mid-1930s was restricted by a dearth of new dwellings. This was well documented and was seen as a significant social problem. A Joint Parliamentary Committee on Social Security was appointed in 1941, in anticipation of the resurgence of social frustration once the war was over. It recommended that improved housing for all Australians, and the abolition of slums in cities and towns, become priorities. The evident need for more data and planning across a range of social and economic concerns led to the formation in 1943 of the Department of Post-War Reconstruction, under the energetic and gifted H. C. 'Nugget' Coombs. As part of its remit the department created a Commonwealth Housing Commission to inquire into the housing situation nationwide and to make recommendations.

The Commission recorded that there was a substantial shortfall in the number of dwellings needed to house Australia's population adequately. It also entrenched the idea of housing as a right and advocated for the state's involvement in providing housing for those low-income workers for whom market provision had failed.[1] This was not unusual for the time and

Sydney Ancher & Partners, Hamill House, Sydney, 1946–7.

it derived from both the European interwar tendency for local government to build and administer housing schemes, and from American New Deal aspirations.

Implementation of the Commission's recommendations proved somewhat trickier. The wartime economy had distorted production of building materials and it took some years for a consumer-oriented market to emerge. As a result houses in the immediate post-war years were restricted in size and a general rule of being extremely economical, even frugal, prevailed: indeed the period has been characterized by Freeland as one of 'Austerity'.[2] However it also fostered an idealism, held in abeyance by the war years, among younger architects.

Typical of this trend was the young architect who had served as Executive Officer for the wartime Housing Commission, Walter Bunning. Educated at the Sydney Technical College, crucible for so many of the city's early modernists, Bunning spent the years from 1936 to 1939 abroad as a travelling scholar of the New South Wales Board of Architects. Through the war years he practised the arguments he had imbibed overseas in a series of critiques of new architecture, but his work with the Housing Commission gave him a broader canvas. A founder of Sydney's Modern Architecture Research Society, modelled on its English counterpart, Bunning sought to outline a more comprehensive approach to the housing problem that loomed. He published his ideas in 1945 as *Homes in the Sun*, an attempt to combine climatically responsive architectural ideas with a range of housing types and arrangements appropriate to different stages of life. It was part of a suite of similar publications by various architects, all intended not only to provide ideas for new housing but to reinvigorate the debate over the desired direction for Australian architecture, conceived both rationally and historically.[3]

In the aftermath of the war the criteria for this direction were themselves remade in view of a changed set of national imperatives. The decline in immigration from the United Kingdom and Ireland had produced a population almost entirely native-born by 1945, and the results had been disconcerting by some measures.[4] The low birth rate made for a slow rate of population increase, something of a strategic concern after the losses of men in both world wars. The portents of decolonization made for an increasing sense of geographic isolation from Europe and for the strategic acknowledgement of the nation's need to establish independent relations with Asian countries. But perhaps most telling were the lessons of the war itself, when Churchill had to be defied in order to repatriate Australian troops for the conflict unfolding in the Pacific. The impression took hold that for Britain, Australia remained a quasi-colonial source of men and primary products, as opposed to the more appealing prospect of a separate formal alliance with the United States. This turning, enshrined in the 1951 ANZUS treaty between Australia, New Zealand and the United States, left its mark on Australian self-image and foreign policy into the present.[5]

Thus the tenets of post-war reconstruction were less bound by historical loyalty than previously and they derived from many sources. The experience of interwar Britain gained by a generation of architects inspired some affection, but the austerity of British post-war reconstruction seemed needlessly severe when compared to the American embrace of a materialistic lifestyle that was the recompense for returned servicemen there.

Despite this view, the late 1940s in Australia were marked by a matching paucity of private capital and economic activity. This was distinct from the public purse, which had grown dramatically as a proportion of GDP. At Federation, taxation at all levels of government was about 5 per cent of GDP. This increased with the introduction of income tax in 1915. On the eve of the Second World War taxation was 11 per cent of GDP, but five years later it had doubled to 22 per cent, effectively setting the base for the welfare state to follow.[6] Private-sector recovery took longer and was boosted by the huge demand for Australian commodities during the Korean War (1950–53), which in turn stimulated imports. This process broke the insularity of the country in trade terms and in the cultural terms that followed.

Post-war Domestic Trends

In architecture the trends of the 1930s continued to play themselves out despite the hiatus of the war years. A number of architects saw war service in units that could use their skills.[7] By the end of the war, though, the idealism that had been formed in the 1930s, but had found few outlets, had supplanted the innately conservative nature of the interwar generation. Though small, the Australian Modern Architecture Research Society (MARS) group emulated its English parent in its exposition of rational design principles.[8] Indeed it was the rise of rationalism as a practice that most defined the post-war years. It sat initially on *sächlichkeit* roots observed by travelling scholars in the European public works of the 1930s, but the gestation period of the war allowed rationalist practice to be remade for Australia conditions. Typical of the trend was Sydney Ancher, whose technical skills were informed by his travels before the war. He enlisted in 1940 and spent two years in the Middle East as a surveyor. Having experienced European modernism through the 1931 International Building Exhibition in Berlin, he was also exposed to the vernacular of Palestine and the German-influenced modernism of 1930s Tel Aviv. On his return to Sydney after the war he bought five building plots in a pocket of the northern suburb of Killara, in Sydney's stockbroker belt. Ancher's sites, however, were in a small picturesque valley on the edge of the suburb, and the houses he built were far from the Tudor revival houses dotted through the suburb and closer to the Mediterranean-inspired houses that had arisen in the wake of the opening up of the North Shore by the Harbour Bridge from 1934.[9]

The houses Ancher designed in Maytone Avenue, Killara, are noteworthy for the particular confluence of influences and historical associations that they incorporate. The overall tenor is of white brick construction, with flat or pitched roofs. Despite his admiration for Mies van der Rohe, they are firmly material, with the proportion of window to wall taking its cue from the Georgian Revival popularized by Wilson in the same locality. The effect, though, is distinctly modern, with openings varying by purpose, and the detailing strives towards an unadorned seamlessness. The balance struck by Ancher is telling: the houses present as progressive while retaining a link to the classicism of the Georgian, a conscious weighting that deftly negotiates the lingering distrust of modernism and its cosmopolitan fellow-travelling ideas. His judgement was affirmed by the award of the Sulman Medal to his first house in 1945.[10]

Ancher's work was mirrored by that of Arthur Baldwinson, who had begun experimenting with modest houses based on his experience in London, working for Australian expatriate Raymond McGrath and the partnership of Gropius and Fry. His post-war houses display similar sentiments to those of Ancher's, commencing with his 1948 design for the home of Sydney's pre-eminent architectural photographer of the twentieth century, Max Dupain. While carefully responsive to its woodland site, the composition of massing owes a debt to Gropius's predilection for angular elements to offset rectilinear massing. Baldwinson's own 1954 house in Greenwich, a harbourside peninsular suburb offering challenging sites, has an even more simplified palette of materials and a variant of the linear plan. Generally this plan type arranges living and bedroom spaces to the north, but in Baldwinson's house the view is the greater determinant. The upper volume slides over the lower volume and has vertical cladding to accentuate the separation between the two. The result carries a greater degree of abstraction than is generally evident in Baldwinson's work, which often featured sandstone walls as a cipher for Sydney topography and materials. This signalling of local awareness binds the work of Ancher and Baldwinson: the former through historical resonance, the latter through a material one.

The idea that post-war reconstruction (and its implicit rewarding of returned service men and women with a richer life) could be rationally configured became widespread and took on a broader programme. The Commonwealth Government held on to the tax base that had expanded

Arthur Baldwinson, Max Dupain House, Sydney, 1952.

through the war and national research institutions like the Council for Scientific and Industrial Research were enlarged. In a pattern that was born in the early part of the century, the domestic house in Australia became the most responsive and agile incubator of architectural ideas, while the government sector moved towards building the components of the emerging welfare state, and the private sector mounted a swift capture of the technically ambitious classical purity inspired by Mies.

Commercial and Public Architecture

After the great exchange windfall of the Korean War, Australian capital looked to events in the United States as apt models for development. There was little major building until the 1950s, but that decade saw the emergence of distinct types of city buildings that owed a great deal to building across the Pacific. The forerunner of these was the 1948 competition for Anzac House, the Sydney headquarters of the Returned Services League (RSL). With the prestige of the armed services at an historic high, the building

Bunning & Madden, ANZAC House, Sydney, 1956.

was conceived as both office accommodation and memorial to the Second World War. The winners were Bunning & Madden, the firm founded by Walter Bunning, now in private practice with ex-public works colleague Charles Madden. The building was finally built to a different design on an alternative site in 1956, but it pointed to an office architecture that was predicated on the rationalist frame as the essential ordering device for a new generation of structures.[11]

As built, Anzac House was significant in demonstrating the space opened for modernism by the war years. The RSL was both a social and a commemorative institution, but it was not particularly progressive. The building was an exercise in grid-generated spaces, with the pattern of structure dominant and running through as a free-standing frame at the uppermost level. Window and balustrade subdivisions followed as smaller increments of the grid. The link to Sydney's colonial-era public buildings, with their Georgian proportions and verandah shading, was easy to make, but more important was the reiteration of proportion as a critical architectural component. A mathematically based system was not only compatible with rational architecture, its identification with the visual rules of the Greek revival gave it historical respectability.[12]

For these reasons the building draws on seminal works that rest on similar aspirations, and it has more than a passing resemblance to Giuseppe Terragni's Casa del Fascio (1932) in Como. This irony could be circumvented by pointing to many other examples of building frames whose careful proportions came to stand for rationalist practice generally. The precedent cited for the building was the 1948 Equitable Building (now Commonwealth Building) in Portland, Oregon, designed by Pietro Belluschi.[13] The international influence of this building has been poorly acknowledged, but its pioneering use of air conditioning and its distinctive expression of frame and window produced more than one homage in Australia.[14] Indeed Belluschi visited Australia in 1956 as the keynote speaker at the Australian Planning Congress in Perth.

In the field of commercial building the Melbourne firm of Bates, Smart & McCutcheon had few peers in the 1950s. Their first exposition of the curtain-wall clad frame, drawing on the recently completed Lever House in New York, was for their returning clients Mutual Life & Citizens Assurance (MLC) in North Sydney (1957). Situated in a traditional low-rise suburb split by the approaches to the Harbour Bridge, the building began the conversion of the area from houses to an office precinct separated from the city centre by the harbour itself. With its long arcade carved into a platonic building mass of flush windows and spandrel panels, the MLC showed the willingness of the architects to address the street identity of the building with bold, reductive logic. Grasping the essential elements of the Lever House model, with its dematerialized exterior and standardized internal condition graded by distance from the window, it proved a fruitful model for subsequent versions. The most striking was the Imperial Chemical Industries (ICI) building in Melbourne, completed in 1958. On the fringe of the Melbourne central business district, it also marked an acceptance of a rationalist logic and aesthetics in the post-war remaking of that most Victorian of cities.

For these reasons the two buildings were landmarks in the field of commercial architecture in Australia and their execution also demanded technical innovation. Bates, Smart & McCutcheon produced a suite of buildings in both Sydney and Melbourne in which the detailing of their curtain walls was honed. First among these was Wilson Hall at the University of Melbourne, replacing a much-loved 1879 building that was destroyed by fire. After some controversy the university committed to a new design, which opened in 1956. Described by architect and critic Robin Boyd as 'the most beautifully fitted jewel-box', the interior was bounded by a fully glazed facade to the east, while the timber-lined western wall continued through a coved transition to the ceiling. The southern wall, as the focus of the interior, was dominated by a large mural by Sydney artist Douglas Annand representing the *Search for Truth*. As Philip Goad has noted, Wilson Hall draws its detailing from beyond the strict functionalist tradition, and as such marked the end of the economics, and aesthetics, of post-war austerity.[15]

This in itself proved ambivalent, since sensibilities shaped in an environment of scarcity were reluctant to confront the possibilities inherent in modernism as style, as well as ethic. Wilson Hall took its cues from humanist modernism, as represented by the 'other modern tradition' documented

Bates, Smart & McCutcheon, MLC Building, North Sydney, 1956.

Bates, Smart & McCutcheon, ICI House, Melbourne, 1955–8.

by St John Wilson. He draws attention to the parallel modernism that sought to subvert or soften the harsher aspects of rationalism, as practised by Alvar Aalto, Gunnar Asplund and Frank Lloyd Wright among others. This distinction, proposed by St John Wilson in 1995, was keenly felt among Australian architects of the 1950s.[16]

Wilson Hall initiated a fertile period for Bates, Smart & McCutcheon, as they moved to confirm their local expertise in curtain walling. A modest building for ICI facing Sydney's waterside hub of Circular Quay marked

the start in 1956. There was, at this stage, intense experimentation with composite curtain walls that incorporated both glazing systems and a mix of materials, including fine corrugated sheets, for the spandrel cladding. This is evident in both the Sydney ICI House and in the subsequent MLC Building. The curtain walling pattern produces an effect of some visual complexity and subverts the tendency to view the glazing and spandrels as alternating bands. The corrugated sheets also prefigure the later charging of this material with regional significance, drawing on the widespread use of corrugated iron in the nineteenth century.

In Melbourne the firm moved towards a purer version of curtain walling. Using the smaller Hume House as a prototype, the detailing of Melbourne's ICI building follows the Lever House model more completely, with both spandrel and windows glazed and differentiated only by colour and proportion. Yet the vertical organization of all these buildings retained a compact modernist expression: the ground level was inset, with exposed columns creating a Neoclassical colonnade, the bulk of the building retained the continuous surface of the curtain wall, and the uppermost floor was either undifferentiated or had fins contrasting with a recessive abstract entablature. The classical references continued with the choice of cladding stone for the columns, facings and stairs, which was generally travertine. As a group these buildings represent the powerful coalescence of a corporate modernism, with rigid and abstract forms now the physical embodiment of progressive capitalism. The effacement of sentiment was well noted, not always favourably – indeed, at the very moment of the acceptance of corporate modernism, the counter-tendency, as we shall see, was in the ascent.

Beyond Commerce

While these may have been the most visible, and indeed the largest, of the manifestations of a resurgent economy, concerns from the early 1940s continued to make themselves felt. In Melbourne the fascination with compact housing and apartments on the European model produced landmark buildings such as 'Stanhill'. Designed by Frederick Romberg in the 1940s, it was finally completed in 1950. As unique as it is distinctive, 'Stanhill' is an amalgam of interwar modernist devices and motifs blended together by Romberg with an eclectic touch. The composition of parts also plays to their individual expression, from the semi-autonomous stair to the horizontal balconies and the egg-crate punctuations to otherwise solid-walled sections and spandrels. Its eclecticism has drawn attention from the date of its completion, but it cemented Romberg as a pivotal figure in Melbourne architecture and it helped validate apartments as a housing form.[17]

Bates, Smart & McCutcheon, ICI House, Sydney, 1956.

Perhaps the most important of Melbourne buildings of the period, in terms of entrenching a popular notion of modernity in architecture, was the swimming pool built for the city's public relations triumph that was the 1956 Olympic Games. A collaboration between Kevin Borland, Peter McIntyre, John and Phyllis Murphy and engineer Bill Irwin, the pool is an exercise in structural ingenuity and the kind of efficiency much prized by the generation of post-war architects. The enclosure is achieved by tensioning the roof truss through the weight of the angled spectator seating. This makes for a lighter roof structure and the two elements are stabilized with vertical steel tie rods secured into the ground. The resulting combination appears to effortlessly roof the pool, while providing well-poised seating and a building of didactic clarity.

Collectively these buildings revealed a singular dynamism in Melbourne architecture, with the debate over the direction of the discipline oscillating between functional imperatives, with a strong sense of economy, and a more playful view that could point to the boom economy of the late 1800s and the occasionally showy buildings it produced, as proof of a long-standing tradition of diversity. Sydney was constrained by the need for

Borland, McIntyre, Murphy & Murphy, Olympic Swimming Stadium, Melbourne, 1952–6.

Frederick Romberg, Stanhill flats, Melbourne, 1945–50.

lip-service to be paid to its classical inclinations, as refracted through its Georgian roots. While Ancher's houses demonstrated how this might be achieved at the domestic level, the new corporate modernism in Sydney also allied itself to those aspirations.

This impression, that Sydney and Melbourne had distinct architectural identities, was voiced in 1947 by perhaps Australia's best-loved architect of the modern era, Robin Boyd. Born in 1919 into a cultured Melbourne family of artists and writers, Boyd had the confidence to define both principles and direction for the field he had chosen for himself, architecture. His literary skills gained him influence through the student publication *Smudges* from 1939 and he sought work with Roy Grounds, from whom he imbibed an acute sensitivity to affectation, and a view that there was a continuous thread of good sense that could be discerned in Melbourne's architectural history. This thread, Boyd argued in his 1947 publication *Victorian Modern*, surfaced despite the excesses inflicted on Melbourne's architecture by the affluence of the gold rushes. Boyd asserted that the city was indeed different

Robin Boyd, Gillison House, Melbourne, 1951.

from Sydney, and bore no loyalty to the Georgian colonial-era buildings venerated in the northern capital.

The proposition of an architecture native to Victoria seemed both historically natural and manifest in developments between the wars, and Boyd crystallized its history, already loosely accepted. He established a lineage for the tradition through Desbrowe-Annear, Robert Haddon and Walter Burley Griffin, and he identified 1934 as a seminal year in the pivot to modernism in the state. Key players in this were Leighton Irwin, Arthur Stephenson and Roy Grounds, and Boyd's view has remained a popular one, as well as having elements of a self-fulfilling schema.[18]

Torn between a view that modernism had a social mission and an enduring distrust of populism, Boyd nonetheless served as director of the Royal Victorian Institute of Architects Small Homes Service, which aimed to disseminate contemporary ideas of architecture and modern living beyond the traditional client base of architecture. This belief in the innate logic of rational and climatically responsive design was a hallmark of the post-war years, and saw proponents like Walter Bunning take to publications like the *Country Life Stock and Station Journal* to persuade country folk of its universal validity.[19]

Boyd's experience, as charted through his journalism, was one of increasing frustration at the inability of his ideas, and those of other modernists, to gain wide purchase. He read avidly and had an exceptional grasp of international building. His Richardson House of 1954 bridges a small stream as a logical response to building on the site, but it is also a knowing reworking of Amancio Williams's Casa del Puente house of 1946. Boyd cast his net for inspiration wide: his Gillison House of 1951 is an exercise in efficient ingenuity at every level, from the diagonal window frames that serve as structural bracing, to the compact in-line plan so suited to Australia's southern states. This plan seeks to arrange adjacent living areas facing north, with services on the southern side. The resulting linear form can be adjusted to keep out summer sun, but to admit lower-angled winter sun into the interior. It became a staple of post-war design, and could be subtly reconfigured to suit different conditions.

By the early 1950s Boyd had developed his characteristic ambivalence, born of the desire to innovate imaginatively, but set against his dislike of ideas added to buildings to hide an abiding insecurity on the part of both architect and society at large. In 1952 he published *Australia's Home*, a history of housing in Australia within which was folded Boyd's views on the status of its architecture generally. His conclusions could be cutting, and as a history of popular taste it is hardly sympathetic: 'Australian building was brought up in the strict school where art meant painting and perhaps sculpture, but nothing more. Music was in another category. Any creative activity which involved the thinnest thread of commerce was suspect.'[20]

The idea of architecture as having integrity as an artistic practice was thus made explicit, and while it may not have exhibited consistency, it determined who Boyd sought out as exemplars and partners. In 1953 he joined with two of Melbourne's most eminent practitioners, Roy Grounds and Frederick Romberg. Romberg had the prestige of his 1940s apartment designs, with Stanhill a stylistic summary of the formal and planning tenets of a European-derived modernity, despite protests about its use of scarce post-war building resources. Grounds continued to bring his distinct touch to his 1950s work, and in 1954 he completed his own house, with four adjoining rental flats. The house was modest but influential, comprising a square plan with an inset circular courtyard. The planning derives from this strict geometric generator, but the amenity of the house lies in the architectural skill of Grounds in using high-level windows to extend the outlook beyond the confines of the defining square. The courtyard, too, is poetically structured with the aid of bamboo and persimmon planting. On view here is the architect's fondness for primary geometries, but the courtyard shows how he sought within this for spaces of transcendent quality, a quest that marks much of his subsequent work.

Accounts of the practice of Grounds, Romberg & Boyd portray an office that was more a collective of distinct designers than a single cohesive entity.[21] Thus authorship of designs, especially in the early years, is easy to attribute. Boyd undertook most of the house design, while Romberg concentrated on institutional and corporate clients. Grounds used the firm as a vehicle to move to larger work. The arrangement avoided a single house style emerging, and Grounds's propensity for experimentation gave the firm's work a diverse nature that only grew over time.

Boyd's fondness for houses, which he used to tease out the distinction, for him, between needless artifice and architectural invention, left a raft of fine houses in Melbourne as testimony to this search. His own house of 1957 in South Yarra is among the best, its twin pavilions either side of a central courtyard linked by a draped roof of cables supporting sections of planked roof where needed. It shows Boyd's propensity to dissolve domestic space from its traditional antecedents in a sustained effort to free domestic life from the dullness of interwar conformity. In this he remained an idealist, and he tried to mask his pointed skewering of popular taste with irony and humour in his writings and cartoons. His best-known work is his 1960 book *The Australian Ugliness*, in which he introduces the design pejorative 'Featurism', defined as 'the subordination of the essential whole and the accentuation of selected separate features'.[22] It appears as excessive ornament and as feature walls that relentlessly draw the eye away from the true nature of the structure. The argument is extensively developed and rests on identifying a deep cultural anxiety in post-war Australia that Featurism attempts to mask. As he pithily put it: 'Two things, then, are essential for the generation of the climate in which Featurism thrives. One is the desire to make things seem other than what they are. The second is the inadequate facilities for the process of camouflaging.'[23]

Trenchant criticism aside, the extent of Boyd's idealism can be gauged from his work for the Small Homes Service, set up in 1947 under the sponsorship of the Royal Victorian Institute of Architects and *The Age* newspaper. The aim was to make architect-designed, modest houses available to the broad public. These would be supplemented by designs from Boyd, as director, and his successor Neil Clerehan. Clerehan in particular developed a fascination for these compact embodiments of what he

Roy Grounds, Grounds House and attached flats, Melbourne, 1953–4, living area and circular courtyard.

termed 'living patterns', and his numerous designs show frugal post-war modernism at its best.[24]

Boyd had sought to define modern architecture in Melbourne as a continuation of a historical thread, and a similar project was undertaken by Morton Herman in Sydney. Herman had been a travelling scholar and part-author of Sydney's first slum rehousing proposal, and his *The Early Australian Architects and Their Work* (1954) gave Hardy Wilson's project a new progressive cast.[25] The years after 1945 also saw a revival of immigration to Australia and the historically low figure for foreign-born residents in the 1940s would slowly increase. The sources of post-war immigration were varied and included many individuals and families from Eastern and Southern Europe. Among these were members of a Viennese family displaced by fascism in the 1930s, who had found their way to Sydney. Their second son, Harry Seidler, had fled the Anschluss in 1938 to join his brother in England. Interned for seventeen months as an alien on the Isle of Man, then transported to Canada, he was released in 1941 to study

architecture at the University of Manitoba. He subsequently studied with Gropius at Harvard, and he attended Josef Albers' Black Mountain course and worked in the office of Marcel Breuer. In 1948 Seidler made his way to Australia via Rio de Janeiro, and a short stint in Niemeyer's office.[26]

Worldly and confident, the young Seidler's first commission was for his parents on a site on Sydney's northern fringe. Employing a plan refined in Breuer's office, and showing the considerable influence of his early employer, the Rose Seidler House launched Seidler's Australian career and proved a fruitful vehicle for the publicity that the young architect sought. The house was the first of three adjacent houses intended for members of his extended family. Flat-roofed, with a central court cleverly worked into a plan that grades from formal living, through informal areas to private bedrooms, the house utilizes a sloping site to ride out towards a gully dropping to distant forest. The square plan and incised court create a modern villa that orients to all points of the compass, as well as creating a sheltered outdoor room. The joy evident in its siting shows the conversion of Seidler from Old World to New: the unbounded horizon is the subject of the dominant views.

Seidler's self-promotion was a consequence of conviction: he bore immense loyalty to the modernist values he imbibed on the American East Coast and in Brazil. For Seidler these constituted principles that had genuine historical agency and he remained loyal to them throughout his career. By 1954 a collection of his work in Australia had been published, prefaced with essays that included an account of the historical imperative for modern architecture, and its fusion with sculpture and painting in the twentieth century. For Seidler the search for architectural and planning consistency that embodied this fusion was the key mission in his work, and in his proselytizing view it should appear in the work of others. He is scathing of the average Australian suburban house as he encountered it:

> The outside is bleak with almost 80% or more of the exterior surfaces solid and only very limited window area for the admission of light and air. The interior reflects this tightly confined atmosphere. By relying on all walls to carry the weight of the floors and roof, the arrangement of rooms becomes a series of tightly sealed little cubicles which paralyse the normal functioning of daily activities.[27]

Robin Boyd (Grounds, Romberg & Boyd), Robin Boyd House 2, Melbourne, 1957.

In these sentiments Seidler echoed those of Robin Boyd, but from a viewpoint less concerned with seeking out the thread of relevant precedents in Australia's history. He acknowledged the suitability of the colonial verandah, but avoided columned spaces in his own work. The difficulty he encountered in gaining approval for his designs through local councils was a source of constant irritation, as it was for Boyd and Ancher. But Seidler did systematically set out the principles that informed his house designs. He proposed three plan types: the bi-nuclear layout, derived from Breuer, that separates a house into living and bedroom wings, or day and night zones; the in-line plan that favours northern orientation; and the compact ring plan for constricted sites where living areas and bedrooms are arranged around a central kitchen.

The most striking feature of the book, however, is the number of houses and projects it contains. It is, as Seidler notes, a summary of his first five years in practice in Sydney, and it contains 37 projects, with at least nineteen completed by the date of publication. While the seminal Rose Seidler House is illustrated in passing, the rest of the completed projects present a remarkably consistent oeuvre that show the manifestation of his principles on a range of sites. A fastidious detailer, the interiors are uncompromising in their composition as planar entities, with different walls comprising glazing, panelling, shelving or stonework. This planar sensibility works against any sentimentality in spatial arrangement, and fosters a transparency to the houses that is liberating in its effacement of the traditional dark interior, but relentless in its intellectual order.

Seidler's reception in Sydney exposed the layering of architectural influences along the dual axes of internal self-definition and international validation. His ideas were a summation of what many travelling architects had encountered and absorbed in the 1930s, when Gropius had been an influence on numerous Australian architects in London. However Seidler had learned to eschew sentiment, and his inclination as an immigrant, and one displaced from his childhood, was to remake the world as he found it. Many of his clients were immigrants as well, and while his modernist houses might demonstrate how to exploit specific characteristics of climate and site, they also served as visions of a historically transcendent identity. If he displayed a fondness for any historical context it lay in Italy, where he saw al fresco traditions and public spaces that seemed more relevant to the climate of southeastern Australia than the British-derived ones. Of the world of Viennese interiors there appeared little trace.

It seems a truism of 1950s Australia, as elsewhere, that at the very point at which modernism as a cohesive style – and one that could be adapted to domestic, corporate and statist use – was in the ascendancy, its antithesis quickly coalesced. The work of Bates, Smart & McCutcheon introduced a sophisticated, classically evocative, corporate architecture to capital cities. The swiftness of this development testifies to an eye that was cocked towards America, its potential more apt for Australia's development than Europe's. Seidler's work also implied a clean break with the

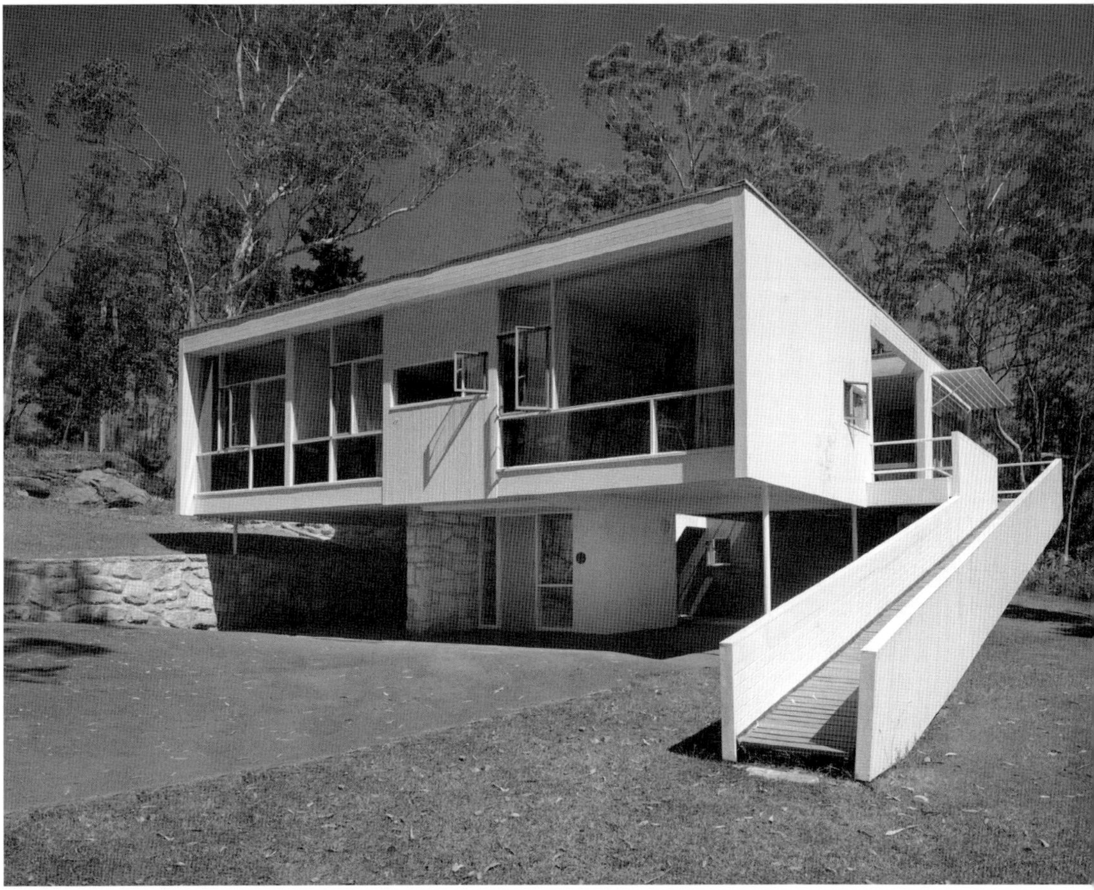

Harry Seidler, Rose Seidler House, Sydney, 1948–50.

politics of European interwar modernism, as he framed it as a rational version of New World optimism that could shake off historical burdens. But for native Australian architects this skirted the more complex issue of locating their work within a meaningful, historically constituted identity. As we have seen, this issue went not only to matters of perceived authenticity, but to claims of cultural leadership. The politics of post-war reconstruction were open to a rational remaking of identity, but the idea of an international modernism simply substituting for a local identity, however poorly constituted, was unsettling.

The reaction was evident in Melbourne from the revival of the building industry after 1945. Boyd's grafting of modernism onto Victoria's history is one thread of evidence, but there were other attempts to make buildings that were in some way intensely site-specific. In Ivanhoe, a locality with a

Peter and Dione McIntyre, McIntyre House, Melbourne, 1955.

long tradition of countercultural experiments in living, Peter McIntyre designed a house that snugly coils around two large eucalyptuses, its extruded form making little concession to convention. The idea was to preserve the trees and to have the house simultaneously deal with a falling site. The date of the Snellerman House, 1954, shows that the Melbourne post-war technique of combining geometric purity with a dominant site-derived idea was already gaining traction. In 1955 Peter and Dione McIntyre built their own house on a riverside site in Kew. Using a visible trussed form to define the building, the resulting structural attributes allowed the house to traverse the difficult topography. Boyd's Richardson House can be seen as part of the same tendency towards a dominant idea, albeit one that Boyd could also pillory mercilessly and hilariously in his later writings like *The Great Great Australian Dream*.[28]

The Reaction to Rationalism

The search for alternate traditions within a contemporary idiom accelerated after 1955, as Australia's acceptance of its geographic location became woven into public and private life. For travellers to Europe the voyage by ship provided a visceral sense of distance, and ports like Bombay (Mumbai) and Colombo introduced passengers to India and Ceylon (now Sri Lanka). Travelling abroad remained a rite of passage for young architects, and while London remained a popular base for touring Europe, other destinations beckoned. By the 1950s animosity towards Japan was declining, and the country was rediscovered as a potent source of pre- and early modern art and architecture. For Australians the resonances with Japan – China was effectively closed following the Communist victory in 1949 – were numerous. It reinvigorated the idea that Australia must invariably become of the east, in some fashion. Initially given form by Hardy Wilson, the search for precedents that could be worked into a nascent Australian modernity in architecture would eventually cover much of Southeast Asia. However at the outset Japan proved fascinating for architects like Neville Gruzman, who toured there extensively in 1955. On his return he experimented with fusing Japanese motifs and colour schemes with contemporary Sydney influences, in an effort to create an architecture of greater evocative effect, or poetics, than that of the abstract-leaning Seidler or the Georgian-inflected work of Ancher. The Goodman House of 1956 presents an early example of Gruzman's attempts to introduce his Japanese experiences and observations to Sydney. A dominant roof twists upwards at the northeast corner in a manner reminiscent of the traditional Japanese

Neville Gruzman, Goodman House, Sydney, 1956.

treatment of hipped eaves. The column and post construction of the houses also evokes Japan, as does the dark brown staining used on the timber framing.[29]

In this turning away from the rationalist-inspired post-war architectural movements, which encompassed both the *sächlichkeit* of state building and housing provision and the restrained classicism within corporate modernism, it was inevitable that both the humanism of Alvar Aalto and the charm of Frank Lloyd Wright's work would become reference points for a maturing post-war generation. The collective pursuit of alternative traditions, and their identification with a peripheral identity yet to play out, was widespread and concurrent without being articulated by a single practitioner. The experience of the war had forced a realigning of Australian loyalties away from Britain, and the sense of the country finding its way within its region saw efforts at national level to understand and engage with Asia. For architects involved in small-scale work, Wright's work served as a useful medium to re-evaluate their architectural aspirations. He had two perceived links with Australia, the first through his work with the Griffins, who had become more enmeshed in the national mythology as the Canberra project stuttered forward, and the second through his Japanese sojourn in 1905, and the six years he spent from 1917 directing the construction of the Imperial Hotel, Tokyo. This, combined with his status as a national architect attentive to landscape, rounded out his appeal in Australia in the 1950s and '60s.

The coalescence of these ideas, varied but defined by a collective anti-rationalist bent, has led to one of the enduring debates in Australian historiography. It revolves around whether the houses that emerged in the 1950s and '60s constituted a coherent school, and it touches on a number of issues of periodization and the identification of distinct and cohesive styles. The difficulty is that there was no central formulation of the principles of the movement, which came to be called the Sydney School, first by Robin Boyd in 1967 and later in a more comprehensive way by Jennifer Taylor.[30]

Taylor's argument rests on the emergence in the late 1950s of architects whose work seemed to have little local precedent, either in the prevailing interwar houses or in the English scene of the 1930s. What appeared from 1953 onwards was a neo-Wrightian school with transcendentalist overtones, suffused with aspects of Aalto and the structural logic of the Californian Case Study houses sponsored by John Entenza through his publication *Arts and Architecture*. These fed into a reinvention of everyday life that accompanied the affluence of the decade, as car ownership expanded, and finally dismantled, the tram city. Previously remote suburbs became accessible, and the idea of the house as a node of consumption and leisure took

Peter Muller, Audette House, Sydney, 1953.

root. The dwelling shortage identified by the wartime Royal Commission was whittled away, largely by the vast numbers of owner-builders who mastered lightweight construction – timber framing clad with premade sheeting inside and out – to quickly build new modest tract houses that came to dominate the expanding Australian suburbs. In a country of historical labour shortages, the lessons of these techniques were not lost.

The earliest exponent of a Wrightian view was Peter Muller, and in the Audette House he worked through a desire for integrity in his use of materials and a close fit to site with a composition of rough-laid bricks, broad timber eaves and balustrades, and a framing system to brace and hold continuous areas of glass. The house was in the Griffin development of Castlecrag, and it continued the principle of altering the topography as little as possible as it is layered down the fall to the north. While striking and, on publication, catalysing of sentiments embodied in the profession at large, it was followed in 1954 by a more modest, subtle and compelling house for Muller himself on Sydney's northern peninsular suburb of Whale Beach, an area with stunning natural attributes and a distinct microclimate.

The remote and elevated site made for difficult building, but the outlook inspired a house of great openness. Facing west towards Pittwater, the house enclosed a modest brief of family living in a set of discrete pavilions linked by a set of split and layered roofs. Although born and educated in Adelaide, Muller had spent two years abroad on a Fulbright Scholarship at the University of Pennsylvania. He was familiar with developments in California, and he cites the work of Jack Hillmer as an inspiration. Indeed the roof elements, stepped and planar, of Hillmer's 1951 Ludekens House can be discerned in Muller's. What the Sydney house achieves, though, is an intimacy with its surrounds as existing trees and rock formations are entwined in the plan.

The evident debt to figures like Wright and Hillmer masks a more earnest search on Muller's part. The attraction of the anti-modernity discerned in Eastern writings and philosophies should not be underestimated. In the early years of his practice Muller employed Adrian Snodgrass, a young architecture student who became widely influential in academic, and practice, circles through his scholarship of Buddhist architecture.[31] These interests coalesced with local practice in the 1950s, and by 1954 Muller was reading Ananda K. Coomaraswamy (1877–1947), the Ceylonese Tamil philosopher and writer who played a major role in introducing the art of the subcontinent to the West. Coomaraswamy served as curator in the Boston Museum of Fine Arts, a base he used to introduce the aesthetics of Indian art, and Eastern art more broadly, to American and English artists and academics. His writings are occasionally marked by a strident anti-Westernism that found a resonance with Australian architects of the 1950s, and Muller's restlessness saw him move between Australia and variously Bali, Sri Lanka, England and France.

Muller's early works in Sydney are thus among the earliest examples of that distinctive coalition of geographical awareness and anti-modernity that has been identified with the architecture of time. It nonetheless arose within an architectural tradition espousing craft as a critical component in opposing mass production, a value that can be traced back to the Arts and Crafts movement. Thus a recurrent anti-modernity in the English tradition, remade in Australia through cultural transplantation, re-emerged in the guise of a local movement centred on the Sydney region. Its cohesion that Taylor identified as constituting the Sydney School rests on a common response on the part of these architects to their location, and a desire to reinvigorate a culture of resistance using the tools at hand.

If Wright was a cipher for a broader incorporation of Eastern motifs and site-specific building form, then his influence was counterbalanced by a reinvention of Australian life in terms of a cleansing simplicity. The question here became how minimally might one live in the Sydney climate, with its temperate compass of seasons and abundance of fine days. This was the quest of Bill and Ruth Lucas, who built a small house in the crook of a winding road in the Griffin-designed suburb of Castlecrag. Square in plan with a central court and deck, the house presents as a series of platforms suspended above its undisturbed site. It rests on a steel structure supported on four columns, with extensive use of tension rods to achieve a cantilevering form. Every aspect is informed by clear intentions, from the site preservation to the lack of applied finishes to the radical transparency. For the couple the traditional house appeared both

Peter Muller, Muller House, Sydney, 1955.

physically and psychically defensive, symptoms of a cultural insecurity. In response their house exhibits transparency not only to its natural surrounds, but to neighbours and passers-by. Its radicalism is as social as it is architectural, and echoes the idealism of the Griffins in establishing the suburb.

The Lucas House was completed in 1957, for Taylor a seminal year in the evolution of what, in retrospect, might be regarded as a recognizable regionalism. In addition to the Lucas House the year also saw the completion of two houses that exhibited influences from the Case Study houses disseminated through *Arts and Architecture*. The first, by Sydney Ancher, showed a progression from his early masonry-heavy houses to one that exhibited a primary structural logic, with an interior showing strong influences of the traditional Japanese house. The Ancher house shows a clever

Bill and Ruth Lucas, Lucas House, Sydney, 1957.

Bill and Ruth Lucas, underside of Lucas House showing minimal structure, Sydney, 1957.

variant of the in-line plan, with a western orientation that demands a deep verandah which in turn becomes a colonnaded allusion to Georgian roots.

The second house, by Sydney Technical College graduate Russell Jack, bends a version of the in-line plan around a sharply falling site. In a reversal of the Lucases' philosophy, Jack uses brick infill panels and clerestory windows to preserve the sanctity of domestic life from the street, while the single room-deep spaces open to the wooded side. Described by the architect as exhibiting the human touch, he consciously sought to imbue it with a measure of craft, and it was an ongoing work for the period of his family's occupation.[32] Again the influences of Wright, Japan and Aalto's tactile progressions are evident.

For Taylor, these are the seminal buildings of the aesthetic school she identifies. They are indeed varied, as are their provenances. Muller's education was through the fledgling course at Adelaide, but his time in America provided alternate sources and gave him the confidence to undertake a reinterpretation of those sources. Ancher and Jack were both graduates of the Sydney Technical College, their interests shaped by the technical challenges attaching to site, history and modernist poetics. Lucas was a graduate of the University of Sydney, which perhaps accounts for his more radical view on the challenge of the Sydney dwelling, his critique of contemporary

Bryce Mortlock (Ancher, Mortlock & Murray), Badham House, Sydney, 1960.

housing taking in a rejection of consumption in general, and an ascetic view on living.

The desire to hew out a distinctive way of living was particularly pronounced, in Taylor's view, in Sydney, because of its lack of a modern tradition. This seems disingenuous. The city did indeed have one, but it was captive to the arguments of Wilson and Wilkinson. Ancher had come closest to articulating it, but in the work of Bryce Mortlock this Sydney tradition meshed with Miesian aspirations. The Badham House (1960) in the southern beachside suburb of Cronulla is exemplary in this regard. Mortlock joined in partnership with Ancher in 1952, but as was the case in many offices of the time, individual partners continued to design buildings under sole attribution. The Badham House is more opulent than most preceding ones designed in the practice, and accommodates an affluent suburban programme akin to its Californian antecedents. Mortlock wished to range more broadly than Ancher in exploiting the growing range of building materials on the market, and he juxtaposed these materials by using each according to its innate logic. The house also departs from Miesian precedents with its deep layering of space, with a large roofed and screened porch attaching to the living room. A central court lights the inner circulation, again showing the influence of Case Study plans.[33]

Curiously, the Wrightian references continued to multiply as more architects found in the American's work new themes to mine. Muller used the later Wright, especially the Marin County Government Center, as the inspiration for a remarkable house on the inlet of Pittwater for an emerging

Sydney Ancher, Ancher House 3, Sydney, 1957.

industrialist. 'Kumale' sits on a clifftop site, and Muller exploited circular plan elements to create a centrifugal composition about a central, dome-covered foyer that intersects with four secondary forms, including a swimming pool. The massive circular columns that mark the major ambulatory spaces evoke Wright's abstract bio-mimicry, and the presence of water and internal planting add to this illusion. It was a unique structure for a building industry barely capable of this level of invention, and it has few local imitations. In conception it was intended as an exercise in a geometric organicism, and despite its allure the house was too internally focused to inspire a profession looking to connect with natural settings.

One further student of Wright emerged in the period, and his work was more studied through his first-hand experience of Usonian houses. After travelling in America, Bruce Rickard returned to Sydney in 1957 and the slides he brought back served as an inspiration to colleagues like Gruzman. His enthusiasm for Usonian space is evident in his family house in northern Sydney of 1959. Composed of broad eaves, raised clerestory sections, and countervailing stone and glazed walls, Rickard's interlocking domestic spaces served as an alternative to the in-line plan

Peter Muller, Kumale, Sydney, 1956.

Bruce Rickard, Rickard House 1, Sydney, 1959.

emerging as a Sydney trope. His subsequent work shows a broad range of variations on this technique, and his feel for siting remained a hallmark of his work.

At the risk of oversimplifying things, it might be said that by 1960 a trend had emerged in Sydney that sought some resistance against both universal commercial culture and the placelessness of tract suburbia.[34] In Melbourne, by contrast, the tradition of the architectural *idea* remained dominant, its very looseness capable of assuming many forms. This characterizes the work that emerged from the coalition of Grounds, Romberg and Boyd through the decade. In a competition in 1956 Grounds had secured the commission for Becker House, the home for the Australian Academy of Science. The scheme shows his affection for unadulterated forms that also meet programmatic requirements. His own house had shown how to place a circle within a square: in Becker House he showed how a dome, its perimeter scalloped to create supporting arches, could accommodate peripheral naturally lit spaces and a raked central plenary lecture hall. The geometric strength of the scheme resonated with the scientific community for its strict order, and the building remains a Canberra landmark.

This followed on previous commissions that the firm had undertaken in Canberra, including two houses by Robin Boyd for the growing intelligentsia attracted to Canberra by its research culture, conducted at the Commonwealth Scientific and Industrial Research Organisation (CSIRO) and the Australian National University. The first, in 1953, was for the historian Manning Clark and his wife Dymphna. A year later Boyd completed a house for microbiologist Frank Fenner, another of the astonishing array of talent that the city attracted in the post-war years. The first is a modest barbell-shaped plan, with a raised study famous as the space in which Clark's magnum opus, *A History of Australia*, was written between 1955 and 1987. The second is a variant with two parallel

Roy Grounds (Grounds, Romberg & Boyd), Becker House for the Australian Academy of Science, Canberra, 1956–9.

Robin Boyd, Manning Clark House, Canberra, 1952–3.

pavilions, sporting asymmetrical pitched roofs and a glazed linking entry hall. Both showed the association of modernism with a progressive state and its institutions, in a Canberra still to be fully consolidated as the national capital.

Multiple Modernisms

As the 1950s progressed, the diversification of Australian economic life gave rise to different types of buildings. On Sydney's southern fringe, near the suburb of Lucas Heights, a precinct devoted to Australia's fledgling nuclear industry was built as a series of discrete buildings by architecture firms who were expanding into state-sponsored work: Collard & Clarke, Bunning & Madden, Stephenson & Turner, and Edwards Madigan & Torzillo. The complex housed a reactor built to the design of the British DIDO reactor at Harwell, but the most significant single building was the canteen, lecture theatre and study block for the Australian Institute of Nuclear Science and Engineering, designed by Bunning & Madden. Drawing from precedents such as Becker House and Richard Colley's Civilian Defense Building and City Auditorium in Corpus Christi, Texas, the building utilizes long-span steel bowspring arches to create a column-free dining space, although the

Bunning & Madden, Liner House, Sydney, 1959–60, mural screen at mezzanine level by Douglas Annand.

form is compromised by the placement of the kitchen and service areas, which undermine the illusion of the floating roof. In part this was the result of the hectic construction schedule, which saw many of the buildings quickly designed and built between 1958 and 1960.

Bunning & Madden's most subtle work from the period was the commercial Liner House, for the Wilh. Wilhelmsen shipping line of Norway. A slender infill office block in the sandstone-clad thoroughfare of Sydney's Bridge Street, the building takes its cue from Gordon Bunshaft's New York work for its transparency and curtain wall treatment. However the facade has a distinctive Sydney inflection in that it is set back some 1.22 metres (4 ft) from the street alignment, and has a set of horizontal shading louvres that give depth and contrast. The ground floor contains an elegant shipping hall, with a mural by Douglas Annand and a sculptural spiral stair to the mezzanine level. The facade framing continues through to the topmost level as a free-standing grid, defining the building's form as an abstract volume dictated by proportion, and filled out through a Cartesian demarcation of space. This schema had appeared in their earlier Anzac House and its symbolism was reprised in Liner House. Again, it represented a contemporary manifestation of the essential elements of colonial Georgian

Bunning & Madden, Nuclear Science Institute and Canteen, Sydney, 1960.

architecture, with the slender framing standing in for columns, the louvres for verandahs, and the emphasis on proportion for the rationalist principles that remained associated with the modest classicism of the colonial era. As in Ancher's work, Sydney's distinctive take on modernism had to be deradicalized by grafting it onto historical antecedents.

Melbourne held fewer inhibitions and it nurtured a wide range of approaches to post-war modernity. Roy Grounds continued to push for a distinctive architecture of geometric primacy, and his design for the National Gallery of Victoria has a monumental aspect reinforced by the extensive bluestone facade with its single arched piercing. The crafted interior, with a central court, mirrors the internalized space of his own earlier house, magnified to public proportions. Its effect has been criticized as intimidating, but the awkwardness that can be read into Grounds's larger commissions resurfaced in later years as a reference for a certain architecture of deliberate discomfort.[35] The building's Great Hall has a magnificent stained-glass ceiling by artist Leonard French, and is an exceptional place for reflective repose precisely because of its inward focus.

Boyd also showed that he remained abreast of developments internationally by rediscovering Japanese architecture, albeit with a different emphasis to his Sydney contemporaries. In 1962 he published a volume on Kenzo Tange for an international audience, in which he emphasized the symbiotic relationship between modernism and Japanese traditional building. Seeing in Tange something of his own predicament – the searching for models from Europe and the U.S. with which to remake something of the East – Boyd notes the embrace of Le Corbusier's concrete idiom in Tange's work and the occasional mannerism in how this is executed. Ever alert to the architectural idea, and the degree to which it might be pitched, Boyd's book conveys a regionalist reading of Japan as a fellow nation struggling for contemporary expression.[36]

One recurrent modernist theme that had a broad attraction in Australia in the 1950s was that of the intersection of geometry and architecture. When combined with engineering principles, this had the potential to eliminate excessive structure through the use of non-trabeated forms that reduced bending moments. The Bunning & Madden canteen is one example, as is Grounds's Canberra building. The ingenuity of McIntyre's work at the domestic scale, and in the association that produced the Melbourne Olympic Pool with engineer Bill Irwin, gave structurally ambitious solutions a particular currency. This was vividly illustrated in the crafted public arena of the Sidney Myer Music Bowl in Melbourne's King's Domain, designed by Barry Patten of Yuncken Freeman Brothers, Griffiths & Simpson. Again engineer Bill Irwin consulted, and the result is a seminal tensile structure draped over two compression masts and clad

Roy Grounds, National Gallery of Victoria with stained-glass ceiling by Leonard French, 1959–68.

in aluminium-faced plywood. The structure covers the stage and front seating, but the arena opens to a vast grass seating bowl beyond. Developed from ideas modelled by Patten and his assistant Angel Dimitroff, the Bowl prefigured the work of Frei Otto at the Munich Olympics by some years. For Boyd it embodied the tenets of the Melbourne School as he identified them: 'a great structural-functional idea carried out with an enforced austerity and a cavalier technique'.[37]

The self-conscious identification with distinct schools, whether Boyd's wry Melbourne one or Jennifer Taylor's later Sydney variant, reinforced the focus on the architecture of southeast Australia and the claims of its two largest cities to national leadership in architecture. Both cities remained conscious of the flaw in their respective arguments: their climates were hardly representative of the country as a whole, nor were their histories. While Australian speech exhibits relatively small regional differences in accent or usage, the compass of the continent presents climatic variations

Yuncken Freeman Brothers, Griffiths & Simpson, Sidney Myer Music Bowl, 1956–9.

Bates, Smart & McCutcheon in association with Conrad & Gargett, MLC Building, Brisbane, 1955.

that are masked by an apparent cultural unity. The massive post-war absorption of immigrants and the historical marginalization of the aboriginal population have common manifestations across the country. But climatic differences between Hobart and Brisbane are significant, and any outlook that acknowledges climatic appropriateness as a factor in assessing architectural worth cannot ignore them.

The evolution of a Queensland vernacular, which took in northern New South Wales as well, had become evident by Federation, and continued into the twentieth century. Indeed many distinct architectural techniques of this northern region appeared as early as 1846. Brisbane, of the major cities, sits uniquely close to the tropics, with Sydney and

Edwin Hayes (Hayes & Scott), Pfitzenmaier House, Surfers Paradise (Queensland), 1953.

Perth at 34°s and 32°s, respectively. At 27.5°s Brisbane makes the transition from temperate to subtropical weather, with discernibly greater heat and rainstorms. The Queensland house of the 1930s – deeply verandahed, high roofed and elevated above floodwaters – was distinct from the brick and tile houses that passed for domestic solidity in the southern capitals and in the wealthier Brisbane suburbs. Its architectural evolution had the effect of a cultural irritant, an example of the exigency that architecture in Australia had sought since Federation. Brisbane, after the war, had seen the construction of several office buildings using masonry construction in combination with framed egg-crate facade treatment for sun control. Local firm Conrad & Gargett partnered with Bates, Smart & McCutcheon for the design of the MLC Building on the corner of Edward and Adelaide Streets in one such exercise, but similar facade treatments were employed as far south as Adelaide. As in the rest of the country, however, it was the detached house that was most amenable to experimentation in form and climatic control.

Among a generation of adept practitioners in the 1950s in Queensland, two practices stand out for the range and quality of their domestic work: Hayes & Scott and Dalton & Heathwood. A 1959 publication by the Queensland Chapter of the Royal Australian Institute of Architects attempts to locate modern work in the state historically, and in terms of a commitment to the contemporary. Hayes & Scott feature prominently, their evolution of a modernist response to the climate already well established.[38] In part this may be due to Campbell Scott's role in preparing the book, but the firm undoubtedly served as both laboratory and incubator for a generation. Notable employees included John Dalton, Robin Gibson and Don Watson, who would all make a mark in the coming years.

Formed in 1946 by Scott and Edwin Hayes, the partners maintained separate workflows and houses can be attributed to each separately. Hayes had spent his childhood in Southport, then a holiday town for Brisbanites situated where the Nerang River meets the sea. It is now the administrative centre of the burgeoning city of the Gold Coast, but in the 1950s the houses built by the practice, generally from the hand of Hayes, attracted a clientele interested in the modernist vision of how one might live well in

Campbell Scott (Hayes & Scott), Jacobi House, Brisbane, 1957.

a setting devoted to leisure. In 1953 he completed a beach house at Surfers Paradise for repeat client Ethne Pfitzenmaier, an elevated house with two uneven pavilions split by a breezeway. The butterfly roof sheltered both the pavilions and the extensive undercover decks that comprised the rest of the building form. Hayes's 1958 Herford House in the same suburb presented a more polished, serene vision of a seaside house, elevated and with strip glazing that modulated glare, and showed an acquaintance with Seidler's Sydney work. Its deftness, though, implies a more universal view that reveals the firm's admiration for the work of Breuer.[39]

Scott worked mainly in Brisbane, and the more demanding climate away from the sea made the issue of sun control more pressing. The extensive roof overhang provided a well-tested solution, and in the Jacobi House of 1957 Scott used a large pyramid roof to shelter an ingenious invocation of the regional Queenslander. With overhangs on three sides, the square

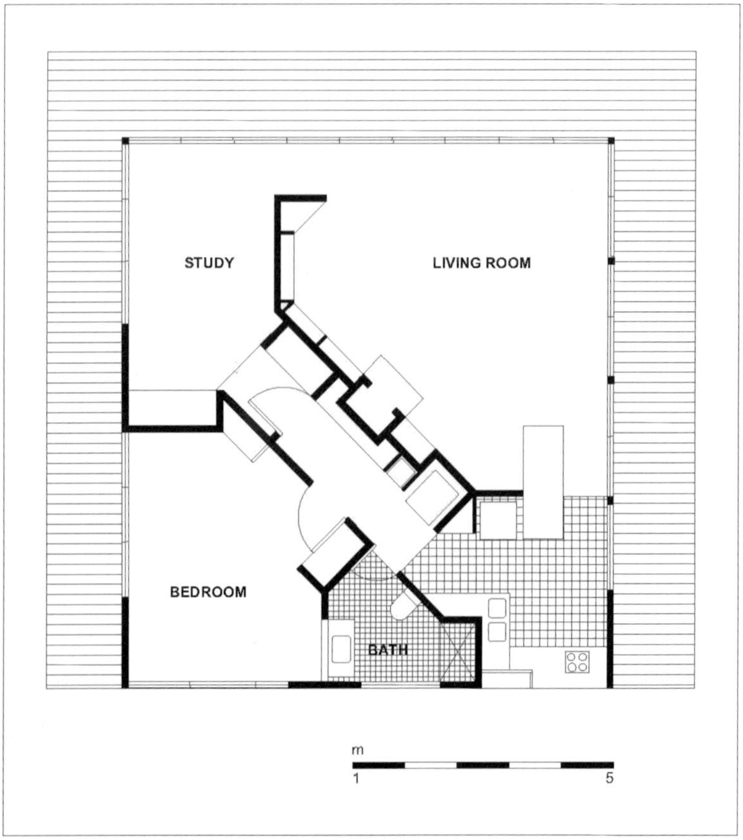

Campbell Scott, Jacobi House plan, Brisbane, 1957.

plan has a short diagonal internal passage that creates two major triangular rooms. This plan owes something to Le Corbusier's early work, with its inventive efficiency. Overlaid on this is a structure designed to free the house exterior of perimeter columns. Deep diagonal beams span from a central core to the corners, and slender steel support columns allow the horizontal lines of deck and eaves to predominate.

The Jacobi House was a particularly effective demonstration of the post-war principles of modesty and efficiency repackaged as an elevated container of intellectual repose. Indeed it was the clearly abstract design of these houses, their principles distilled through a rational sublimation, that accounted for their appeal. The same approach underpinned the winning design for the 1957 Plywood Exhibition House by John Dalton and Peter Heathwood, both ex-employees of Hayes & Scott. The win launched their practice and, as Elizabeth Musgrave notes, the house emphasizes their ongoing interest in climatically relevant design. A deeply shaded and extensively screened box on a recessed base, it evidently refers to Ancher's colonnaded classicism in idealized form, as well as to the building efficiency of the Case Study houses.[40] This device reappears in Mortlock's Badham House in Sydney two years later.

The impetus for a rational modernism in Queensland had external sources as well as local. European events had delivered to the state the Viennese-born Karl Langer in 1939. Langer had worked for Behrens and had a modest profile in Europe, and he also had the distinction of a doctorate in art history. Politically progressive, and with a Jewish wife, Langer left Austria and arrived in Australia in 1939, finding his way to Brisbane. His expertise was soon recognized and he found teaching work during the war, but had to wait for its end to take up opportunities offered in planning. In 1944 Langer had turned his training to the issues of building in the sub-tropics, and his technical pamphlet of 1944 titled *Sub-tropical Housing* was a counterpart to housing guides such as Bunning's *Homes in the Sun* and John D. Moore's *Home Again*.[41] Langer's argument rested on a technical analysis of the degree of roof overhang needed to shade openings at Brisbane's latitude, as well as the physiology of living in a hot climate. He added a range of house plans that presented variations on generic types for different orientations: an in-line version, a court type, a ring plan and two L-shaped configurations. They show his experience in compact planning, and his reworking of the house types to connect with adjacent outside spaces and exploit breezes influenced numerous post-war designs. He also proposed an urban planning configuration to maximize the advantages of the plans.

Langer found consulting work across Australia, but his best-known built work was the Lennon's Hotel at Broadbeach, just south of Surfers Paradise.

Karl Langer, Lennons Broadbeach Hotel, Broadbeach (Queensland), 1953–7.

Completed in 1956, the five-storey structure catalysed development in the area and remained its tallest structure until 1960. Built for a perceived luxury market, it had private sports facilities, one hundred guest rooms and could also accommodate conferences. But the owners had misjudged the market and the resort town that developed around the hotel aimed to meet popular taste, initially with a ribbon of private holiday houses following the coast. Nonetheless the building remains seminal to the story of how the Gold Coast grew into a linear coastal city now rivalling Canberra in size.

The late 1950s also revealed the talents of James Birrell. Melbourne born and trained, in 1955 he was appointed City Architect for the extensive Brisbane City Council, which takes in its core and most of its suburbs. Birrell was deeply influenced by Roy Grounds as a teacher, who left him with a taste for formal experimentation. He also cited Griffin as a model for his practice, and who inspired his view that individual pieces of architecture should sit in an encompassing designed landscape.[42] These themes informed his design for the Centenary Pool on an elevated site on the city fringe. The swimming pools and equipment are carefully worked into the topography, but the complex is distinguished by an elegant free-form elevated restaurant that provides a sensuous focus in the manner of Niemeyer. In a city some distance from swimming beaches, and prone to subtropical heat, the complex drew multitudes looking for relief in summer. The popular pool raised expectations of civic design, as Birrell had intended: his library designs in the suburbs of Toowong and Annerley were also instrumental in reviving the ambition of its public architecture.

Looking back, Birrell painted an image of Brisbane in the 1950s as underfunded and with a backlog of public works. Like Perth and Adelaide, its economic structure was distinct from the larger southern capitals of Sydney and Melbourne, home to an additional layer of national capital formation and governance. However by the 1950s the prevalence of overseas and local journals made for the wide dissemination of architectural

James Birrell, Centenary Pool, Brisbane, 1959.

ideas and these were taken up as they were presented – with a sunny idealism. Thus Scott and Hayes could experiment with modern houses as long as they had a clientele who sought out the modern as style rather than polemic, with the latter worked into the buildings as climatically sensible design. Although influenced by international examples, the best Queensland buildings of the time are very good indeed, their ambition not subject to the anti-modernity prevailing in Sydney. Not surprisingly Birrell, like Hayes & Scott, trained and influenced local architects who would go on to significant careers.

While Brisbane could at least count on rail and road connections to Sydney and further south, Perth developed in unique isolation despite a culture not markedly different from the East Coast. Historically the city had felt that its governance and direction was as likely to come from London as from eastern Australia, and an undercurrent of separatist leanings had persisted since Federation. In 1933 a referendum for Western Australia to secede from the Commonwealth was approved by a sizeable majority, but was not implemented. Perth's isolation gave it a measure of independence and was not always regarded as a drawback. The same magazines arrived in Perth as elsewhere, and images and ideas were taken up with equal enthusiasm. The same path was trod to Europe, and occasionally to the United States.

Indeed it was to the latter that third-generation architect Geoffrey Summerhayes travelled after graduating from the Perth Technical College in 1950. The following two years were spent at Princeton on a fellowship, under the guidance of Jean Labatut and in the footsteps of Robert Venturi, who Summerhayes recalled as 'always talked about'.[43] Work at the Perth Technical College, like its technical counterparts elsewhere, was modernist in principle, but viewed as a relatively straightforward set of techniques to be mastered. What Summerhayes imbibed at Princeton was the significance of history as a way of layering the process of design. On his return to Perth Summerhayes played the role of a seminal modernist, at the same time as he grasped it as a contingent phenomenon. His own house in the progressive enclave of The Coombe, completed in 1961, has all the signs of a house detailed to enforce a platonic cohesion. The thinness of the roof plane, and the single-brick walls used on edge as privacy planes, together with the floor-to-ceiling glazing and geometrically precise internal fittings all serve to downplay the core structure as a determinant of form. The street facade is exceptional: two broad planes of painted brickwork intersected by a recessed glazed entry porch reached by a flight of floating stairs.

While it presents the modernist object as an ideal, the subtlety of Labatut's influence can be discerned in a more complex work built by the practice in 1957. It is the chapel for the St Louis Jesuit School in Claremont, and its historical resonance, as Michael Markham has pointed out, is

Geoffrey Summerhayes, Summerhayes House street entry, Perth, 1961.

complex. For Markham the transition from a Mediterranean-influenced composition – long a Perth preoccupation – to a glazed southern facade has something of the transpositions of Venturi, as well as traces of the keen interest Labatut had in the experience of church architecture as a counterpoint to rationalist post-war space.[44]

Yet in the rationalist mode Perth also boasts one of Australia's finest interpretations of the office block, Council House. Won in competition in 1960 by the new firm of Howlett & Bailey, the building opened in 1962. Jeffrey Howlett, as lead designer, had trained at the Architectural Association in London after growing up in India. On moving to Melbourne he worked for Bates, Smart & McCutcheon for five years from 1956, in the period when the firm refined their curtain wall designs. Armed with extensive technical knowledge, Howlett reinvented the curtain wall for Perth by introducing a layer of T-shaped shading elements. That these remain separate, yet held in a tightly patterned matrix, gave the building its unique appearance of sun-shielding without the enclosure of a full *brise-soleil*. This allows the glazed box to remain evident, lending a lightness to the composition despite its modelled depth. At ground level the intersection of glazing with structure is particularly deft, and the building has retained the sort of contemporaneous feel reserved for buildings of exceptional craft.

The work of Summerhayes and Howlett laid the basis for a Perth architecture that multiplied the lessons of their seminal work, as we shall see in subsequent chapters. Adapting to isolation, the self-referential nature of a remote city that cultivated international ties as it saw fit gave the place a clear inflection on the modern, with both practices serving to further this. Howlett had moved from Melbourne to Perth for family reasons, but others arriving in the post-war stream of displaced Europeans were unconcerned about its remoteness. As on the East Coast, these included European-trained architects who arrived with well-formed ideas that were pursued with the vigour of the newly unbound. One of the most eclectic of these was Bulgarian-born Iwan Iwanoff, who trained in Munich through the war years from 1941 to 1946. He arrived in Perth in 1950 and worked for the firm of Krantz & Sheldon, a practice known for designing large apartment

Iwan Iwanoff, Schmidt-Lademann House, Perth, 1958.

Howlett & Bailey, Council House, Perth, 1963.

blocks. After a stint in Melbourne to secure registration, he returned to Perth. His architectural ambition became evident in the houses he designed independently, beginning with the Schmidt-Lademann House for the then German consul in Perth. A flamboyant piece of raked-roof modernism with an attenuated structure extending beyond its confines, the house shows Iwanoff's tendency to accretion and complex composition. It presages a career marked by unique experimentation with building materials and techniques, and in time his work found a deserved recognition.

One can view Perth as a microcosm of the Australian experience of the post-war period to 1961. The major shift of the time – from an economically and militarily exposed country to one of affluence and social idealism – set in train cultural developments visible to the present. The American influence was absorbed with little angst, and it sat alongside European precedents without undue concern about making the distinction between the two. Heady on economic optimism, the first task for architecture was to consolidate this into modes of practice hinted at in the 1930s, but held back by the war and its aftermath. The momentum of this outlook would continue well into the next decades, among the most fruitful in the country's ongoing self-definition.

chapter four

The Very Good Times, 1962–80

No architectural saga encapsulates the transition in Australia from post-war idealism to relative affluence as well as that of the Sydney Opera House. Not only is the building among the world's most recognizable, but its design and construction have also been the subject of numerous accounts, from the professional to the popular.[1] It remains among the most complex and difficult buildings ever constructed, as well as a key monument indelibly associated with the city's identity.

All of this is exacerbated by the unlikeliness of the project and the uncharacteristic generosity that accompanied its fulfilment. As Robin Boyd had lamented, the interest in architecture in Australia to the 1950s was confined to the profession and moneyed enthusiasts, with some curiosity on the part of the public for exhibition houses as demonstrations of a lived modernity that they might aspire to.[2] In a deeply practical country whose bourgeoisie was still sorting out their cultural penumbra, public architecture devoted to the arts was not part of immediate post-war concerns. The Sydney Symphony Orchestra (SSO) had been strengthened in 1947 by the appointment of Eugene Goossens as conductor and director of the New South Wales State Conservatorium of Music. Born in London, much of his career had been spent with American orchestras and he was lured to Sydney after fifteen years in Cincinnati. His ambition to raise the standards of orchestral, chamber and operatic performances in Sydney was timely, given that the city was yet to find its way to the international exposure that Melbourne garnered by securing the 1956 Olympics.

Goossens found a willing ally in Joe Cahill, Labor Premier of New South Wales and a proponent of public funding of culture as part of an enriched public domain. An Opera House Committee was established in 1954, composed of interested parties and advised by the New South Wales Chapter of the Australian Institute of Architects. Henry Ingham Ashworth, Professor of Architecture at the University of Sydney, was a member of the committee and would play an enduring role in the building's realization.

Jørn Utzon, Hall, Todd & Littlemore, Sydney Opera House, 1957–73.

The initial competition was for two halls: a larger one seating over 3,000 for concerts and grand opera, and a smaller one holding 1,200 for more intimate opera. The site chosen was the first natural promontory east of the Harbour Bridge, then occupied by tram sheds. Thus the city's own cove, lined by Circular Quay, would be bookended by the Harbour Bridge and the Opera House. The ambitious competition, conducted according to recognized protocols, drew considerable international interest and at its close on 3 December 1956 some 217 entries had been submitted.[3] The judging, by Ashworth, New South Wales Government Architect Cobden Parkes, Leslie Martin of the London County Council and Eero Saarinen, took place over the summer and on 29 January 1957 a young Dane, Jørn Utzon, was declared the winner.

The competition brought old fracture lines to the surface. The imprimatur of international validation through a credible competition was much valued by a section of the architectural profession, and by a state government intent on altering the perception of New South Wales as a cultural backwater in national and international terms. There were also local architects who felt that the competition should have been restricted to Australian firms, based on an inverted parochialism that resented the desire for international validation. Among these, Walter Bunning stood out as a persistent critic of both the design and the process that unfolded. In addition, the performance expertise of Goossens was lost earlier that year when he left the SSO and Australia after being arrested at Sydney Airport with pornographic material, an interest of his piqued by an affair with a Sydney occultist.[4]

Utzon was requested to team up with an experienced engineering firm, and he chose the London-based Ove Arup & Partners. His scheme clearly held technical challenges, but it was regarded as among the cheapest to build. Utzon had proposed a superstructure based on self-supporting shells, a technique that had wide currency at the time with the work of Félix Candela in Mexico, Saarinen himself with his TWA Terminal at Idlewild, New York, and the little-known Uruguayan Eladio Dieste, whose work perhaps most closely mirrors Utzon's aspirations. Saarinen saw few challenges in Utzon's shells, which he anticipated would be thin, light and easy to construct.[5] The scheme relied on a massive base that rose up towards the open harbour to accommodate tiered seating. While creating a headland form, it required that patrons pass by the stage areas on the way to their seats, restricting the space for stage wings and forcing complex solutions for prop changes and stage management.

In the ensuing story, few aspects are beyond dispute. The construction occurred in three phases: the base, the shells, and the enclosure and construction of the halls. Utzon oversaw the first two. The last was undertaken by the team of Hall, Todd & Littlemore, acting for the New South Wales Government. The initial idea of self-supporting shells of minimal mass proved impossible, and the final structure has great elegance but consists of a series of massive ribs that collectively make the roofs – a cumulative strength rather than one derived from a single geometric principle in the form of a parabola or ellipse. The move to shells generated from spherical geometries made the analysis and construction of the shells possible, but Arups summarized at least eleven versions that were considered before the final one was documented in 1962–3.[6] The technical problems of casting, erecting and cladding these ribs occupied a further four years. Utzon's involvement ceased at the end of February 1966, when he famously wrote to Davis Hughes, Minister for Public Works for the conservative coalition, that 'you have forced me to leave the job' due to non-payment of his fees. It seems this was not intended as a resignation, but it was taken as such. Nonetheless negotiations between the architect and the New South Wales government continued for some weeks to see if Utzon would return under changed arrangements, but to no avail. The architect and his supporters insisted that he retain full control: a meeting at Sydney Town Hall to press this view featured placards stating 'Utzon in Charge' and was organized by a committee that named itself using this phrase.[7] The events took place during a fortnight of high drama that included more Australian conscripts being committed to the war in Vietnam and the effective ousting of President Sukarno in Indonesia.

In April 1966 Utzon left Australia for the last time. The team to replace him had Peter Hall, a product of the Public Works Department, as designer, with David Littlemore and Lionel Todd drawn from private practice to oversee documentation and construction. They completed the design of the cascading glazing enclosure, and the plans for the two halls and smaller performance spaces.

At its core the issue of architectural control in the project was a defining one – the status of architecture, and the architect, as the final generator and arbiter of building form and detail in the execution of a *Gesamtkunstwerk*: a comprehensive whole with a cohesive guiding aesthetic. Utzon's view was that the building should be of the highest order, that is, one that embodied the best solutions he could conceive for each part. His method of contemplative designing had produced the ribbed solution to the shells, and he had worked out the glazing system and the internal structure of the halls in principle. He assumed that these would play out in a process of design and redesign, as the shells and their cladding had. His drawings reflected this process, and the construction documentation for the first two stages had been largely undertaken by Arups. The prevailing practice in Australia, though, was derived from the English system of competitive tendering, which aimed for unfettered market principles in theory. This entailed producing a complete set of documents for builders to tender on, allowing any competent builder to win the work if they could commit to building the works described in the documents more cheaply than their competitors. However this method entails long lead times to refine all components and describe them in detail. The Opera House commenced, for political reasons, before most of the superstructure had been resolved, with the result that costs could never be accurately ascertained.[8] Locked into an ambitious building whose progress was subject to public scrutiny, the various governments responsible for its progress could only persist towards a conclusion.

Sydney architect Harry Seidler's role in the saga shows how these opposing views – that the building should proceed primarily as an expression of Utzon's refined sensibility, with costs and documentation in train, or that he should be sidelined as an adviser to speed completion and contain costs – polarized the profession. For Seidler the retention of Utzon was critical, as his leaving would be a victory for the parochial pragmatism Seidler had fought through the courts in gaining approval for his own designs. Utzon also had exceptional credentials for those holding anti-rationalist sentiments in the profession: the architects who were building Wright-inspired houses around Sydney. He admired the American, and he also sought inspiration in traditional Mayan architecture and in ancient Chinese construction texts. The whole premise of the Opera House design, its reworking of the land form and its division into a base and a superstructure of formal and sculptural complexity that clearly flew in the face of rationalist principles, was a deliberate challenge to pragmatic geometric solutions. In an age struggling to hold to poetic notions of space other than those rooted in the classical tradition, the building assumed enormous potency.

The building's shortcomings, its failure to accommodate the required audience numbers and the lack of ancillary space to the stage areas, have been comprehensively overshadowed by its successes. It remains an ensemble of remarkable appeal, the quality of its construction still evident. Its iconic life is almost unparalleled, and it transformed the status of architecture in Australia briefly, as it became allied to the seemingly boundless idealism prevailing when it was opened by Elizabeth II on 20 October 1973. The final cost exceeded AUS$100 million.

How the state of New South Wales, aided by an ongoing lottery of 496 draws that raised almost the entire construction cost, could underwrite a building of this magnitude is a sign of the ambition of the post-war state in general. Neither opera nor classical concerts have a notably wide following in the city, but the building has been used for many events including massed school choirs; it now has a string of restaurants and bars built into its approaches, and its shells host spectacles of light projection. The effect of the building has been enormous but almost accidental, its unique stature among modern cultural buildings worldwide having emerged through the saga of its ambition and construction. Australia had changed between the conception of the building and its opening: by 1973 the Opera House symbolized a new cultural maturity, in promise if not in deed, predicated on a unique vision crafted from non-mainstream roots – Danish, Australian and the pre-modern exotic – in a feat of exceptional precision.

A Productive Disquiet

Architecture, too, was enjoying a period in the 1960s where ambition stood at arm's length from cost. The support Utzon garnered was an expression of this, although there was a sector of the profession that found his method irresponsible. But the moral high ground was with him, and among his most committed supporters was Peter Kollar, a lecturer in architecture at the University of New South Wales. Kollar would spend his career trying to articulate a trans-historical role for architecture, albeit one that was compatible with aspects of the modernist tradition. He had a sponsor in the dean of the faculty, Frederick Towndrow, whose academic writings articulated the perceived limitations of Functionalism. Kollar expanded on these themes, and an abiding ambition to define an architecture capable of deep meaning can be gleaned from his published statements:

> Beyond the physical and human plane there exists a vast realm that contains man's deeply rooted desire to reach higher than himself . . . When architectural thought is focussed upon this plane, it unveils some aspect or part of the perennial Truth, recognisable beyond its own time and context with Universal validity.[9]

Others made complementary points. Milo Dunphy, an influential teacher and avid bushwalker, decried the spread of suburbia and the effacement of the natural settings that were the playground of his youth. Collectively these sentiments fed into a growing disquiet with functionalism. As we have seen, much of what happened in Sydney domestic architecture from the 1950s was an attempt to transcend this tension. Domestic and public architecture took different turns from commercial work, which was seen as formulaic and based on classical models whose appeal was wearing thin.

The result was a flourishing of the Wright-inspired work evident in the 1950s, and attempts to fuse it with techniques of dematerialization to effect a unity of house and site. Neville Gruzman was among the most inventive: his Holland House (1962) is a composition of Wrightian roof

Neville Gruzman, Holland House, Sydney, 1960–62.

planes mirrored by a series of floor planes, with the intervening walls almost entirely glazed. Set on a virtual cliff, the drama of the structure was engineered by Miller, Milston & Ferris, who also worked on the Opera House glazing in 1963.

Alongside this admiration for Wright a parallel influence derived from European post-war frugality also appeared. Exemplars like Le Corbusier's Jaoul houses had reinvigorated the textural aspect of building, which found favour with the post-war desire for economical construction. The democratization of architecture aided this. While the Californian tendency was to pursue refined, detached houses as the architecture of everyman,

European designers sought to combine a working-class vernacular with the modernist principles of integrity in how materials were used. Taken a step further, this approach could unify frugality with a labourist aesthetic, where the process of construction became the ethical basis for the ensuing form, marked by the display of that very process. In practice this meant eschewing applied finishes and revealing as much of the structure as possible. This intent was recognized from the outset: in 1958 the English *Architectural Review*, in a piece on Stirling & Gowan's Ham Common Flats, noted that they were part of an approach that included the Smithsons' Sugden House of the previous year:

> What emerges from all these examples, and even more forcefully in the flats illustrated on the following pages, is an attempt to face the economic realities of dwelling construction in England today, and to extract from them an architecture that is workable in plan and grouping, and an aesthetic that is affective, rather than merely sufferable.[10]

Within a year architect Tony Moore had applied these principles to his own house at North Sydney. The exposed brickwork and dark timber structure had a robust textural quality that sat easily in bush settings, and two more influential houses of this ilk followed. In 1962 Ken Woolley produced an inventive variant on a falling site, whereby he created a series of cascading floor levels steeply retained on clinker walls. The roof consists of four monopitch tiled planes resting on an exposed post and beam structure, which also holds the intervening glazing. Internally the functions follow this schema, where a series of small room-platforms with little separation allow the structure to predominate.

In 1963 Peter Johnson, partner in McConnel, Smith & Johnson, built his own house in Sydney's northern suburbs that showed how the English precedents had matured. Using the same palette as Woolley, Johnson's house has all the hallmarks of English good sense and practical invention, but writ large for a bushland site. The monopitch roof gives a freedom to the plan unconstrained by hip-roof geometries, but with the practical advantage of good water shedding. The split level introduces a spatial syncopation, as well as eliminating intermediate stair landings. And the finishes have natural variability, while needing little maintenance.

Invariably attention also turned to the unselfconscious structures of the colonial period, as the mining of all precedents for a perceived authenticity continued. In 1969 Philip Cox, John Freeland and Wesley Stacey published *Rude Timber Buildings in Australia*, but the thesis of reinvigorating a rural tradition had been demonstrated in 1964 with Philip Cox and Ian McKay's C. B. Alexander College at Tocal in New South Wales. A dedicated agricultural college in the Hunter Valley, the low-set complex evokes both farm and cloister, punctuated by a shingled spire to the chapel. Its extensive use of structural timbers gives it an exemplary rectitude in its construction, and its version of authenticity thus rests on a reworked vernacular, an honesty towards materials and a spatial organization that has the humanist aspirations of Aldo van Eyck's work.

With each claim on authenticity, a moving construct valid only until the next demonstration, architecture in Sydney added to the collection of work that has been termed the Sydney School. In 1965 Clarke Gazzard & Yeomans completed the Wentworth Memorial Church, a small chapel on the now urban estate of one of the colony's earliest champions, William Charles Wentworth. Designed by Donald Gazzard, the carefully placed church platform is integrated into an approach path that slowly reveals the building. The assembly forecourt, whitewashed walls and topographic sensitivity lean more towards a European pre-modern vernacular, with overtones of the Mediterranean as well as Aalto's craft in siting. Gazzard was assisted by a young Richard Leplastrier, whose time working with Utzon had left him with a strong feel for craft, and the innate logic of a considered solution. These would become the touchstones for a later generation of Sydney region architects.

Ken Woolley, Woolley House 1, Sydney, 1962.

Peter Johnson (McConnel, Smith & Johnson), Johnson House, Sydney, 1963.

Tocal and the Wentworth church were for religious clients, whose reforming tendencies accommodated the aspirations of the architects to produce works of poetic and humanist resonance. They have both become key works in the extension of these sentiments from domestic work to institutional buildings. But the 1960s and '70s were the high point of public architecture in Australia, with state government architectural offices producing work of the highest ambition, alongside key private practices that garnered government contracts. Often identified with international

Philip Cox and Ian McKay, CB Alexander College, Paterson (New South Wales), 1965.

Brutalism, the work showed a continuing debt to the training undertaken by influential Australian architects in London in the 1950s.[11] They absorbed the techniques of off-shutter concrete first pursued by Le Corbusier, but later taken up by the Smithsons and championed by Reyner Banham.

The perceived integrity of unadorned concrete was a major factor in its uptake in Australia. Subject to no artifice, and showing extreme durability, the technique quickly gained appeal in a construction industry where highly skilled formworkers could translate the plastic nature of concrete into complex forms. For perhaps two decades labour costs made delicate concrete construction viable, in a happy confluence of intent and means. For integrity, above all, informed architectural debate, as the profession sought to add its voice to a state rivalling the private sector in resources and prestige. The work of economist Thomas Piketty has underlined how historically unusual this period was in its effective redistribution of resources through progressive income taxes.[12] Affluence also opened the door to social idealism, and entrenched racism towards Aboriginal Australians was exposed by the Freedom Ride, an activist tour of towns in New South Wales by a busload of students from the University of Sydney in 1965.[13]

Three versions of late modernist integrity, derived from English pragmatism, Wrightian naturalism and Eastern traditionalism, played their roles in Australian architecture of the 1960s and '70s. In a country and time not marked by intellectualism, these influences made a direct appeal to the disquiet that attended widespread and rapid commercial development. If anything, the prevailing intellectual tradition was a robust progressive libertarianism, carried abroad by thinkers like Germaine Greer and Clive James. To read the latter's reminiscences is to be reminded of the dull pragmatism that marked wider society at the time of his leaving.[14] In his memoirs he remarks that sailing through Sydney Heads on his way to England 'was like being born again'.[15] What persisted in architectural circles, though, was the abiding fascination for perceived authenticity. Heidegger featured more prominently in the debate than Marx, but it is possible that Coomaraswamy eclipsed them both.

Don Gazzard (Clarke Gazzard & Yeomans), Wentworth Memorial Chapel and forecourt, Sydney, 1964–5.

The sentiment for authenticity was nationwide and has sometimes been so loosely identified with the Sydney School that it is possible to identify representative buildings in all cities. This is the result of conflating an intention with its manifestation, and while Sydney may have been an incubator, the same three tendencies can be found across the country. It was occasionally identified as regional, as in the assertion of a local identity over a national, or international, one, but the fracturing of national identity into progressive and conservative camps undermined any expectation of a cohesive cultural voice. This was prefigured by the tension between Utzon and New South Wales minister Hughes, but the strong showing in the 1969 Federal election by the Labor party, infused with Gough Whitlam's idealism, revealed the progressive ascendency. When Labor won power in 1972 it marked the end of 23 years of conservative government.

Architectural Ambition in Public Works

In architecture the period saw a flourishing of public works, with large-scale buildings showing the same idealism as smaller ones. Among the beneficiaries of public building was the Sydney practice of Edwards, Madigan, Torzillo & Briggs, whose suburban library at Dee Why on the Northern

Edwards, Madigan, Torzillo & Briggs, Warringah Civic Centre, Sydney, 1971–3.

David Turner (NSW Government Architect's Office), Ku-ring-gai College of Advanced Education, Sydney, 1968–72.

beaches combined a massive brick and precast concrete exterior, moulded with a Stirling-esque logic to draw light in, with a steel-framed interior. Clearly conceived as an adjunct to the topography, it exploited features of the new suburbia whose density was low enough to conserve natural features. It was complemented some years later by an adjoining Civic Centre by the same architects, again demonstrating a sense of drama in siting and form. Indeed this illusion, of the city in the bush, underpinned the finest product of the New South Wales Government Architect's office, the Ku-ring-gai College of Advanced Education on a hilltop above the Lane Cove River. Less than 10 kilometres (6 mi.) direct from the city centre, the area had proven rugged enough to resist subdivision. The college complex, designed by David Turner during J. W. Thompson's tenure as government architect, was carefully mapped onto the site by Allan Correy. It surmounts the crest of the hill and cascades down on five levels, with an ancillary hall and dance studios. While the exterior has a complex and meticulously executed system of sunshading, with distinctive suspended fins, the interior reveals an embrace of the humanist underpinnings of Brutalism. A long internal street forms the social spine, feeding the major rooms and creating a space that is intensely animated to carry the building's social programme. The concrete work displays a full range of finishes, with board-marked textures

Peter Hall (NSW Government Architect's Office), Macquarie University Library, Sydney, 1967.

to the exterior and coffered structural ceilings internally complementing the suspended forms and dramatic spans. The confluence of craft, social programme and landscape forms a compelling ensemble, with landscape designer Bruce Mackenzie ensuring the fine-grained integration of the building with its surroundings.

Across the valley the new campus of Macquarie University was incrementally taking shape, as part of the nationwide founding of universities that followed the establishment of the Australian Universities Commission in 1959. Of its distinctive ensemble of original buildings, the work of Peter Hall can be seen in the Library Building (1967), which has an inverted walling system where light is admitted diffusely around panel perimeters, and the detailing shows the influences of Kenzo Tange's teasing of structural articulation. Hall's talents had earlier shaped Goldstein Hall (1964) at the University of New South Wales, where the combination of concrete and brick had been used to create a building with distinct cardinal faces, the north showing a broad sweep of glazing, and the western face having hit-and-miss concrete panels to give depth and shade. His appointment to the team to complete the Opera House was based on genuine precocious achievements in public works.

There remained nonetheless a trace of the rationalism that accompanied the rise of early Australian modernism. Walter Bunning was a persistent critic of Utzon's Opera House scheme, having little feel for the opposition that had coalesced against the views he had espoused in

Peter Hall (NSW Government Architect's Office) with Schmaeling & Partners (documentation), Goldstein College, The University of New South Wales, Sydney, 1962–4.

the brief incarnation of the Australian Modern Architecture Research Society (MARS) active through the war years.[16] For Bunning rationalism was at the core of modern architecture, and a modern Neoclassicism was its fitting expression. When the firm was awarded the commission (with T. E. O'Mahoney) to design the National Library in Canberra, Bunning responded to Prime Minister Menzie's preference for something consonant with the classical orders by designing, with Noel Potter, a deeply classicist colonnaded structure.[17] It employed a distinctive motif of the time, popularized in Max Abramovitz's Philharmonic Hall in New York (1962). This entailed using a series of perimeter columns rising to roof height, but with a linking beam set at first-floor level to define a visually separate low-scaled ground floor. A similar device is used with intimate effect in the Reid Library at The University of Western Australia, by Cameron Chisholm Nicol (1964). In time these references declined, to be

Bunning & Madden in association with T. E. O'Mahony, National Library of Australia, Canberra, 1961–8.

Cameron Chisholm Nicol with G. Stephenson and R. Johnson, Reid Library, The University of Western Australia, Perth, 1964.

replaced by the aesthetics of authenticity that met the transcendent claims of classicism with a phenomenology of gentle antipathy.

Perth had built on the exceptional credentials provided by the work of Summerhayes and Howlett & Bailey, among others. The advent of a concrete-inspired aesthetic can be traced to the Hale Memorial Hall, designed by Marshall Clifton, with Brand Ferguson & Solarski in association. Serving as a memorial hall for school alumni killed in action, it heralded a period of Western Australian architecture of remarkable quality. Clifton was best known for his Mediterranean-inspired pre-war houses, but it was Tony Brand who grasped the potential of concrete construction in the sharp light, white sand and limestone outcrops of the city's coastal plain.[18]

Also involved in the Hale Memorial Hall was R. J. 'Gus' Ferguson, who would go on to become another skilled exponent of the distinctive limestone-imbued concrete perfected in the Perth region. The institutions of higher education in the city were enlarged in the 1960s, and provided

R. J. Ferguson in association with G. Stephenson, Law School, The University of Western Australia, Perth, 1967.

a series of case studies for the distinctive amalgamation of the city's Mediterranean credentials, as expounded by Clifton, and a sympathy for the ambitions of English public works of the time. While these had a presence on the East Coast, in Perth they acquired a New World idealism that transcended the pragmatism of the English models. The addition of limestone to the concrete gave it a lighter hue consonant with the local stone formations, and the chalkiness was offset with the use of terracotta tiles for roofing. Ferguson authored one of the seminal buildings of this type, the Law School at The University of Western Australia. The building is also distinguished by narrow cantilevered verandahs, and a central court with brick paving and timber windows that again provide a crafted counterpoint to the concrete walls. The detailing of the roofs reprises that of the interwar Winthrop Hall, with rafters and purlins exposed and the underside of the terracotta tiles shown as part of the ethic of the valorization of construction.

Across the Swan River at Bentley a new campus took shape from 1961 onwards, designed by Haydon Williams and Vin Davies of the Public Works Department. Conceived as a series of courts with linking walkways, the campus shows an astute awareness of the demands and potential of sharp sunlight. There are numerous screens to mitigate glare, and there is a careful handling of the transition from full sun to dark, almost numinous, interiors. The Architecture Building, designed by Davies and completed in 1971, shows this approach at its most ambitious. A Brutalist exterior, marked by a strict gridded window pattern and enlivened with sculptural elements inspired by Le Corbusier, gives way to an interior street and atrium with muted natural light and a prodigious sense of vertical movement. The lowered light is a mark of the confidence of the work, being more subtle than its East Coast equivalents. Remarkably Davies had never left

Vin Davies (WA Public Works Department), Architecture Building, Curtin University, Perth, 1971.

Australia before designing the building. He attributes his sources to the Smithsons, Paul Rudolph's Yale Architecture Building, Wright and Le Corbusier, all gleaned from publications.[19] What the building lacks in compositional refinement it makes up for in its worked interior volumes and its handling of light. As in Ferguson's work, there is a keen awareness of construction logic and durability, and the same mastery of concrete. Other buildings on the campus echo these attributes.

The works of Ferguson and Davies are strong statements in an evolving idiom, but they are also imbued with a strict structural and compositional order that hews close to Neoclassicism. Perhaps their import was yet to be evident – and some of the best buildings yet to be built – but when photographer Harry Sowden produced his influential survey *Towards an*

Tony Brand (Forbes & Fitzhardinge), South City Beach Change Rooms and Kiosk, Perth, 1970.

Howlett & Bailey, Perth Concert Hall, 1973.

Australian Architecture in 1968, he concentrated on the works of local Perth firm Cameron Chisholm Nicol. While they too were adept exponents of the deep-shaded facade and exotic Brutalism, it was ultimately Tony Brand, working with Forbes & Fitzhardinge, who produced the most exuberant works of the era in Perth, and perhaps Australia. The small City Beach Kiosk of 1970 is a playful piece of late Le Corbusian-inspired architecture, with its use of highly intelligent curved geometries in both plan and section prefiguring the Spanish work of Enric Miralles. The East Perth Train Station is a building with an uncommon degree of articulation, to powerful effect, but the front facade of the now demolished Masonic Centre (1967), with its discrete boxes and entry under a massive sheltering roof, has a play that shuns any overriding organizational system. This plastic facility is Brand at his best.

The swansong of the remarkably fecund period of concrete building in Perth came from Howlett & Bailey. Their design for the Perth Concert Hall,

Iwan Iwanoff, Marsarla House, Perth, 1977.

opened in 1973, continued the firm's interest in trabeated and rectilinear structure. The Concert Hall has a series of Tange-influenced concrete portal frames that hold up a deep roof structure with expressed concrete purlins. Separated from the volume of the hall below, the structural system has transcended the tight utilitarian logic of early Brutalist work and has tipped into mannerism. This seems fitting in a city whose architecture had explored so wide a range of concrete systems and expressions, and had earned the right to self-reference, with the Concert Hall having an affinity with Brand's Masonic Centre.

In the domestic sphere the string of beachside suburbs that developed from the 1960s fostered a range of modernist houses. The Commonwealth Games of 1962 had proved a happy opportunity to encourage a popular view of modern architecture, with centrepieces such as the Perry Lakes stadium complex and the athletes' village.[20] The fine detailing of Summerhayes was much emulated, and exposure to the Indian Ocean gave much of the city a feel of proximity to the elements. More than any other Australian city Perth cultivated the idea of lifestyle, drawing on both Old and New World precedents. The mercurial Iwan Iwanoff continued to produce houses that oscillated between a vigorous suburban modernism and a highly personal investigation, following Wright and Scarpa, into the decorative potential of imaginatively detailed blockwork. His own house at Floreat Beach shows these techniques, which also served to create permanent ventilation when courses of blockwork are slid in plan. His work is another example of an architecture following a line of inquiry formed elsewhere, but given due credit for its ambition and singular determination. However, like many immigrant architects elsewhere in Australia, Iwanoff's work was difficult to graft onto the prevailing trends, incubated in common concerns, that distinguished Perth architecture in the 1960s and '70s.

The strength of Perth architecture of the period can be gauged against that of Brisbane. While the 1950s had seen a strong trend to invention in southeast Queensland, later decades produced a small collection of inventive work from practitioners already established. James Birrell was appointed as campus planner and architect to the University of Queensland in 1961, and in the following four years he designed a suite of noteworthy buildings on the campus that show his capacity to reinvent an aesthetic for each project. His three major works – Union College, the J. D. Story Administration Building, and the Agriculture and Entomology Building – each present a refined version of his fascination with material. The first, Union College, adopts the English Brutalist ethic of frugality, but with a proportioning that reveals Birrell's astute compositional eye. The Story Building, reprising some of the sculptural tendencies evident in his earlier Centenary Pool, adopts a sweeping curve to anchor a structure based on repetition of elements, with precast units and a modified curtain wall held in a tightly gridded frame, and bookended by sculpted external stairs. This was Birrell's version of the office block, but conceived within a tactile rather than transcendent aesthetic regime.[21] The Agriculture Building carries this materiality furthest, using richly variegated bricks to create an orderly series of blocks where the brick, on occasion, encloses stairs and services with curved walls that are corbelled and rhythmically punctured.

In broader terms, Birrell's work at the university can be read as part of a move to make larger institutional buildings with the same emphasis of the phenomenological over the abstract that characterized houses of the era. It was a distinction that was easier to make in government service than in private practice, where the progressive tenor of capital overrode the obsession with integrity. In a few cases there might be a displacement, with a city building taking on the attributes of the burgeoning campuses. This was the case with the New South Wales State Office Block, designed in the office of the Government Architect by a young Ken Woolley. Completed in 1967, the building departs from its commercial contemporaries in the sacrifice of usable floor area for an enclosing sunshading system comprising extended floor plates and vertical metal-clad perimeter fins. The arrangement gives shaded depth to the facade, which both relieves heat load and mediates between the Georgian antecedents of state government architecture and the vertical steel sections of the Miesian skyscraper. Nonetheless the building comes down on the side of mass as opposed to a dematerializing curtain wall and entry colonnade, as evident in the concrete elements that constitute the entry sequence and seating.

Adelaide, caught between architectural cultures elsewhere in Australia that had experienced periods of clear self-definition, gained some seminal buildings in the 1960s. The Reserve Bank Building of 1965, by Rolf Jensen with the Commonwealth Department of Works, was a concerted exercise in making a building whose interiors and exteriors were set against the prevailing tendency for what Jensen termed 'filing cabinet featureless office buildings'. Also rejected was the open *Bürolandschaft* (office landscape) arrangement then gaining currency, in favour of discrete working areas. The elegance of the fluting to the side elevations, and the depth given

James Birrell, J. D. Story Administration Building, The University of Queensland, Brisbane, 1963.

James Birrell, Hartley Teakle Building (Agriculture and Entomology), The University of Queensland, Brisbane, 1969.

to the main facade, were intended to counter the anonymity and regularity of the rationalist office block, perceived by the architects as driven by economics. The structure is enclosed by an elegant filigree screen above street level, and the lift motor room and tanks at roof level were housed in a recessed top level, surmounted by a capping slab. The side elevations have a subtle concave sweep, again to counter any perceptions of rigid geometric form.[22]

The legislation that established the Reserve Bank of Australia in 1959 stipulated that its operations be housed in its own premises. Under the early directorship of the ubiquitous H. C. 'Nugget' Coombs, who steered so much of Australia's post-war institutional development, new buildings were designed for all capital cities. The Sydney building was completed in 1964, on a prominent site on Martin Place.[23] The last of the suite of capital offices to be completed was in Hobart, where again a premier site was garnered for a quality building in the refined rationalist mode that marked all Reserve Bank buildings. The Hobart office opened in 1977, although the design had taken some years in the Commonwealth Department of Works, with P. Tate as the project architect. The strongly gridded facade, again employed as a rationalist cipher, reprises the Sydney modernist technique of using proportion as a device to link the new with the classical proportions of early colonial work. Given Hobart's founding as Australia's second city in 1804, and its early stock of civic buildings, this alignment carries local relevance, as does the cladding of Tasmanian sandstone. A recessed balcony at the third level provides a subtle civic focus to the street.

The expression of the frame is given some complexity with the stylized trabeation scheme superimposed on the grid and evident in the floor plane

Ken Woolley (NSW Government Architect's Office), State Office Block, Sydney, 1962–5.

Rolf Jensen with the Commonwealth Department of Works, Reserve Bank Building, Adelaide, 1965, now a site of Flinders University.

continuing through the rebated corners. This reiteration of rationalist composition through an aesthetic doubling, as it were, of the underlying design principles marks the self-conscious endgame of Reserve Bank design: a knowing elaboration of the iconography that had held such promise in the 1960s in ushering in a modern, refined state institution.

Car Park
ndis

Sydney Progressivism

The tension between a corporate modernism and one that wilfully sought a materiality through mass and texture continued to play out in the main cities. Sydney's first modern skyscraper, and the first to exceed the 45-metre (150-ft) height limit in place since 1912, was the AMP Building (1962) fronting Circular Quay, by Peddle Thorp & Walker. With a curved facade that recalled the shape of the original quay, it presents a bronzed curtain-walled highlight to a precinct revitalized by the nearby Opera House project. Its classicist format created a finely scaled podium and tower with an intimate colonnade and courts at ground level, and a recessed viewing deck at topmost level surmounted by a slender roof slab. The curving of the building, against type, gives a dominant orientation to the facade, and it singles the building out from others that appear as extrusions of a rectilinear grid. Yet the sensed divide between a specific locality and the placelessness of modern commercial towers could not quite be overcome, even with so distinct a gesture.

The opposing embrace of materiality produced two other significant government buildings in Sydney, both from the firm of McConnel, Smith & Johnson. Its dominant principal, Peter Johnson, had shown his hand in his own house at Chatswood, so the extruded mass and heavily shaded facade of the Metropolitan Water Board can be seen as the migration of his sympathies from domestic to city scale. In the later Commonwealth Law Courts, adjoining Sydney's premier collection of historic Georgian buildings, the use of precast panels and non-regular facade openings continue the idea of a defined building mass from which openings are subtracted, rather than the minimal enclosure of the curtain wall.

These buildings, and their embodiment of Brutalist techniques as a cipher for authenticity, threw into sharp contrast the work of Harry Seidler. After successfully establishing himself as a domestic architect, Seidler partnered with Dick Dusseldorp to change the face of commercial office development in Sydney. Dutch-born Dusseldorp had been sent to Sydney in 1951 by construction company Bredero's Bouwbedrijf. Within a decade he had founded the Civil and Civic construction company, and secured the contract for Stage 1 of the Sydney Opera House, the extensive podium. His transforming insight, though, was to create a finance arm that would allow large-scale projects to exceed the scope of the prevailing pattern of the single owner-developer.[24] His landmark scheme was Australia Square, an office tower and public plaza that amalgamated some thirty properties. The finance vehicle was Dusseldorp's Lend Lease corporation and the urban vision was Seidler's, founded on his contention that Sydney's historic street network played little role in fostering a mixed urbanity of work and leisure.

Commonwealth Department of Works, Reserve Bank Building, Hobart, 1977.

McConnel, Smith & Johnson, Metropolitan Water Sewerage & Drainage Board Building, Sydney, 1965.

The main commercial component is a circular tower of fifty storeys, with a structure designed by Pier Luigi Nervi. It absorbed the bulk of commercial office space, with the remainder taken up in an elevated thirteen-storey linear block enclosing the plaza to the east. The plaza itself is modelled on traditional Italian precedents, and is cobbled and shielded from the traffic of the major flanking thoroughfares. Positioned for midday sun, it remains among Sydney's most successful eating squares, contained entirely within a commercial precinct. It was a model that would inspire Seidler in subsequent developments, and its reinvention of the Sydney block gave the architect great credibility in the commercial sphere.

Peddle Thorp & Walker, AMP Building, Sydney, 1959–62.

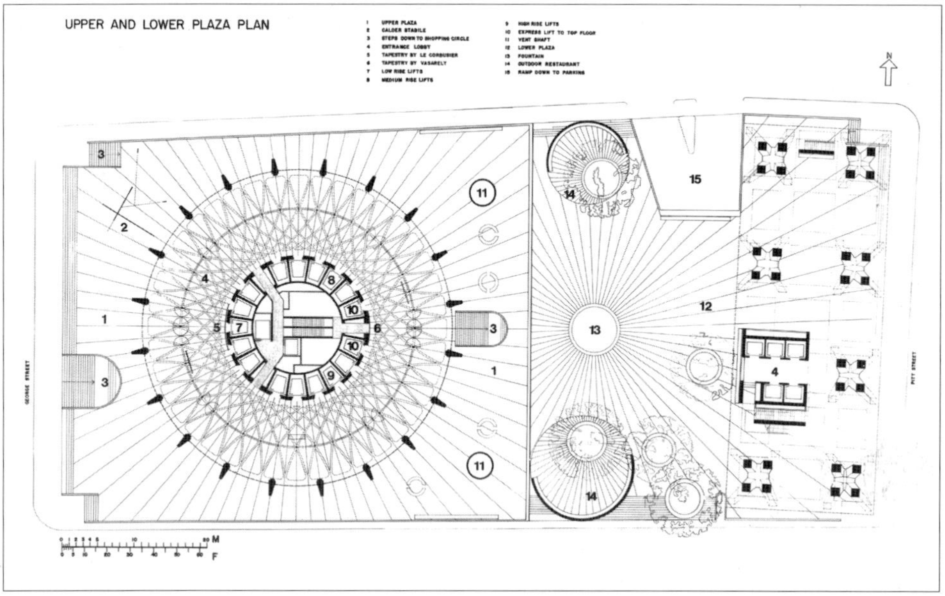

Harry Seidler & Associates, Australia Square plan, Sydney, 1961–7.

Seidler had never quite subscribed to either the search for a material authenticity or the transcendent object of the Miesian tradition. His loyalty to a set of principles, absorbed from an émigré community in North America but European in origin, continued to underpin his work across all scales. Having undertaken the intellectual effort to formulate a consistent viewpoint, inflected by his brief experience in Brazil, Seidler considered that the issue of integrity could be played out through a rational matrix that encompassed all aspects of architectural practice. The acute economy of means that ran through early Brutalism in Sydney is absent in his work. Instead he pursued its techniques as part of his textural palette, in line with his view that exuberance, too, has a part to play in architecture. Only this sensuality could have provoked his design of Australia Square, although it is important to differentiate this quality from the Wright-derived tactility of domestic work of the time. Seider's sensuality is deeply visual and his spaces are marked by the rationalist tenets within which they were generated.

His own house in Killara, completed in 1967, exhibits all of these qualities. Set in a wooded suburban site that retains an air of seclusion, the house works around a split-level plan that allows it to fall away from the road. The internal palette of materials – brick, concrete, quartzite floor tiles and timber-lined ceilings – are used with the signal rawness of the time, aided by a Breuer-influenced sense of contrast. The planning shows

Harry Seidler & Associates, Australia Square tower viewed from plaza, Sydney, 1961–7.

Seidler's fondness for rectilinear order, with wall planes continuously projecting the gaze outwards. The broad concrete balustrading and eaves pay homage to Breuer, as do the scattering of stone walls. The refined detailing is at odds with the pragmatic roots of Peter Johnson's 1963 house, for example.

Precisely because of this distinction, Seidler was untroubled by the question of how the integrity of materials should be honoured in their usage. It also allowed him to approach each project he undertook as a continuum

Harry & Penelope Seidler, Harry and Penelope Seidler House, Sydney, 1965–7.

of concerns, from the creation of outdoor dining spaces on the Italian model, to the structural potential of concrete, to the evocative textures and colours of quartzite and granite. Added to this was a sculptural tendency never quite free of primary geometric patterns. In Australia Square these came together in a limited number of elements, with enduring success. His next venture using the same development model was more complex, with mixed results.

The development model pursued by Dusseldorp had profound effects on Sydney commercial real estate. It foresaw the massive mutual funds that would be harnessed to create multi-site complexes, a financial prerequisite for the visions of development that borrowed heavily from the 1960s Metabolist movement in Japan. In the original, building megastructures followed a semi-organic order of growth: in the Sydney version the acquisition of separate sites provided the impetus for multi-block developments. This represented a new phase of capital accumulation and ownership, and it allowed Seidler to speculate, with investments clients like the MLC, as to how the city could be reconfigured at a mega-scale. In the 1970s in Sydney's core, as in other cities of its size, the target of activist counter-modernity was the dominance of the car. Seidler, working with the city council, produced schemes for the separation of pedestrian and vehicular traffic, using elevated walkways and a reconfigured urban grid that could view buildings as free-standing objects on this new raised plane.[25]

Such was the depth of the antipathy towards cars that these massively ambitious schemes were seriously considered both from an urban planning viewpoint and from an investment one. The remaking of the city was never cohesively undertaken, but it left a legacy in the form of underground shopping streets, pedestrianized thoroughfares like Martin Place, and consolidated redevelopments like the MLC Centre that adjoins it. The move to eliminate cars from Martin Place came independently through architect/planners like Don Gazzard.[26] Seidler's proposal simply exploited this by connecting a series of pedestrian levels to the traffic-free street, and by breaking the wall of street-aligned buildings that prevailed. Again, using an amalgamated site, Seidler decanted the office space into a single faceted tower, set to the south to allow the public plazas to face the sun. In one move the severe unity of Martin Place was broken, replaced by a sunny centrepiece that eroded the distinction between street, public space and private domain. The various levels of the eating areas make the spaces less comprehensible than Australia Square, but the cobbled plaza again emphasized the potential for outdoor eating in Sydney, and it prefigured the contemporary merging of work and leisure.

Seidler retained an antipathy towards the preservation movement, initially founded in Sydney on a fondness for the Georgian with all its

Harry Seidler & Associates, MLC Centre, Sydney, 1972–7: wall sculpture adjoining *Wrestling* by Josef Albers © Josef & Anni Albers Foundation.

attendant colonial associations.[27] The deference paid to these antecedents by Sydney modernists left Seidler bemused, despite his appreciation for the best of these buildings. This estranged him from some in the profession, but he had enduring relationships with commercial clients and his propensity to experiment continued throughout his career. As with other immigrants, his work, while widely admired, was rarely emulated.

Singular Practitioners

In failing to attract followers, Seidler was not alone. In 1955 a young Italian architect, Enrico Taglietti, was sent to Sydney to install an exhibition promoting the Milan Triennial. The following year he set up practice in Canberra, seeing the city as a blank canvas. Still to assume its modern form, the city was a trace of Griffin's original plan, with the construction of its signature lake still some years away. Taglietti had studied at the Milan Polytechnic, and worked in the summer of 1954 coordinating the teams of the 10th Triennial, where he encountered leading modernist architects and painters. He remained enthralled by Canberra and produced a unique body of work in the city that reflects the interest in organic architecture promoted by Bruno Zevi in the 1950s.[28]

Taglietti was ignored by Harry Sowden in his 1968 volume *Towards an Australian Architecture*: for Sowden, he sits apart from the mainstream of Australian architectural historiography. By the mid-1960s he had built both public and private commissions, but his Giralang Primary School of 1974 made his contribution impossible to ignore. It is a summary of his ideas as developed in Canberra, marked by a tendency to countermand the strictures of grid-based architecture. With elements canting and chamfering, and arcs and semicircles appearing in plan and elevation, his work defies the tenets of rectilinear reproducibility that gave modernism egalitarian credentials in Australia. While Taglietti used the materials that prevailed in public works of the time, his distinctive iconography and formal play precluded his work from being emulated, since it had, as a matter of intent, become highly personal. This experience further delineates how the core of architectural identity in Australia comes to be continuously remade. It favours not only work that incorporates elements of architecture that resonate with broad cultural significance, but versions of that work that are amenable to reproduction by other architects. In other words the seminal work will recur in various versions at the hands of more or less skilled practitioners. Taglietti has deliberately proofed his work against this tendency.

This accounts for the uptake of English Brutalism, and Wrightian themes by groups later identified as parts of schools or tendencies in

Esmond Dorney, Young House, Hobart, 1959.

Australia. If architecture were to assume a wider social significance, then these modes of working would have to prove pliable and attractive and to become an expression of the egalitarian intentions of the age. Outstanding works of architecture benefit a single client, while appealing movements that are widely emulated benefit many.

The singular vision is not only the province of the immigrant. A prominent example of translocation reveals the differences within regions, in this case between Melbourne and Hobart. Following service as a pilot in the Second World War, Melbourne native Esmond Dorney moved to Hobart, where, in Gerard Reinmuth's words, 'he devised a series of guerrilla-like interventions in the local built environment and landscapes'.[29] Dorney built and rebuilt his own house atop a gun emplacement overlooking the suburb of Sandy Bay, and the last version remains a prominent landmark. His best-known house is the Young House in the same suburb. This is a good representative of the steel-framed structures with singular curved geometries that Dorney designed. In part this was due to early experience working for engineers, but it only became a distinctive mode on his move to Tasmania. The structural stability of the steel arch allowed unobstructed glazing to the west to take in Hobart's extensive water views, and the high latitude made heat gain less of an issue than elsewhere in Australia. The

Enrico Taglietti, Giralang Primary School, Canberra, 1974.

Esmond Dorney, Pius x Church, Hobart, 1957.

same logic of maximizing views, framed by geometric structure, marks other houses by Dorney. Tasmania's history of frugality – doing more with less – was also a factor, as evident in the small Pius x Catholic church in Taroona from 1957. The combination of steel frames and minimal structure, using a vaulted form, renders this small building unique in its economy and clarity.

In Sydney Hugh Buhrich emerged as a figure of some interest, based on his own two houses in the extension to the Griffin's subdivision at Castlecrag. He had fled Germany in 1938 with his architect wife Eva, the couple arriving in Sydney on the eve of the Second World War. Neither had their degrees recognized, despite an education under Hans Poelzig and Otto Salvisberg in Germany and Switzerland. Eva worked in drafting and journalism, and advocated for a refined modernism in the 1950s and '60s with articles published in the *Sydney Morning Herald*. The couple's first house (1947–52) showed a learned and refined grasp of modernist space, with a distinctive sculptural spiral stair at its core. The second house, overlooking the waters of Middle Harbour, achieved the rarest

Hugh Buhrich, Buhrich House 2, Sydney, 1968–72.

of things: a collection of forms and devices both distinctive and without misstep. A simple in-line plan on a floating concrete base orients to the water. This is surmounted by a sinusoidal roof clad in copper above and timber below. The non-regular geometry of the roof acts as counterpoint to the rationality of the plan and supporting structure in an exquisitely judged ensemble: a regionalist school, as it were, in one building.

On a larger stage, the career of John Andrews demonstrated that it was possible to work on both sides of the equation: to be both singular and to produce buildings that could be emulated. Andrews, from Sydney, graduated from the Sydney University architecture programme in 1956. His early experience was with Edwards, Madigan, Torzillo & Partners, but he won a scholarship to the Harvard Graduate School of Design, and in 1958 a group design with fellow students for the Toronto City Hall Competition was promoted to the second round of judging. Further experience at John B. Parkin & Associates in Toronto established Andrews as a designer of uncommon invention, and taught him the elements of North American detailing and practice. After extensive travel in 1961 Andrews returned to Toronto, and the following year he was appointed designer for Scarborough College, part of the University of Toronto.[30]

The successful implementation of his Scarborough design was followed by a series of major commissions that allowed Andrews to develop an architecture that displayed a number of influences. These included Brutalist aesthetic tenets, the didactic structures of Louis Kahn and the attenuated plans with functions clearly grouped and delineated that these two sources, and the Japanese Metabolists, advocated. Andrews was acutely aware of the social programme implicit in Brutalism as the critical humanist counterweight to its rawness, something evident in Aldo van Eyck and Herman Hertzberger as well. Both of his best-known North American works after Scarborough, the residences at Guelph University and his widely publicized Gund Hall, which houses the Harvard Graduate School of Design, have embedded social patterns as generators of their planning and form.

When Andrews returned to Australia in 1969 it was to a buoyant economy for both public- and private-sector building. His work in Ontario and Boston had prefigured the growing ambition for buildings of substance, loosely defined, that were sought in the wake of the large budgets committed to buildings like the Opera House and Australia Square. Like Seidler, Andrews saw little distinction between the architectural integrity demanded either by public or private money, or by large or small projects.

As Paul Walker and Anthony Moulis have observed, Andrews's formative years owe more to his education at Harvard under Josep Lluís Sert

John Andrews International, Cameron Offices, Canberra, 1970–76.

than to the English tradition, and he extended the social programming in his buildings beyond their confines by making spaces that enrich the greater urban experience.[31] His work is marked by a confidence, filled out by his touring and from the validation of his work in the highly competitive North American sphere. While his public works in Australia display many elements in common with buildings emanating from various government offices, it is the degree of programmatic articulation that he introduces that separates his work from his contemporaries. While working on the Cameron Offices complex in Canberra, his firm secured the commission for a large office tower on one of Sydney's most prominent locations, at the corner of King and George streets. Both of these schemes, as completed, are unique in their attitude to site and programme.

The Cameron Offices design commenced in 1968 and was completed in 1977. Only a fragment of the building remains, but when fully occupied it comprised seven office modules, each arranged around a long central court that was extensively landscaped to provide a shaded outlook to individual workspaces. Themes for landscaping ranged from deserts through

John Andrews International, Woden College of Technical and Further Education, Canberra, 1977–81.

to alpine streams, complete with fish, representing the unique collection of Australian biomes. The building structure uses massive concrete T-beams, from which building parts are suspended, the whole standing astride the courts in a mannered version of a framed mega-structure far removed from the frugal roots of English Brutalism. The modules are linked by an elaborate pedestrian route holding vertical circulation and shops, so that the building could be woven into a discrete walking route separated vertically from the vehicular traffic of adjoining and intersecting roads. This was intended to be linked to the larger plan for Belconnen, a satellite centre to Canberra.

For Andrews this was his most ambitious work, exceeding in scale and complexity even Scarborough College. It is an exposition in ingenuity, intended to meet specific needs like the expansion and shrinkage of specific departments, the delivery of mail by cart, and numerous entry points so wings can be subdivided into separately accessed units. For these reasons a high-rise solution was rejected early on, with the whole complex housing a large population that was intended to animate the internal street and the surrounding area. A didactic vision of singular complexity, its ambition to reinvent the office building as a dense pedestrian mat is unmatched in Australia.[32]

Like much of Canberra, the building assumes an intensity of use that cannot be realized in the prevailing grid. The city had developed at very low densities, its suburban character fostered by a generous road network that linked the multiple centres intended to decentralize working and shopping. From the filling of Lake Burley Griffin in 1963, the city slowly assumed its modern form, punctuated by architectural works of uncommon generosity and complexity like the Cameron Offices or the built fragment of Andrews's vision for the Woden College of Technical and Further Education (1981), a concentric design with top-hung structure and a central lift and stair tower servicing its surrounding wings through concrete and plexiglass walkways. Elaborately conceived and again deeply didactic in its separation of functions, with the structure designed to minimize supporting columns at ground level to deal with rare flooding, the full vision of repeating modules with filigree stainless sunshading was never realized.

The King George Tower in central Sydney provides a contrast to the institutional work Andrews undertook. His first commercial project, its development came in the wake of Australia Square and concurrent with Seidler's scheme for the MLC Centre. With the prevailing view in favour of pedestrians, and amenable to building form that distorted the city grid to maximize light, or views, Andrews proposed a truncated square, almost triangular in plan, that leaves the corner free of building. A simple structure with a column grid and three vertical cores, it derives its identity from the fine stainless sunshading that shields the office glazing. This was determined, in part, by the construction process: being at the perimeter, the shading structure was designed to put the least stress on the central crane as it was lifted into place.

The truncated plan of the tower allowed sun into the street corner itself, which was sunken through a cascading set of circular seating pods. Lowering the corner plaza removed pedestrians from street traffic, with the intention of creating spaces of repose to counter the bustle of this major intersection. Only partly successful – the change in level discouraged potential users – the building played its role in subverting the dominant pattern of building to the street alignment. This brief moment of counter-urbanism, also championed by Seidler, reveals again how sentiment had shifted against the car to the extent that prevailing urban legibility could be surrendered to spatial reinvention.

AMERICAN EXPRESS

Pragmatic Local Variants

John Andrews International, American Express Tower, Sydney, 1971–6.

The compulsion towards authenticity in the 1960s, in its many guises, has a distinct geography. Its seems to have been prevalent in the mid-southern latitudes, centred on Sydney and Perth. In Queensland the house was reinvented along climatic lines to deal with summer heat, a function of the low latitude. John Dalton's work exemplified the period, with his Graham House of 1966 deriving its section from a diagram of air movement drawn through a central clerestory bank of windows. The language recalls Aalto, with timberwork and brick that has an affinity with Sydney architects like Gazzard and Woolley, but the genesis of the design is found in its climatic performance. The period also saw the emergence of Robin Gibson as a mature designer, with his design for Mayne Hall at the University of Queensland merging the precedents of the glazed aspect of Wilson Hall in Melbourne with the structural clarity of the Perth Concert Hall. Gibson employed the simple devices of massive roofs, and mass concrete, to control heat gain in his Brisbane buildings. His finesse with these materials would have ample expression in subsequent public buildings.

John Dalton, Graham House, Brisbane, 1966.

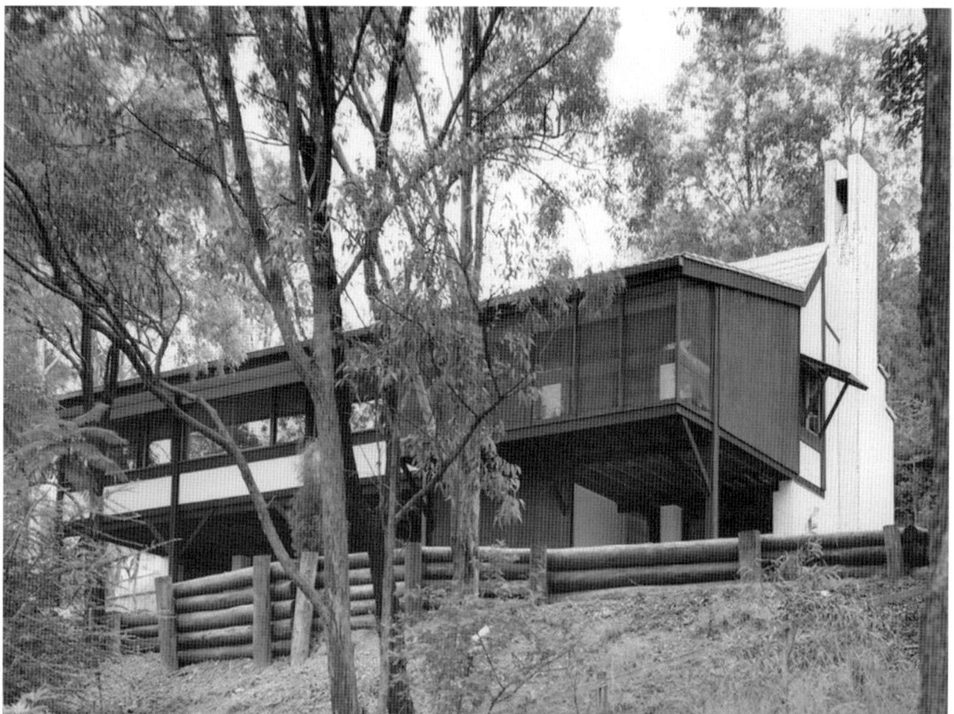

Yuncken Freeman, Victorian State Offices and Premier's Office, Melbourne, 1962–70.

Melbourne, as the most southerly mainland city, seemed less concerned with issues of authenticity. As Boyd had observed, Victorian architecture was characterized by ideas, with less emphasis on the legitimacy of a site-specific building response. While some commentators have proposed that by the 1960s Melbourne had lost its position in the vanguard of Australian modern architecture, the city may have simply been historically unsympathetic to the rising architectural obsession to give meaning – understood as both uncovering the *genius loci*, and defining the main current of a nationalist iconography – that prevailed in the temperate latitudes.[33] The reproduction of Brutalist tropes was widespread in the city, but intellectually distinct. Always more permeable than its counterpart capitals, Melbourne's city centre retained its varied character as it shaded on all sides to its suburban surroundings. Seidler had tapped into Sydney's aspiration for new patterns of consumption, but the history of Melbourne office towers lies in the innate logic of the tower form and its unfolding expression. As Giorgio Marfella has chronicled, this led to ongoing collaboration between key Melbourne architectural firms and leading American ones, to better exploit the formulas that defined the successful commercial tower.[34]

Robin Gibson & Partners, Mayne Hall, The University of Queensland, Brisbane, 1973.

Yuncken Freeman, BHP Building entry foyer, Melbourne, 1967–72.

The role of Bates, Smart & McCutcheon in refining curtain wall construction in Australia has been noted, but it was the firm of Yuncken Freeman who refined the square tower plan that represented the most efficient ratio of exterior wall to enclosed floor area. Among their earliest works of this type is their winning design for the State Government Offices in Treasury Place, on the edge of the central city grid. Designed in 1963, and completed some six years later, the ensemble of two buildings, one of sixteen storeys and another of six, is a compelling reworking of the rationalist grid into an object whose regularity and visual depth propels the building towards Manfredo Tafuri's utopia of form. This is aided by the subtle handling of the lowest level, to mediate between the pristine ambitions of the office blocks and the undulations of the ground plane.

The aesthetic here is noteworthy, as it transcends the strictures of classicist antecedents while still evoking their credentials in proportion. Neither fully instrumental in controlling the sun, nor overtly historicist in their trabeated form, the buildings present a version of the office that derives visual strength from being considered in the round, as opposed to one composed of discrete elevations. This potential inheres in the square plan, but here it is brought to fruition. This objective was revisited by the same firm some years later in their BHP House (1972).

As Philip Goad has argued, BHP House is the most notable corporate high-rise of the Miesian tradition in Australia.[35] Designed by Barry Patten of Yuncken Freeman, the design was undertaken with the close involvement of the Chicago office of Skidmore, Owings & Merrill (SOM). This was an arrangement with good precedent, since the 1960 Shell Building and the 1965 AMP Tower and St James Building bore the hand of the San Francisco office of SOM. The former was designed by Buchan Laird & Buchan in association with SOM, while the latter was documented by Bates, Smart and McCutcheon to the design of SOM. Both buildings are adjacent to the BHP House site. However the collaboration between Patten and SOM was of a different sort. A team from Yuncken Freeman worked in the SOM office utilizing the expertise of Fazlur Khan, whose innovations had produced the structure for the John Hancock Center in Chicago. Bill Irwin, whose work on the pool for the 1956 Melbourne Olympics had established him as a structural innovator in his own right, also visited Chicago. The team's exposure to Mies van der Rohe's projects, and to the new generation of massive U.S. high-rise projects under construction or recently completed, led to the design of BHP House using a structural core, and a perimeter that combined structure and glazing to form a stiff outer carapace, with floors free of internal columns spanning between the two.

The client, BHP, has been previously mentioned as a major driver of Australian industrialization, especially in the interwar period. By the 1960s it was the unrivalled leader in steel manufacturing in the country and the building was intended to showcase the material. Patten, whose ingenuity was already on display at the Sydney Myer Music Bowl, led his team through the iterations that resulted in the tower as built, a glass and steel edifice characterized by three belt trusses spanning two floors each, and adding to the stiffness of the facade. The generic space created by the column-free floors made for a pristine office environment, allowing fitouts of great variety between the uninterrupted floor and ceiling planes. The facade grid has been worked into regular vertical and horizontal proportions, with additional strength and modulation provided by external engaged columns running the height of the building. The plan is perfectly square, in a comprehensive demonstration of the tendency in the city to align

Skidmore, Owings & Merrill in association with Bates, Smart & McCutcheon, AMP Tower and flanking St James Building, Melbourne, 1965–9.

Roy Grounds (Grounds, Romberg & Boyd), Victorian Arts Centre, Melbourne, 1969–84.

efficient form with the prevailing city grid. Unlike Sydney's experiments in fracturing urban form, BHP House demonstrates the subtle relations to alignment and geometry that have maintained the integrity of Melbourne's urban grid.

The effect was heightened by the adjoining AMP Building and its lower L-shaped counterpart (1965). The AMP tower, of SOM design, has a similar alignment to BHP House and uses its site configuration to allow the tower to emerge as free-standing, with both buildings sitting within implied internal plazas set back from the street. In a demonstration of the swiftness of the late-modernist dialectic, at the completion of BHP House its very

refinement was a lightning rod for the counter-modernist sentiment that was in the ascendant.[36]

The period also saw the protracted saga that was the design of the Victorian Arts Centre. Grounds had been appointed architect for the complex in 1959, and after completion of the National Gallery of Victoria the design for the theatres was revised to suit the difficult geology of the site. Grounds had envisaged a large spire surmounting the complex, and the iconic significance of the Sydney Opera House lent credence to the idea of demarcating the complex within the city. The second phase opened in 1984, with the distinction of embodying a design conceived some 25 years earlier. The result is dominated by geometry and was taken to show Grounds's limits as a designer, but came in subsequent years to be a reference point for the distinctly Melburnian reaction to the strictures and tenets of institutional modernism.[37]

Ken Woolley (Ancher, Mortlock, Murray & Woolley), 'Lowline' Project Home for Pettit & Sevitt home builders, Sydney.

David McGlashan (McGlashan & Everist), interior, Heide 2, Melbourne, 1965.

While the city may not have held fast to the pursuit of authenticity, it fostered individual exponents of the associated materials and construction ethic. Foremost among these was Graham Gunn, who worked in both the domestic and institutional Brutalist modes. His work for Merchant Builders, designing standardized home plans for repetitive supply, continued the ambitions publicized by John Entenza in California in the 1950s for affordable architect-designed houses. The counterpart to Merchant Builders

Jack McConnell (Hassell, McConnell & Partners), McConnell House, Adelaide, 1967.

in Sydney was the firm of Pettit & Sevitt, which offered designs by leading architects like Ken Woolley. His 'Lowline' design combined an expressed timber frame, its form implying the economies of standardization, with the textured natural finishes of domestic Brutalism.

In a moment of particularly refined sensibility, McGlashan & Everist designed a house for prominent art patrons John and Sunday Reed, around whom a bohemian circle of artists had coalesced. The house, completed in 1967 on the outskirts of Melbourne, blends elements of utilitarian detailing with a sophisticated spatial sequence that on occasion looks to the landscaped grounds through large windows. The combination of spatial compression relieved by volumetric generosity, woven through with a complex movement sequence, is highlighted by the simple, almost severe detailing. It is marked by a blend of deep roof planes and spaces designed for an inventive domestic life, with living patterns that defy convention. Now part of a small museum complex, the house neatly transcends its antecedents in one of the high moments of Australian modernist architecture.

In another seminal exercise in mature regional modernism, Jack McConnell built an elegant version of the urban Adelaide house in 1967. Partner in the influential local firm of Hassell, McConnell & Partners, the house presents a restrained, stripped-down version of the double-storey verandah to the street. This conceals a lofty studio and sitting room overlooked by a bedroom gallery, but the distinctive response to site and climate lies in the rear court and garden, divided into pool, colonnade and grassed courtyard. At the rear is set guest accommodation and parking, in a site treatment much emulated in later Adelaide houses.[38]

The city's best examples in institutional architecture of the period came from the firm of Dickson & Platten, exemplified in their Union House for the University of Adelaide. Inserted into the heart of the historic campus, it links the upper and lower levels through a series of walkways and stairs that give onto student facilities. This interpretation of the movement and sociability vital to the Brutalist vision is enhanced by the finely articulated concrete detailing, echoing contemporary work in Perth. The building highlights the ubiquity, albeit with subtle variants, of this trend to embody in public buildings an architectural version of the wider aspiration to institutional integrity.

The passing of this style of architecture, hastened by the growing cost of off-shutter concrete, would be complete by the early 1980s. The monumental social idealism of the early 1970s found its denouement in the dismissal of the Whitlam government in November 1975 at the hands of

Jack McConnell (Hassell, McConnell & Partners), McConnell House ground and first floor plans, Adelaide, 1967.

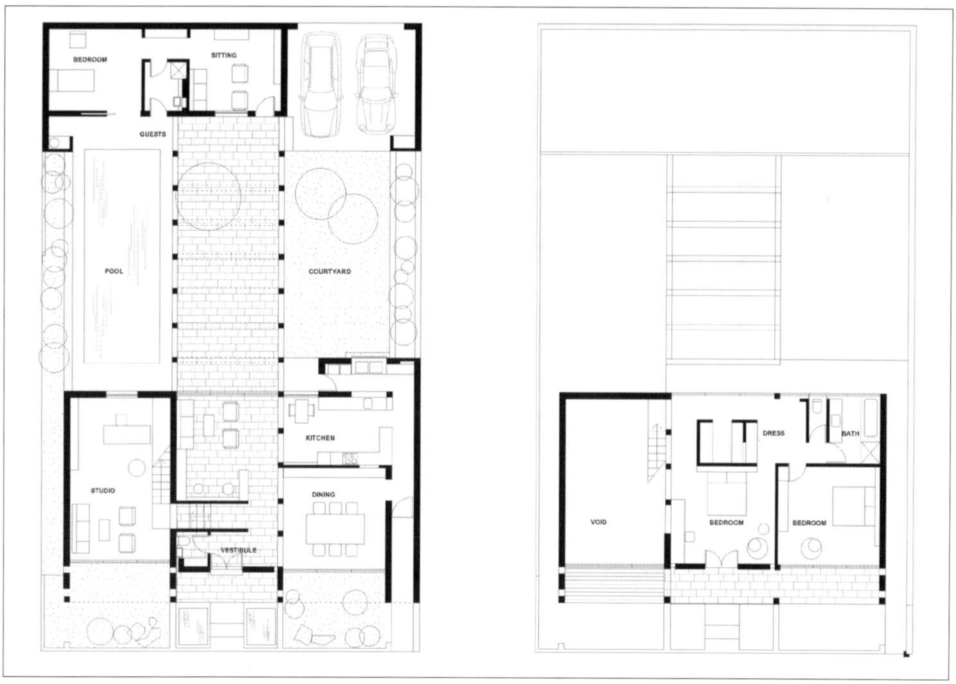

Dicksen & Platten, Student Union, University of Adelaide, 1969–73, detail of roof structure.

the governor general, Sir John Kerr. Whitlam had been the embodiment of progressive social values, linking for the first time the aspirations of the urban intelligentsia with older working-class Labor traditions. His election also terminated Australian military involvement in Vietnam as an American ally, following the gradual withdrawal begun by his predecessor Sir William McMahon in 1971. His opponents cultivated the perception, during his term in office, of profligate spending to support social schemes, with the suggestion that this was done irresponsibly. The fate of public architecture in the country followed a similar course some years later. The early promise of Brutalism, its combination of dignity with apparent frugality, shifted to a mode of building that became increasingly expensive as expectations for the quality and physical articulation of *in situ* concrete rose. In the early 1980s some of the finest works in the materials were constructed, but they were already the swansong of a period where a revitalized idea of integrity marked the final attempt to resurrect the promise of modernism as the style of a progressive historical mission.

The redefinition of Australia in post-war terms was, in effect, complete by 1980 and it left behind numerous buildings as testimony to the entrenchment, indeed the flowering, of the welfare state and its distinctly Australian egalitarian sentiments. By 1980 demands on the tax base had multiplied to include a wide range of social programmes, which invariably brought pressure to bear on public building budgets. Projects in train would continue into the 1980s, but the costs of idealism were under scrutiny, and gains made under the easy profitability of the 1960s and '70s were at an end. In a period that had seen Sydney and the smaller state capitals in the ascent architecturally, and Melbourne searching to translate its idealism of form into something more visceral, the subsequent era brought about new alignments and a revitalization of the southern capital's role in defining a local view of architecture's historical mission.

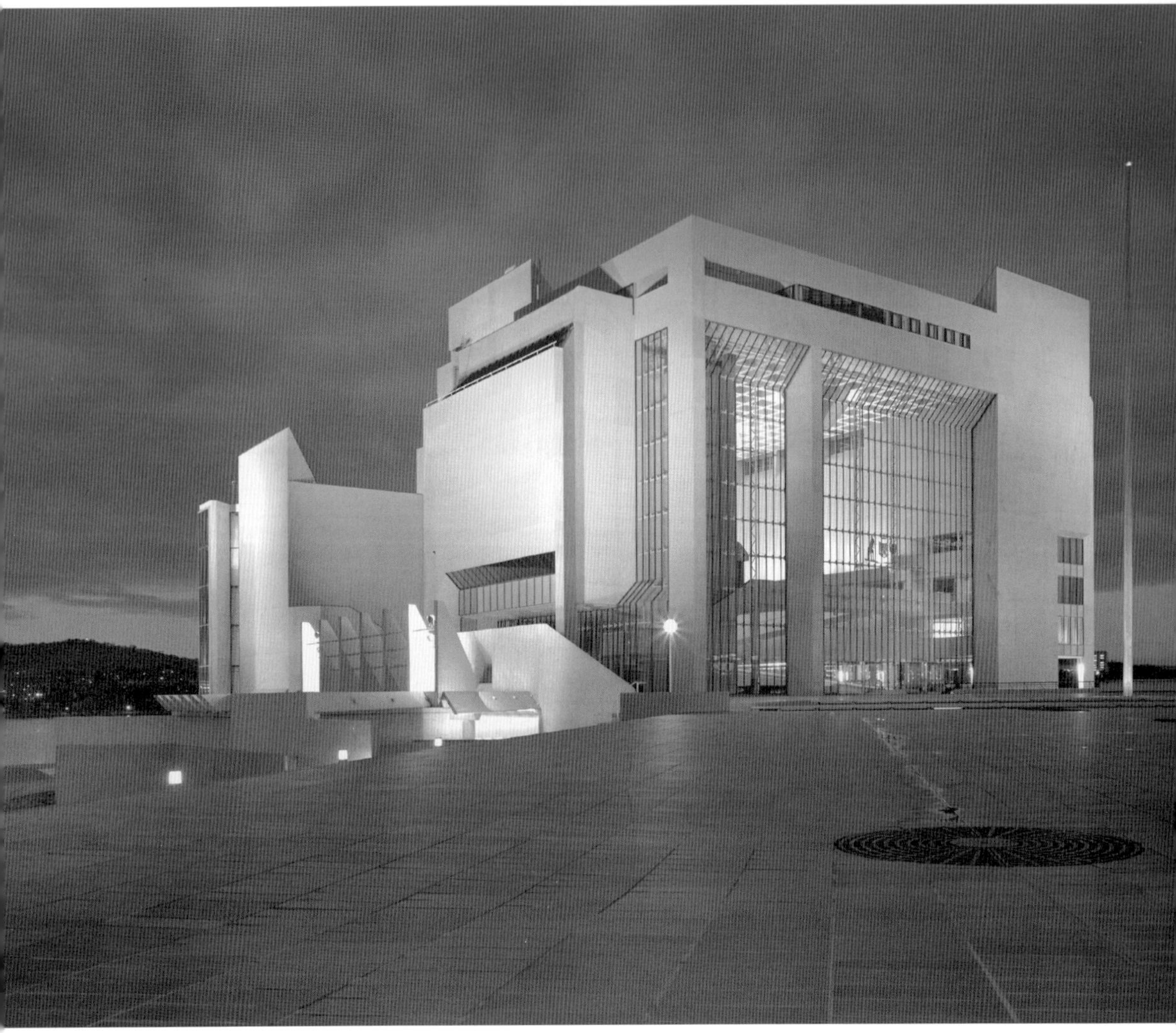

chapter five

The Fragmentation of Identity, 1981–99

The political events that ensued in the wake of the Whitlam government and its dismissal encapsulated the sharp turns in social policy that characterized the shift from the long post-war boom to the politics of neoliberalism. Malcolm Fraser was elected prime minister in 1975 in a landslide, at the helm of a conservative coalition. The Whitlam years of political idealism left their imprint on the national consciousness in the form of a broad social confidence that the subservient reflex of the second Menzies period (1949–66) had been effaced, and even conservative politics now wore a distinctly Australian face. Fraser was classically liberal by inclination, and his stance on Apartheid won him wide trust as a mediator. But he was from the grazier class, and his old view of national identity emphasized individual effort.[1]

Despite his political alignments, Fraser saw out the last of the Whitlam building projects, such had been their momentum. Key among these were the two exemplars in Canberra of the new idealism: the High Court of Australia and the adjoining National Gallery. Designed as part of the civic precinct of Parkes, the High Court was won through competition in 1972 and completed in 1980. The National Gallery opened two years later. Both were the work of Sydney firm Edwards, Madigan, Torzillo & Briggs, formed in 1948 by the three first-named principals. The buildings have the imprint of Col Madigan, who inclined to sculptural concrete work over the more rationalist leanings of Jack Torzillo. With Maurice Edwards they were social progressives of post-war hue, a generation whose idealist aspirations found a ready outlet in the Whitlam reforms. Bluff and prone to straight talking, Madigan's persona masked a sensitive and imaginative feel for architectural space and form.

Despite some claims to the contrary, the Opera House did have architectural progeny. They came not through direct imitation but through adoption of specific aspects of the project in subsequent buildings. The High Court and Art Gallery take from the Opera House the idea of buildings of the public realm executed to the highest degree of craft, consistent with a public realm that embodies the highest aspirations of the nation. While this may seem like naive political economy, it produced some of the finest off-form concrete in the world. Both buildings are a world away

Edwards, Madigan, Torzillo & Briggs, High Court of Australia, Canberra, 1974–80.

from the realist economics of Brutalism. They are made to the tightest possible tolerances, a practice honed of necessity in the making of the Sydney Opera House.

The High Court comprises three courtrooms held within a large concrete and glazed container, their forms secondary to the loftiness of the bounding space and its attendant structure. A massive ramp connects the various courts vertically, with low balustrades giving its passage a sense of drama in a building of some knowing theatricality. The sobriety of the courts themselves, incorporating finely worked timber panelling, is offset by the major artworks that unfold across the interior surfaces. It is a vision of the court expressing profound contemporary relevance, as ultimate guarantor of a state above sectarian or class interests. There is little recourse to the classical antecedents of state courthouses, and the prominence of the artworks reflects the growing view, implied if not acknowledged, of art as the secular repository of the mysterious.

It is this aspect that links the High Court with the National Gallery. They are true Whitlamite structures in their effort to create an ahistorical precinct of form, where the iconography inheres in the meticulous detailing and engineered plasticity of concrete as a material of high architecture. The spaces of the National Gallery are occasionally mannered in their structure, but are mute to content, as befits a collection intended to play

The Architects Partnership (Heffernan, Nation & Viney with Hartley Wilson, Oldmeadow, Eastman & Walch), Australian Antarctic Division Headquarters, Hobart, 1979–80.

Edwards, Madigan, Torzillo & Briggs, Australian National Gallery, Canberra, 1968–82.

an avant-garde role in the national consciousness. Like many Canberra buildings of the era, the complex separates pedestrian and vehicular traffic in a vertically layered parti giving users ambulatory freedom, unencumbered by services.

While these buildings transcended the rough-and-ready ethic of Brutalism in their meticulous detailing, another tendency was becoming evident at the start of the 1980s. This was the reinvigoration of the machine-derived techniques of early modernism, whose potential had been dramatically demonstrated with the opening of Piano & Rogers's Centre Pompidou in Paris in 1977. The most compelling early example of this approach in Australia was the Australian Antarctic Division Headquarters in Kingston, just outside Hobart.

Although Australia is generally characterized by its warmer latitudes, the city of Hobart at 43°s has a temperate climate and is the gateway to the country's vast Antarctic claim. The Antarctic Division is now part of the Department of the Environment and Energy, and operates three permanent research stations on the Antarctic mainland. The Division's headquarters were designed in 1979–80 as a collaboration between the Commonwealth Department of Housing and Construction and the Tasmanian consortium of The Architects Partnership. This latter team comprised two firms: Hartley Wilson, Oldmeadow, Eastman & Walch, and Heffernan, Nation & Viney. This arrangement was not unusual for Tasmania, where firms and individuals associate easily for projects or periods of time.

Ray Heffernan had been producing distinctive houses referencing Wright and Richard Neutra since the early 1960s, but Michael Viney and Bob Nation had absorbed the lessons of late modernism, with Nation attending the University of Toronto in 1971–2 as a postgraduate.[2] While better known for their houses influenced by the New York Five, under Viney's direction the Antarctic Division Headquarters took on a language of hermetic precision with the four original buildings clad in a unique aluminium and glass assembly. While evoking the need for complete enclosure in Antarctica itself, the complex also has suspended enclosed links between buildings that reinforce both the sense of a contained interior and the precise fabrication of the late-modern strand championed by Piano and Norman Foster.

While the curtain wall and its steel-framed progeny would persist, meticulous concrete work – at the moment of its most compelling demonstration in the High Court and National Gallery – would soon be in decline. Partly this was to do with the cost of construction, and partly with the rapid fracturing of its attendant political programme. In 1983 Fraser's conservative alliance was defeated by Labor under Bob Hawke, who ushered in an era marked by a pragmatic vision of effecting class cohesion. Financially the state could not continue to spend its way to satisfying various class aspirations, and Hawke, with the aid of his treasurer Paul Keating, set about reforming the economy.[3]

Hawke and Keating turned away from the model of class antagonism that had been part of the modern Anglophone tradition and looked to states where labour and capital made a coordinated effort to meet their respective goals. While Hawke was a master of populism as a political unifier, Keating brought a cultivated, if conservative, view of aesthetics to the political arena despite his lack of formal education. Together they cemented, at the highest levels, a distrust of avant-gardist tactics in the pursuit of political progress. This accorded with the tenor of the times, as solutions were negotiated between unions and capital in a careful bid to remake an economy no longer buoyed by the profitability of the long post-war boom.

Andrew Andersons (NSW Government Architect's Office), Captain Cook Wing, Art Gallery of NSW, Sydney, 1972, viewed from the original 1909 building by Walter Liberty Vernon.

The effect on architecture was twofold. On the one hand the state began to withdraw as the sponsor and builder of quality housing and public buildings. On the other the symbolic regime that proved the swansong of

modernism, one that derided populism and espoused singular architectural visions, found itself under attack. This was not, of course, confined to Australia, but its local dynamic was shaped by an increasing cultural confidence expressed in the popular music scene and in the distinctive Australian film industry that was emerging. These latter two were particularly important for a country aiming to establish a post-colonial culture with tools largely fashioned along European and American lines.

At state level the decline of the powerful design office of the New South Wales Department of Public Works can be read through the career of Andrew Andersons, who had joined in 1964. His early design work included the refined concrete of the extension to the New South Wales Art Gallery (1972), and he later assumed design responsibility for the New South Wales Parliament House and the new wing to the State Library. However, he left public service in 1988, as the relative autonomy of the public design office quickly eroded, and private firms tendered for public projects.

Modernism Fractured

The conflicting impulses that shaped the new era can perhaps be best illustrated through the work of Philip Cox, who proved to be a particularly astute reader of architectural trends and tendencies from the 1960s. His work at Tocal, with Ian McKay, has been mentioned as a representative example of robust contextual design incorporating timber framing, inspired by agricultural buildings of the nineteenth century (see Chapter Four). With the assault on abstract composition that accompanied the new pragmatism of the 1980s, Cox was well placed to extend his interests in the Australian nineteenth-century vernacular into his contemporary work. Generally avoiding the idle geometric overlays that characterized the early attempts of post-modernism, Cox drew on Sydney's Victorian typologies to reinforce the city's debt to the period's urban form and its constituent parts. As in many parts of the world, the threat of losing parts of the city previously considered ubiquitous, but unremarkable, galvanized a preservation movement that had previously been concerned only with individual buildings. Cox's work allayed preservationist fears while creating a template for continued development. He demonstrated this with small- and large-scale projects. His redevelopment of the Haymarket precinct for the University of Technology Sydney in the early 1980s was seminal in its retention of specific parts of the streetscape, notably a corner bell tower and portions of shopfronts, as historic fragments in a development tied together with massive banded brickwork walls. At an opposing scale his infill houses in the historic Miller's Point area for public tenants showed his propensity to rationalize historic elements of streetscape into a modest but reproducible palette, following Aldo Rossi's examples in the Po Valley and Veneto.[4]

Leveraging on this formula of historically aware redevelopment, the same firm designed the Darling Harbour Exhibition Centre (1988), using the didactic structural approach of Piano & Rogers and contemporary works by Norman Foster. Here the appeal was to the Englishness of this approach as suitable for a prominent but neglected site, an association exploited through a certain calculated iconoclasm that extended at least back to Paxton's Crystal Palace.

Given the rediscovery of the Victorian city, valued now for its typologies of shopfronts and terrace houses that yielded a rational kit of parts for the city, it was inevitable that there would be a turning again to the traditional European city. This was true of Sydney more than Melbourne, which had maintained its urban structure more completely, and which still boasted acres and acres of intact Victoriana. Metabolist urban ideas,

Philip Cox, Richardson, Taylor & Partners, Market Three Campus, NSW Institute of Technology, Sydney, 1984–7.

Philip Cox, Richardson, Taylor & Partners, Millers Point Infill Housing, Sydney, 1982.

and the trend to separate pedestrians from traffic, disappeared within half a decade.

These developments had myriad international counterparts, but again the local manifestation in Australia encompassed specific historical shifts that gave it a distinct inflection. The most telling, in Sydney, was the retreat of the debate over authenticity from the corporate sphere. The attempts at high-rise towers that made raw concrete a material of integrity quickly lost currency, replaced by a new internationalism that matched the currency flows unleashed by the floating of the Australian dollar in 1983. The post-war idea of the nation state as the incubator of social progress gave way to a revitalized concept of self-interest as the driver of a hidden but emergent collective good. The effect on Australian architecture was to generate a culture of searching self-awareness, and it disliked much of what it found.

The method that dominated architecture at its most confident in the 1960s married a progressive outlook to the conviction that buildings and cities could be remade in a fashion that corrected historical deficiencies.

The dubious aspects of this view were offset by the boldness of its projects, their relative successes and failures demonstrating how uncertain was the balance struck between idealism and a desire for the familiar. It took a period of extraordinary growth and confidence to sustain this idealism, and when growth ceased the failures moved sharply into focus. The city, viewed as a gridded matrix that could accommodate diverse outlooks, supplanted the modernist city of collective ambition remade with bold planning. Within architecture the deeply held tendency to reflect climate and local

Philip Cox, Richardson, Taylor & Partners, Sydney Exhibition Centre, 1985–8.

building traditions suddenly seemed to be tinged with parochialism, and the techniques of post-modernism had a brief but widespread flowering as part of the process of diluting the concept of authenticity.

The result was a fragmentation of architecture into contending approaches, with distinctive yearnings, that mirrored the interwar years in their range and diversity. The shift became evident in the work of Melbourne-based Daryl Jackson, whose partnership in the 1960s and '70s with Evan Walker had produced confident public buildings in sculpted off-form concrete such as the Canberra School of Music (1976). When the partnership broke up in 1978, Jackson quickly moved on from his strong Brutalist credentials to a reductive geometric formalism that reprised historical details, though in the abstract. The St Patrick's Diocesan Centre in the regional centre of Ballarat shows this approach in the context of strong Victorian-era precedents.

While Jackson, along with Philip Cox in Sydney, may have sensed the shift towards historical reference that occasionally lapsed into the literal, the field of possibilities in the early 1980s proved remarkably diverse. Sydney, in line with its classicist leanings, moved quickly to

Daryl Jackson Evan Walker Architects, Canberra School of Music, 1976.

Daryl Jackson Architects, St Patrick's Diocesan Centre, Ballarat (Victoria), 1982.

reassert these in a number of ways. The first, already noted in Cox's work, was the reinvention of Sydney typologies with some degree of faithfulness in a spirit of urban repair, following Leon Krier.[5] This nostalgia for an intact early industrial city was as far back as the city could plausibly go, since it was young and achieved urban cohesion relatively late. Firms like Allen Jack+Cottier, also well-credentialled in late modernism, adopted a similar approach. Exploiting this eclectic view of history, the partnership of Wendy Lewin and Alec Tzannes designed the Henwood House in the gentrifying suburb of Paddington. Where Cox had opted to stylize the terrace house typology into its masonry mass with attached verandah, the Henwood House introduces a simple masonry version of the urban dwelling, using proportions and mouldings to establish contextual credentials. This diversion from type made for wider intimations of urbanity, recalling both European capitals and the attached urban dwellings of American East Coast cities.

For many architects, this turning to history magnified the disquiet that had always attended the rationalist triumph. Rationalism as a practice had proven an appealing and useful adjunct to post-war nation building, but the limitations of its reductive solutions for social and urban ills were thrown into sharp relief. This opened the gates to many forms of practice, with relatively few practitioners holding to their late modernist

Lewin Tzannes, Henwood House, Sydney, 1982–5.

principles of design. Predictably Harry Seidler was one who did, and his confidence in architecture to transform portions of cities in both form and usage was given currency through projects such as Riverside in Brisbane (1986), an office tower set among dining venues and a boardwalk. Seidler here demonstrated the appeal of the Brisbane River as a backdrop for leisurely dining and drinking, in a transposition of the urban spaces in his Sydney developments of prior decades. The popularity of the Riverside complex attests both to his conviction that Australian cities are limited

Harry Seidler and Associates, Riverside Centre, Brisbane, 1983–6.

in amenity by their inherited morphology, and to the changing nature of work under the resurgent appeal of capitalism in the 1980s. Outdoor cafes and restaurants became ubiquitous from the late 1980s across the country, and work became defined less by where it took place than by its gradual merging with eating and drinking. Riverside was a significant catalyst in this process for Brisbane, its urban configuration drawing patrons from the street, through the site, to the river.

The commercial appetite for Seidler's methods was undiminished and he rounded out the decade with two large and inventive projects in Sydney. Grosvenor Place (1990) shows the development of the large office tower as an investment vehicle along the lines first trialled in Australia Square some 25 years previously. The tower floors of paired, offset crescents about an eye-shaped core have a compelling logic where unobstructed office space and views are maximized, and building time is minimized. The consolidated ancillary spaces and retained buildings at ground level provide the suite of restaurants and small food and drink outlets that constitute Seidler's public realm, albeit on private ground. The Capita corporate headquarters building presented a more difficult problem, its constrained site producing a shaded undercroft at street level, with a restaurant tucked well away from the footpath. This is partly a result of shifting office space from the lower to the upper levels, a strategy emphasized by the asymmetrical structure tied together by massive exposed diagonal bracing. While not entirely successful, it shows an architect at the height of his commercial game, his ambition of subverting the street-wall alignment of buildings at pavement level fully in evidence.

Yet these went against the grain, with the prevailing sentiment in favour of reconstituting the traditional city even as its functions became increasingly uniform. In Sydney the 1980s reaped the sites vacated by industry and power generation, as these moved beyond the city and in many cases overseas. In Melbourne the Spencer Street Power Station, opened in 1892, closed in 1982 and was subsequently demolished. All Australian cities experienced these shifts, and have been reconfigured from the 1980s to replace industrial urban and city-fringe sites with housing, retail and offices, supplemented by education. The demands of these building types are modest in formal terms, and their treatment encourages surface overlays on an often predetermined logic of circulation, wall to floor-area ratio and building depth limited by a maximum distance from natural light.

Melbourne firms seemed better placed to exploit these conditions. The firm of Denton Corker Marshall, formed in 1975 by John Denton, Bill Corker and Barrie Marshall, expanded from urban planning and design into large-scale commercial work in the 1980s. Their urbanist roots gave the firm the capability to approach each development as a city fragment.

Harry Seidler and Associates, Capita Centre, Sydney, 1985–9.

Each was embodied with an idea of how such buildings might collectively heal a city torn, at that moment, between newfound historical respect for the prevailing Victorian grid and the imperative of commercial redevelopment. The firm showed particular skill in bundling these components as urban collage, combining the post-modern tactic of maintaining pre-existing facade coursings and building heights with contemporary high-rise towers, the whole tied together by skilful articulation to maintain a clear relationship between building masses. The result is a method that discriminates finely between the tower as an ideal form and its inevitable concessions to context. The key here is that the towers do not project their idealized form as a universally valid model, but rather as mediators between history and the commercial logic of the office block.

Beginning with their 1985 No. 1 Collins Street, a literal grouping of old and new buildings that imbued the new with a skilful neutrality, the firm went on to build significant urban buildings that all negotiated the fine line of urban compromise. This approach is shown with 101 Collins Street (1991) – a large office building of some 130,000 square metres – set back from the street so that continuity is maintained with the addition of a low podium to the footpath. A more ambitious scheme won the competition for two new towers in central Sydney, together with associated development on an irregular island site that called for the retention of a row of terrace houses fronting Phillip Street, and an attached museum. The towers, named for early colonial governors Phillip and Macquarie, utilizes deep transfer beams to cantilever over the back of the terrace houses. Few schemes display the valorization of history during the period as completely as this complex, with a massive structural effort required to avoid impinging on the nineteenth-century terraces. The attached museum is devoted to Sydney's history and faces a new square that helps to preserve buried remnants of Australia's first Government House.

The location and nature of entry foyers in the firm's work is also distinctive. Worked into the interior according to the dictates of each site, the spaces nonetheless reprise the ambition of the towers themselves in their striving for geometric clarity within complex sites assembled from both retained and demolished buildings. The result has something of the nostalgia for the grand spaces of the late nineteenth and early twentieth centuries, but with a scale and lighting arrangement that sometimes overshoots the gravitas they intend for these high-end workplaces.

A parallel practitioner of this emerging mode of composite design was Nonda Katsalidis, a graduate of the University of Melbourne. As a director of AXIA, Katsalidis designed the Argus Centre, a commercial high-rise completed in 1993. While it has resemblances to the work of Denton Corker Marshall, Katsalidis has a stronger commitment to the language of high

Denton Corker Marshall in association with Robert Peck YFHK, No. 1 Collins Street, Melbourne, 1981–5.

HYATT
HOUSE
ONE

Denton Corker Marshall (entry and foyer by Johnson Burgee), 101 Collins Street, Melbourne, 1986–90.

Denton Corker Marshall, Governor Phillip and Governor Macquarie Towers (detail showing beams to overall historic terrace houses), Sydney, 1990–94.

modernism and the asymmetrical compositions that mark it off from Beaux Arts tendencies. Thus while the Argus Centre relies on the juxtaposition of precast solids at street level, and a curtain-walled tower above, the decorative elements of the tower evoke the 1930s rather than any nostalgia for a pre-modern symmetry. This has remained a hallmark of his work, a brand of historicism that excavates the modernist tradition for its tropes and optimism.

The 1980s also saw the completion of another landmark building that fused a strong geometric generating diagram with an architectural grandeur that matched popular expectations. The inadequate size of the 1927 Parliament House led to a competition fifty years later in 1979 for its successor on the site Griffin designated for a building devoted to documenting the nation's history. In 1980, after a second stage of judging, the design of

Mitchell/Giurgola & Thorp was announced as the winning scheme. The firm of Mitchell/Giurgola had a distinguished record on the American East Coast, and they partnered with Australian Richard Thorp for the design and construction phases of the project. The guiding hand was that of Romaldo Giurgola, who relocated to Canberra with his family and played a major role in both the design of the Parliament House and the architecture produced by the firm after it was completed.

Giurgola trained in Rome and had excellent academic credentials, having worked alongside Louis Kahn in Philadelphia and subsequently serving as chair of the Architecture Department at Columbia University. The winning scheme excavated Capital Hill and partly remade it as the

Mitchell Giurgola Thorp, Parliament House of Australia, Canberra, 1980–88, entry forecourt.

Parliament House complex, with two back-to-back arcs retaining the grassed slope that surmounted the buildings. Also cut into the slope was a vast entry court, the whole complex being roughly symmetrical and presenting a strong formal presence at the centre of an encircling road system. The site was defined by the city's topography, the formal axis established in Griffin's plan, and the intersection of the offset grids that had resulted from the plan's pragmatic implementation.

The personable Giurgola worked with builders, artisans and artists to create a *Gesamtkunstwerk*, with the finished building displaying both commissioned artworks and extensive use of Australian timbers.[6] The plan emphasized the bicameral structure of the Australian parliament, and the separate houses for Representatives and Senators are afforded equal standing. This imbued the symmetry with symbolic import, and merged with the strong geometric determinants of the plan. The architecture has something of Kahn's monumentality, but undercut by Giurgola's firm insistence on an architecture accessible to popular taste. In contrast to the architecture of the preceding decades, it held no avant-garde messages for the conducting of democracy. Instead it has opulent spaces and materials, on a scale hard to comprehend from within but evident in the dominant presence the building has at the crest of the city's symbolic public triangle.

The return to symmetry came easily to Giurgola as he reprised the Beaux Arts tradition latent at the University of Pennsylvania, where he had spent many fruitful years. Compared to the robust asymmetry of Edwards, Madigan, Torzillo & Briggs's High Court or National Art Gallery, the Parliament House complex shows a marked turning towards the formal devices and plans of the nineteenth century. In this Giurgola read the times well, but the building's strongest aspect is its bold topographic rendering of Griffin's intent. In its interior it sets the tone for the coming decade, that of a new pragmatism where craft supplants the challenges of abstraction, and architecture's critical edge is blunted. In this it paralleled the demise of Whitlamesque idealism.[7]

In the field of public architecture, the Parliament House proved to be an astute embodiment of prevailing sentiment, but it was not a dominant one. In line with the move to enshrine state cultural identities, Queensland embarked on the construction of a large cultural complex on the south bank of the Brisbane River. The design fell to Robin Gibson, a Brisbane architect who had spent time in the London office of Sir Hugh Casson before returning to his home city, where he subsequently set up practice. In his formative years he had worked in the office of Hayes & Scott, and his work retained the learned modernism that they espoused. Early commissions at the University of Queensland established Gibson's credentials for larger work, and his success in the 1973 competition for the Queensland

Art Gallery led to further design work in association with the Queensland Department of Works on the other components of the Cultural Centre: a performing arts complex, museum and state library.

The Art Gallery, completed in 1982, is a counterpart to the contemporaneous Canberra institution. Both are among the last creations of the exceptional period of Australian concrete work. With tolerances and finishes that conveyed an opulence of effort rather than materials, the Queensland Art Gallery also shows an astute judgement in light modulation that attests to an appreciation of latitude and the crafting of public interiors. The Performing Arts Centre (1985), Queensland Museum (1986) and State Library (1988) are all consistent with the materials, finishes and spatial dynamics of the Art Gallery, but differing programmes within have constrained the ambition of making the buildings exemplars of social amenity. The generosity of the Art Gallery remains exceptional as a public space, its internal pool testament to the building's genesis in a period that idealized the public realm.

Thus the 1980s were characterized by the eliding of two tendencies. On the one hand there were practitioners cleaving to a socially informed ambition to democratize private space and to extend the public realm across the confines of private boundaries. This political blurring – brought about through an undermining of the simple spatial markers that distinguished the one from the other – created a spatial syntax that relied on ambivalence. In Seidler's work he invoked the collective medieval urbanism of Tuscan towns as his model for undermining the sanctity of the street alignment as the plane where the private realm commences. Anyone can drift through the MLC Centre forecourt, with only a shift from pavement to cobblestones marking the divide between public space and private. In public buildings, conversely, the divide was contingent on how accessibility was understood in class terms. The Opera House may have been a public facility, but entry required an interest in classical music or theatre, neither regarded in Australia as popular arts. As new cultural centres arose in state capitals, they attested to the rise of the arts as secular vehicles for the numinous, or for those aspects of life not within the economic or productive realm. This called for buildings of the highest quality to entrench the newfound status of culture as a mark of national maturing. Yet while attendance at galleries and concerts grew, they were no match for the flowering of popular culture that took place in cinemas and live music venues, incubators for the Australian bands and film directors who gained international fame in the 1970s and '80s.[8] The state patronized institutional arts, while the pubs churned out worldwide chart-toppers.

The curious status of fine art in late twentieth-century Australia – that of being free, but increasingly associated with national standing – was

Robin Gibson & Partners in Association with the Queensland Department of Works, Queensland Art Gallery, 1975–82.

nowhere more in evidence than when the National Gallery purchased Jackson Pollock's painting *Number 11*, widely known as *Blue Poles*. Bought in 1973 for AUS$1.3 million, then a record for a contemporary American work, its budget was approved by Prime Minister Gough Whitlam.[9] The purchase generated enormous controversy, centring on its price, intrinsic value and indeed the use of public funds to create national collections of art without popular appeal. The issue revealed the public ambivalence over state patronage of the arts, which was accepted as necessary but expected not to go too far. In the best of Australian public buildings from the 1970s and '80s we can discern an idealistic desire to bridge this divide through the exceptional architectural effort expended on art galleries, performing arts complexes and universities. The effort yielded pragmatic results as well: the arts and higher education increasingly underpinned an economy moving towards services and retail.

The counter-tendency of the period was the revitalization of the private sector in the wake of the Hawke–Keating reforms, and the weakening of trade unions as Australia experienced stagnant wage growth from the late 1970s. The pragmatic Laborism of those years looked to a less antagonistic model of labour relations, moving closer to German ideas of negotiated agreements rather than those struck under duress. The economic pressures that precipitated this can be read from the Australian unemployment rate, which rarely exceeded 3 per cent from the 1940s to the early 1970s. By the 1980s it had climbed to 6 per cent and above, where it remained until 2000. Inflation in the 1970s averaged 10.2 per cent, the highest figure for any decade of the twentieth century.[10] The structural shifts that these figures chart also brought a new frugality to government and curtailed wage growth. But the idealism of the post-war state was in sharp decline, and its patronage selective and increasingly corporatized.

The economy of modernism also fell victim to these changes. The equation of results measured against the means employed – modernism was always predicated on an idea of underlying scarcity, even if it was only paid lip-service – shifted towards the economy of the sign, to paraphrase Baudrillard.[11] This occurred at different scales, from an outright embrace of symbolic content as a dominant architectural quality to a version of modernism that conveyed an economy of means as a mark of identity rather than as an organizing principle.

A Regionalism of Politics

In a distinctive move, the shift opened an avenue for a revived political stance in Melbourne. The subtle class composition of the city, and its sectarian history as a major centre for Irish Catholic institutions and class advancement, nurtured a long tradition of anti-establishment sentiments remade for the New World. While they became more diffuse as class mobility broke down old alignments and loyalties, the city still maintained old rages, which motivated both a desire to provoke and a fondness for an avant-garde sensibility. These sentiments were deeply held, and while there has been debate over their literal translation into architecture, they are evident in thinkers of the complexity of Peter Corrigan and Maggie Edmond.[12]

Corrigan graduated from the University of Melbourne in 1966, Edmond in 1969. They commenced practice in 1975 as Edmond & Corrigan, following several years spent by Corrigan in the United States. He undertook a Master of Environmental Design at Yale, where he came to know Robert Venturi and Denise Scott Brown, as well as Steve Izenour. Charles Moore was dean and Vincent Scully a central figure, both being formative influences. Corrigan absorbed not only Venturi's ideas of popular iconography being a valid subject for architecture, but Moore's inventive use of carpentry to construct interiors that hinted at a secular spatial mysticism. Moore derived this from the Eucharistic architecture of Labatut at Princeton.[13] This complex of influences, rooted in a desire to find a contemporary expression for Catholic space and practice, but extending to a larger secular interest in a workaday, compassionate spirituality, can be discerned in both the arguments and practices of Edmond and Corrigan.

In the monograph on their work, Conrad Hamann places a seminal quote from Corrigan at the start:

> The buildings produced by our practice are what I would like to regard as 'poor' architecture (as in 'poor' theatre). Modest means, pedestrian imagery, and bush details are employed in an attempt to make public statements within tight budgets . . . The first Roman Catholic church designed after my New York sojourn was at Mortlake in the Western District of Victoria. Mr Malcolm Fraser was the local member. It was intended to be a rural Australian public building free from squatter romanticism.[14]

The political implication is clear. Fraser was the prime minister who succeeded Whitlam and his home was a large agricultural property. He was associated with the 'squatter' class, Australia's equivalent of a landed gentry so named because of their de facto occupation of frontier land for grazing in early colonial history. The statement sums up Corrigan's ambitions for a community-minded populist architecture, in sharp distinction to the ideological trappings of entrenched class interests as he saw them.

The imagery of the country church has, indeed, little to do with romanticism, and it is a succinct collection of elements for regular worship: a hall with interior lofted towards the altar, with a generous verandah for the spilling congregation. As Hamann has noted, it is a building that presents as both suburban and rural, the two linked in the common elements of socializing that bind both contexts.[15] The immersion in the ordinary, and the ambition to give it a form of intellectual dignity, even a veiled one, would remain as a concern for the firm. The intensity of their work would grow over time, evidence of their ambition to maintain a critique of the reductive nature of modernism and its economy of means. A deep knowledge of architecture, and the spatial tropes of post-modernism, provided ample themes to work through subsequent projects.

A series of buildings designed for the Catholic parish of Keysborough, on the southeastern edge of Melbourne, provided the opportunity for the practice to work through themes and designs in accordance with their notion of 'poor' architecture. In a suburb distinguished by nothing more than an uncanny flatness, the buildings for the parish included a school, housing for the elderly, and two houses relocated and reworked into a club. The buildings have the distinction of being free of the irony that attended some of the early attempts to subvert late modernism. The irregular geometries of the school challenge the repetitive orthogonal economy of modernism considered as both method and symbol, substituting it with a flagrant excess of effort. This allows a continuous play of form and

Edmond & Corrigan, Keysborough Church of the Resurrection, Melbourne, 1976.

planning, creating opportunistic pockets of space in a way that eludes the carefully structured logic of modernism. The church, by contrast, seems achingly modest by contemporary standards. Nonetheless by the early 1980s the work at Keysborough had received national attention, at least in the architectural press. As Hamann writes: 'That was appropriate. The parish buildings had been the most comprehensive onslaught on Australia's prevailing architectural ideology in many years.'[16]

This technique of the reconciliation of fragments surfaces in the Athan House of 1988, built in the town of Monbulk for a large extended family, and it serves as a repository for moments of architectural imagination and recollection. The juxtaposed textures and colours of the post-modern work of Michael Graves, as one reference among many, is here turned to a humanist intent rather than the semiotic games of much of the American work. The Athan House shows two local references re-imagined. The first, as Hamann notes, is the work of the Griffins, with the indeterminate mythologies invoked by its medievalism.[17] The second is the awkward urban monumentality of Grounds's Victorian Arts Centre, initially taken as a sign

Edmond & Corrigan in association with Demaine Partnership, Building 8, Royal Melbourne Institute of Technology, 1991–4.

RMIT
RMIT
City Campus

of his declining judgement but later becoming a symbol of anti-architecture aimed at the formal perfection pursued in the Sydney Opera House.

When Edmond and Corrigan moved to urban-scale work, as they did in association with the Demaine Partnership for the design of Building 8 at the Royal Melbourne Institute of Technology (RMIT), they did so with a full range of ideas for both exterior and interior. Sitting on an incomplete base left over from a John Andrews scheme, the building defies rationalist logic in its circulation and interior organization, while its exterior shows some prescience in anticipating the signature buildings sought by universities in the twenty-first century. The riot of colour and form it presents to Swanston Street reinvigorated the latent antagonism to prevailing taste that had served Melbourne architecture well in the post-war years. It confirmed the status of the practice as a rallying point for Australian architects still yearning for a critical function for their work, in the face of a now discredited modernism and the slow starving of the public realm to the benefit of the private.

Gregory Burgess, Box Hill Community Arts Centre, Melbourne, 1990.

Other Victorian architects used a version of the organic/rationalist antipathy that had motivated architects like the American Bruce Goff. Gregory Burgess reworked this antipathy in a series of buildings through the 1980s and '90s. The difficulty of translating this mode of working to the modern building industry led Burgess to craft an aesthetic that took organic appearances as far as he could, with curved geometries having to be rationalized to suit factory-made components. In his mature works, like the Box Hill Community Arts Centre, these geometries are interspersed with a full range of 'low' materials: corrugated sheeting, plywood, gypsum board alongside brick and hand-wrought metalwork, to create a building of hand-crafted appearance and loose organic association, a pointed rejoinder to precision building. The resonance of the work was wide, perhaps more for the tenor of the age than for the intellectual uniqueness of Burgess's work. The English *Architectural Review* editorialized that he was among the few architects internationally who were 'trying to find ways in which human values can be expressed against the alienating and normative forces of the global economy'.[18] As commentary on these forces, Burgess's work lacks the political sharpness of Edmond & Corrigan's, and cleaves closer to a generic assertion of the countercultural values invoked through the organic.

The most vigorously critical firm to emerge from Melbourne was the partnership formed by Stephen Ashton, Howard Raggatt and Ian McDougall in 1988. The origins of the practice were vividly described by McDougall when the three were jointly awarded the Australian Institute of Architects Gold Medal in 2016. In 1979, as young graduates, they would meet at the Perseverance Hotel in inner-city Fitzroy: 'Our gang – which as well as Steve included Howard Raggatt and me – grew into the Halftime Club, a group of graduates who, angry and ambitious, curious and competitive, established a culture of architectural adventurism for a generation in our city.'[19]

McDougall was drawn to the teachings of Peter Corrigan and the ambitions he held for architectural design as a stage for a theatre of an identity still in the making. The group reacted to the perceived complacency of architecture in the late 1970s and '80s, and their momentum carried them through a series of experiments, individually and when the practice coalesced, that revolved around architecture as meaning rather than process. As it was for Edmond & Corrigan, this search was conducted with an intensity free of cynicism. Rather it was driven by an indeterminate searching for an aesthetic regime consonant with the demise of a humanist economy, and its attendant historical schema predicated on progress.

Fuelled by the recurrent Australian ambivalence towards the legal and moral grounds of the nation's founding, Ashton Raggatt McDougall (ARM) allowed this uncertainty to play out both in the process of their design and in the iconography of their buildings. The results, as intended, were confronting in their intensity of colour and form. The first work to gain widespread attention was their renovation and extension of Storey Hall (1995). The project, from the outset, was loaded with ideological significance, with the firm's website noting that the original hall was built by the Hibernian Australian Catholic Benefit Society, 'at a time when Protestants controlled all of Melbourne's other meeting and speaking venues'.[20] This in part accounts for the prevalence of green throughout the work, but it does not account for the crystalline facing on the upper facade, nor the version that lines the interior of the auditorium itself, nor the powerful geometric elements forming the circulation at entry.

The bold tiling patterns were drawn from the work of mathematician Roger Penrose, who demonstrated in the 1970s that it was possible to cover a surface in a non-repetitive pattern using just two tile shapes. The fascination with complex geometries was, of course, widespread at the time, and held the promise of revealing mathematical properties not immediately evident to an architectural sensibility attuned to repetitive order. In an age striving to transcend the strictures of causality, of the reductive cause-and-effect that underpinned modernist rationalism, the idea of geometric emergence, where hidden rules become manifest, had particular appeal.

The simple idea that nature and modernity have been in opposition has long been a feature of Western architecture and has parallels in other areas of thought. In the English tradition this is tied up with the broader movements of anti-modernity that emerged in the nineteenth century, and takes in the English Gothic Revival and its use of a more complex structural geometry than the trabeated systems of classical architecture.[21] The fascination with geometric systems like Penrose's tiling revives the idea that there is an underlying order in mathematics as an expression of natural rules, but in ways that transcend the grasp of working or instrumental rationalism. This view adopts the mechanics of Darwinism, where a simple set of rules generates almost infinite variety when operating over myriad iterations.

ARM found close historical resonance to this idea in the work of Griffin, who had also embraced a crystalline iconography as part of his critique of modernity.[22] This adds to the strong local sense that also motivates their work, and which resulted in numerous references to Melbourne landmarks, some overt and some veiled, that occur throughout Storey Hall. The building also reprises the intention, already evident in Edmond & Corrigan's Building 8, to create a bold symbolic presence for RMIT as a university of contemporary intellectual relevance.

The political aspect of the firm's work lies in their referencing of marginal groups whose interests constitute an ongoing challenge to the status quo. In Storey Hall this falls to the Hibernian Society and its marginalized

Ashton Raggatt McDougall with Allom Lovell Associates, Storey Hall (centre), Melbourne, 1992–5.

members in nineteenth-century Melbourne, as well as the Women's Political Association who used the hall from 1916. Also keen to negate the often reactionary history of nature-inspired critiques of modernity, the practice embraced computers from the outset as design tools whose sophistication could reveal avenues of innovation in thinking, more than in documenting the process of building.

The firm's work thus continues the local Melbourne tradition of viewing architecture as a potent vehicle for ideas. Boyd had understood this as making each building a sort of localized puzzle, with both local determinants like site and client meshing with broader concerns of abstract geometries or structural systems. McDougall made this explicit: 'we have attempted to understand localism, a non-insular and deliberate provincialism founded partly to ring-fence a safe zone to work in, holding back the onslaught of the international carpetbaggers from the centre'.[23] For ARM ideas are drawn from a wide cosmology, taking in natural systems, historical alignments and mainstream religion to maintain a sense of indeterminate potential in their work. A large component of this is the history of architecture itself, and their referencing of modern architecture is overt in their National Museum of Australia, which will be considered in the next chapter.

Climatic Regionalism

The work of Edmond & Corrigan, and later ARM, magnified the differences in architectural culture between Melbourne and other capitals, notably Sydney and Brisbane. The sense of aggrievement that drove them to seek process over resolution, and to let this show in their work, found little resonance in Sydney, which had invested so heavily in the late modernist paradigm with the Opera House, and its Brutalist contemporaries. Climatic determinism also grows stronger as one moves north in Australia and its effects served as a counterweight to the symbolic demands placed

Glenn Murcutt, Laurie Short House, Sydney, 1972–3.

on Victorian work. Architecture in Sydney in the 1970s and '80s responded to different cues, with topography playing a major role, alongside a stronger awareness of geographic location.

The most recognized vehicle for Sydney's architectural culture emerged from the work of Glenn Murcutt, an early graduate of the architecture programme at the University of New South Wales. Like many of its graduates, Murcutt saw materials and building techniques as critical to formulating an architecture embodying regional intelligence. While the date of the emergence of a distinct regional consciousness in Sydney is difficult to locate, Murcutt's work takes a sharp turn from the collective roots of the Sydney School as defined by Jennifer Taylor. Although the practitioners that Taylor identified had little idea of their collective direction, they did have common roots in the alternative architectural tradition delineated by Colin St John Wilson.[24] The textural qualities of Aalto's work and the interiors of the later Wright houses both served as models for buildings that resisted modernism's universal claims of relevance. This can be observed in the common elements in the work of Gruzman, Rickard and McKay, for example, while pragmatic Brutalist ideas suffuse the houses of Johnson and Woolley. Murcutt understood this tradition well from his time working for Gruzman and Woolley, and indeed it was widely practised in 1960s Sydney. In the late 1960s, however, he rejected what he saw as the sentimentalizing tendencies of those practitioners in favour of a more sophisticated approach to building technique.

While Gruzman and Rickard had invented construction methods to achieve their aims, sometimes with evident deficiencies, Murcutt sought to understand construction itself as a vehicle for his ambitions. Through his father, a self-taught designer, he gained a fondness for Mies van der Rohe and for a reductive approach that sought a poetic appeal through simplicity: 'Eliminate complexity. Minimise the number of joints. Keep it simple.'[25] In the Laurie Short house of 1973, Murcutt adopted steel and concrete for a house on a fire-prone site at the northern edge of Sydney. A muscular steel frame, joined together with meticulous consideration, supports a concrete roof on which water ponds. This achieves both fire protection and thermal stability, as well as preventing the small concrete shrinkage cracks through which water penetrates. The isolated site permits a transparent building shaded by generous overhangs carefully calculated to screen summer sun but to allow winter sun to warm the mass concrete floor. This is the simplest technique for passive thermal control at Sydney's latitude, and it gives a functional extension to Mies's architecture of transparency.

Murcutt's most significant move, though, was to transpose this Miesian sensibility onto an older vernacular tradition. The ambition for this had

Glenn Murcutt, Marie Short House, Kempsey (New South Wales), 1974–5.

been sketched out by Queensland architects in the 1960s, notably Hayes & Scott and John Dalton. However Murcutt shifted the symbolic focus away from modernism to the vernacular itself, so his buildings evoke a historical dimension by raising the status of vernacular materials to accepted components of high architecture. There is a subtle subversion here. Australians have long been conscious of the class associations of various building materials, with weatherboard and corrugated iron regarded as the materials of the urban working class. Wealthier homeowners preferred brick and tile construction, entrenching these as the materials of middle-class aspiration.[26] Murcutt vaults over these developments by conferring a status on board cladding and corrugated iron by associating them with the rural tradition of good sense, allied to the pragmatism of squatter aesthetics. The Marie Short House of 1975 is his seminal work in this social valorization of modest materials.

He continued to refine this insight, and in subsequent work the components of enclosure, ventilation and drainage become magnified to make the functional logic explicit. In the Ball-Eastaway House for two artists in bushland to the north of Sydney, Murcutt teases out the rainwater system to cope with occasional deluges and the tendency for conventional gutters to become blocked with leaves. A vaulted roof is achieved with curved corrugated sheeting, which drains to two large flanking box gutters discharging via large rainwater heads and downpipes. This system determines the section of the house, as it assumes an extruded form with inset voids for side decks and a larger verandah formed by the roof continuing beyond the enclosing walls.

The appeal of Murcutt's work lies in his compaction of many elements, functional as well as symbolic, into deceptively simple forms. Essential to this is his fondness for architectural poetics, or the evocation of

Glenn Murcutt, Ball-Eastaway House, Sydney, 1980–83.

transcendence with a minimum of means. Early travels in Greece gave him models for this, derived from the simple courtyards on Greek islands that counter the often stark nature of their landscape and climate. The Done House (1991), for a prominent Sydney artist, is Murcutt's nod to these experiences, with an internal court of intense white that recalls Josep Antoni Coderch's reworking of the Mediterranean vernacular. The house is unusual in Murcutt's work for its reliance on this central space, his response to a suburban location with close neighbours. More typical is the Southern Highlands house of 1992, which follows an extruded, in-line plan using a steel structure, anchored by masonry walls extending to door-head height. The house is noteworthy for the incorporation of these masonry walls in a body of work previously identified with steel and timber, as Murcutt acknowledged his influences from abroad and sought to move beyond being identified as a regional architect. In the Arthur and Yvonne

Glenn Murcutt with Wendy Lewin and Reg Lark, Arthur and Yvonne Boyd Education Centre, Riversdale (New South Wales), 1996–9.

Boyd Education Centre on the Shoalhaven River, designed with Wendy Lewin and Reg Lark, the larger scope of a complex of buildings to accommodate short-stay groups encouraged an even broader palette. The projecting blades of the shared rooms, with their shuttered and louvred openings, have the ambience of verandah sleep-outs, while the concrete columns of the dining area introduce a monumentality to match the exceptional outlook. The influence of Aalto's tactile use of materials is explicit in a building that leverages off both the site and Murcutt's rural yet precise detailing to connect to international strands of modernist history.[27]

Yet Murcutt also remained within the strictures of Sydney architecture laid down in the 1930s, with its classical taste and hints of an idealized Mediterranean play of form and light. His work is thus situated within the mainstream of the city's historical taste, further adding to its local potency. His incorporation of climatic logic as a determinant of form established an affinity with practitioners to the north, who had long sought a modernism suitable for Australian East Coast conditions. This leaning towards the subtropics found a small laboratory on the peninsula forming the northern extent of Sydney's coastline, its microclimate and idyllic vegetation combining with plateaus and gullies to form powerful architectural cues. It was the site for Peter Muller's house above Whale Beach; it was also where Utzon chose to situate his studio, and the Dane's influence persisted after his departure. Richard Leplastrier had worked on the Opera House and was deeply influenced by Utzon's search for the uncompromised building system that constituted his ideal solution to an architectural problem. In the Opera House this had manifested in the building being conceived as discrete but integrated problems: the podium, the shells, the tiling, the exterior glazing, for example. Working at domestic scale, Leplastrier assumed a similar attitude towards building construction, re-imagining structure and details as idealized systems for drainage, for support or for ventilation. He also had an intense interest in Japanese architecture, having spent eighteen months in the country where he came under the influence of Tomoya Masuda.[28]

Many of the studies done by Utzon were discarded after he left, but they remained influential among those who worked on the Opera House. He had been working on a plywood beam system for the auditoriums, and prototypes were manufactured by Ralph Symonds Ltd. The system comprised U-shaped beams whose upturned flanges were capped by smaller channels with rounded heads. The whole was marked by the elegance of Utzon's eye, giving the system a refinement often absent in architecture that incorporates semicircles or quarter-circles. This validation of curved geometry as part of a classically elegant formal system remained with Leplastrier, and it recurs in his work of the 1970s. For the Palm Garden House at Bilgola (1978) Leplastrier designed a series of attenuated pavilions, with vaulted roofs of copper astride two small enclosed living and bedroom spaces, the whole linked by a circulation spine. Following Japanese cues for integrating the garden and the building, Leplastrier has forgone enclosing the building except where imperative, and the design demands some hardiness on the part of the occupant in dealing with hot and cold weather. The reward is a house of finely graded spaces and landscapes, with a compelling proposition about how one might live in Sydney's relatively benign climate.

The Pittwater peninsula gave rise to other experiments in both form and living. Morrice Shaw worked with both curved roof forms and exposed interiors in the Wave House (1979) on Scotland Island, a sheltered colony in the confines of the large bay of Pittwater. Half a generation behind Leplastrier, Peter Stutchbury emerged from the culture of the sensual re-imagining of coastal Sydney that stretched back through Leplastrier and Muller to local holiday houses of the 1920s. Stutchbury was a graduate of the University of Newcastle, a regional school less than two hours north of Sydney. Grounded in sound building technique, Stutchbury also uses topography and climate to generate buildings marked by a frugal exploitation of the possibilities offered by both. His Israel House of 1991 at Paradise Beach (with Ken Israel) is an exercise in self-contained romanticism to a greater degree than attempted by Murcutt. Stutchbury displays here a signature fondness for vertical living, allowing the dweller to experience the full range of light conditions through the tree canopy. A curved oversailing roof protects the living silo below, whose small footprint allows the retention of most of the trees on the site. Materials are largely lightweight: plywood, timber, steel framing, with generous sliding windows at key locations. The house is a compelling demonstration of the ideal hinted at by Leplastrier: the house as antidote to placelessness and its attendant anomie.

These houses had few counterparts on the Victorian coast, where conditions preclude the sort of unguarded attitude to enclosure that both Leplastrier and Stutchbury worked with. At Sydney's latitude the question of how one might live, understood as a balance between comfort and sensual opportunity, becomes an open one. In Victoria the swimming season is comparatively short, and the southern exposure of the coastline makes for a harsher environment. The coastal house designed by Barrie Marshall of Denton Corker Marshall for his own use south of Melbourne takes enclosure as its starting point, and its massive concrete construction with partial roof planting sits in sharp distinction to the ambitions of its Sydney counterparts. The contrast underlines the climatic variations in a country settled largely on a north–south ribbon of coastal fringe stretching from Tasmania to the northern reaches of Queensland.

Richard Leplastrier, Palm Garden House, Sydney, 1978.

Travelling up the coast, one encounters sugar cane for the first time in northern New South Wales, about two hours' drive shy of the Queensland

border. This is a seminal line, marking the shift to the subtropics and the tropics. In sentiment parts of Sydney aspire to the climatic benevolence of these regions, but Brisbane and its surrounding areas demand that summer heat be taken seriously. The city's distinct post-war architectural culture has already been noted, as has the refined modernism transmitted through Hayes & Scott, Birrell, John Dalton and Robin Gibson, among others. As modernism emerged in the 1990s as a valid candidate for historical revival in its own right, the attraction of a learned re-invention of that tradition marked the first project for the partnership of Brian Donovan and Timothy Hill. Both graduated from the University of Queensland, though some years apart. Their breakthrough project was the C House in the old Brisbane suburb of Coorparoo, designed over a number of years and completed in 1998. The house is a collection of high modernist details and inventions, configured as abutting pavilions around a central courtyard. While the form provides a wide variety of spaces for outdoor living through all parts of the day, the experience of the building is dominated by the intense consideration given to detailing. The references owe much

Donovan Hill, C House, Brisbane, 1991–9.

Andresen O'Gorman, Mooloomba House, North Stradbroke Island (Queensland), 1995–9.

to Carlo Scarpa, but with elements of Queensland regional precedents woven through.[29] It is an instructive summary of the numerous strands that constitute the city's heritage.

The filigree screen to the courtyard is a reference to the work of Brit Andresen, for whom Hill had worked in 1990. Andresen was born in Norway, and after graduating from Trondheim held teaching appointments at Cambridge and the Architectural Association, London. In 1977 she took up a position at the University of Queensland and established a

Russell Hall, Carpenter-Hall House, Brisbane, 1985–6.

practice with her husband Peter O'Gorman. While teaching remained a prime focus, the couple pursued a modest practice designing houses in the Brisbane region. The Mooloomba House on Stradbroke Island, off the southern Queensland coast, typifies their work. Andresen describes it as small and fairly rough, in the tradition of the holiday house that encourages or indeed demands that one live mainly outdoors.[30] The emphasis is on context – the horizon, the light, and the tree canopy that is stylized in the form of splayed timber members and the firm's distinctive timber screens. Partially used for sun protection and partially to define volumes for living without full enclosure, these screens have a decorative cast recalling the work of Mackintosh and Wright. The association extends the houses from simple responses to their circumstances, using local building methods, to works that sketch out ancillary rooms in a manner invoking modernism's early flirtation with primitivism. This is further played out in the contrast between the occasionally rough structure and the strict proportioning system applied to panels and framing for enclosure. The climate here, nearly 1,000 kilometres (620 mi.) north of Sydney, makes the ideal of layered, leisured sensuality easier to achieve.

The house, like its Sydney counterparts, uses local hardwoods extensively. The continued availability of these timbers into the late twentieth century gave architects a durable and malleable material that had all the hallmarks of local identity and usage. While subject to large initial shrinkage, these timbers are extremely durable and over time harden to a remarkable degree. They have been a mainstay of Queensland construction for a century, but have been displaced in commercial building by softer plantation-grown timbers like pine, which shrink less but have much poorer strength and finished appearance. The use of hardwoods is a statement in structural integrity, in the spirit of late Brutalism, as well as a re-affirmation of building craft.

These were tools available to a generation of Queensland architects haltingly articulating what Kenneth Frampton formalized as critical regionalism. There was an element of fantasy, very much part of Andresen O'Gorman's work, that sought to subvert the practical bent of middle-class family life. Towers and elevation gave views and spatial interest, especially in the hilly terrain of northern and western Brisbane. Russell Hall had neatly captured this anti-middle-class romanticism in his Carpenter-Hall House of 1985, an exuberant mix of fun and good sense. The fantastical is offset by generous shading to windows and the very Brisbane construction method of exposed exterior wooden framing, with the single-thickness timber walls fixed to the interior side of the frame.

Many of the houses that experimented with new domestic configurations were designed by architects for their own use. The Mooloomba House, for example, was a retreat for its designers. The appeal of handcrafting, or small-scale fabrication, lay partly in its cheapness, and in the ability of the architect-owner to stage the building process. In Queensland these houses took on more of a proselytizing role, drawing attention to the excessive size and inward-focus of suburban houses, and the potential for making cheaper houses that lent more intense experiences to the everyday. On the Sunshine Coast, a developing area still within easy drive of Brisbane, Gabriel Poole had experimented with minimal enclosure after some years working in the office of Robin Gibson, as well as a London sojourn. Poole looked to emulate the logic of traditional high-set Queensland houses, but through a modernist approach of economy of means.

This enduring question of how minimal enclosure might be, and still serve as useful habitation, had earlier precedents like the Lucas House in Sydney. Poole's exploration resulted in the Tent House at Eumundi for his own use, where his systems approach to building, intended for mass production, combined with the simple expedient of an elevated and shaded platform. The system has the added advantage of needing little site preparation, in distinction to Frampton's observation of the tendency of tract housing to efface natural terrain.[31]

Poole employed two younger architects in his practice who had graduated from the Queensland Institute of Technology (later Queensland University of Technology). Lindsay Clare was a Brisbane native, while Kerry Clare had lived in Sydney and Darwin. Both continued Poole's interest in how natural ventilation and building techniques evolved in hot climates before the advent of air conditioning. Their practice, established in 1979, produced a series of houses in the following decade that played out these concerns but with a different inflection to Poole, who favoured expressing the principles of his buildings and leaving the impression of a project constantly under refinement. The Clares' work from the outset was more polished and marked by a tectonic skill in finding the sculptural qualities in lightweight materials and systems. Their own house in Buderim of 1991 shows lessons gleaned from Murcutt's work as well, in the expression of drainage as a didactic as well as a sculptural element, and the use of an extruded building section to exploit the economy of repetitive elements. The skill of the Clares has been in rationalizing their approach so it can be reconfigured for various building types and scales. They have taken an architecture initially forged in a tradition of opposition to conventional building practice and brought this critique into the architectural mainstream. In recognition of their abilities in this form of transposition, they were appointed as design directors for the New South Wales Government Architect in 1998.

While Queensland served as an incubator of climatically responsive designs, the most demanding challenges on the island continent came at its northern extremities. Darwin had long been the one Australian settlement oriented to Asia, being less than 800 kilometres (495 mi.) from East Timor and the Indonesian archipelago. Its closest Australian town of size, Alice Springs, is nearly 1,500 kilometres (900 mi.) distant. The average daily temperatures are concentrated in a narrow band, with the greatest seasonal variation coming through rainfall and humidity, with wet and dry seasons. The constant heat is uncomfortable without some adaptation, and from 1937 a prototypical house design was developed by Beni Burnett for government accommodation. The designs relied on continuous air movement through the house to promote cooling, and they

Troppo Architects, Green Can project house, Darwin, 1982.

reconfigured ideas of domestic privacy with partition walls stopping short of the ceiling, extensive use of louvres and a plan that arranged sleeping spaces around the perimeter of the building.[32] Even with the advent of domestic air conditioning, the challenge of providing houses that encouraged an accommodation with the climate, rather than sealed-box denial, persisted as one view of how to live in the city.

Following an extensive national road trip, two University of Adelaide graduates, Adrian Welke and Phil Harris, established an architectural practice in Darwin in 1980.[33] Drawn to the challenge of the region, and the frontier mentality that pervaded day-to-day living, the practice, iconoclastically named Troppo, set out to develop prototypical houses in this spirit of local accommodation.[34] The materials were familiar to a generation schooled in the economy of framed and sheeted vernacular buildings, and Troppo's early work uses these materials to capture the inventiveness necessary to emulate Burnett's solutions, and to devise original ones. The firm promoted itself with a degree of irreverence, in line with the general sense of Darwin life being less structured or bureaucratic than the rest of the country. Their Green Can House (1982), a prototype for mass production, used a framed and corrugated sheet aesthetic to create spaces of loft, ventilation and shading as the basic techniques of climatic mitigation. In architectural culture the firm also served as a cipher for a national mythology fast disappearing, one of values-driven experimentation in a context

Lawrence Nield and John Mainwaring, Sunshine Coast University College Library, Sippy Downs (Queensland), 1996.

that recalled the less-regulated building industry of the 1960s. The idea of Darwin and indeed the Northern Territory as a frontier evoked a nostalgia in southern cities for a degree of autonomy already on the brink of extinction.

With the extensive coastal development underway in Southern Queensland, opportunities arose for the application of regional climatic control to institutional buildings. As part of a new university campus, Sydney-based Lawrence Nield partnered with local practitioner John Mainwaring for the design of the Sunshine Coast University College Library. The traditional library of internal spaces is here inverted, with a large screened verandah to the north creating a public-scale version of the filigreed rooms of Andresen O'Gorman, which in turn drew on the louvred verandah of the traditional high-set Queenslander house. Shaded and permeable, the space serves as entry to the main library levels, which are lit through a series of south-facing clerestories. The building employs a facade principle of extensive glazing, whose potential for heat gain is mitigated by equally extensive screening. This wrapping to preserve the transparency of the modernist space, while at the same time shading it with screens for striated light, would become a mainstay of buildings seeking to accommodate the spatial syntax of modernism with the growing call to reduce air conditioning.

Positioning for the New Millennium

While the period to the new millennium saw the demise of public works, and the often excellent design offices run by the states, it was also a time of extensive cultural reinvention. Australia from the 1970s made great strides in popular culture, and the veritable explosion of film-making and popular music that was exported in subsequent decades established a view of the country as shaped through these media. The fecundity extended to architecture, with Murcutt the most internationally visible of Australian architects through the unmistakeable amalgam of tradition and modernity that he perfected. He had never argued for his work as regional, in the parochial sense, since he had always acknowledged his debt to global architecture.[35] His reception abroad says as much about the international architectural press, and its constant search for difference, as it does about Murcutt himself. To assume a position informed by topography and climate is to imagine that it could be successfully replicated elsewhere, and that it therefore has universal validity. While this argument is sometimes disingenuous, ignoring the idealization of memory and history that make up the spatial lexicon of the architect, it provided a way of working grounded in technique that suffused much of the Australian profession. The exception remained Melbourne and to a smaller extent Tasmania, where the essence of regional identity was acknowledged as cultural perhaps more than technical. This view had less interest in transplantation and more in retaining loyalties to a place-specific critical view.

These identities arose in the context of a strong post-colonial pride, with the country moving well beyond viewing itself as somehow a thing of two parts, being both independent and yet tied to Empire. This view declined markedly in the 1960s, in a process that fostered the cultural flowering of the 1970s. It also opened the door to a new generation of immigrant architects, drawn to the optimism projected by Australia abroad. All owed a debt to Seidler, who with entrepreneur Dick Dusseldorp had transformed commercial development in the centre of Sydney through a quality impossible to measure historically: force of will. Immigrants like Buhrich, Fooks or Iwanoff had worked away from the mainstream, but Seidler simply demanded that the universal relevance of his informed modernism be recognized.[36]

For the new generation of immigrants, Sydney presented more eclectic and open opportunities than other capitals. Its classical bent could be

Durbach Block Architects, Droga Apartment, Sydney, 1998.

interpreted in many ways, especially when informed by site or climate. Both tendencies appealed to Neil Durbach, who immigrated from South Africa in the early 1980s. His springboard was winning, with fellow South African Harry Levine, the 1985 competition for the new headquarters for the New South Wales Chapter of the Royal Australian Institute of Architects. He formed Durbach Block in 1993 with Camilla Block, born in Johannesburg but trained at the University of Sydney. The Droga Apartment of 1998 was built on the roof of an existing inner-city commercial building undergoing renovation, and its prominence as urban sculpture, visible from the main train line, underlined the firm's formal credentials.

Drawing on a deep knowledge of the modernist canon, the firm created an apartment of plastic sophistication that took in extensive views of the city skyline. The contrast of intellectual endeavour with the grit of the city's traditional garment district brought some focus back to its potential for seductive urbanity, away from the yearning for a rural idyll.

The awarding of the 2000 Olympic Games to Sydney produced the inevitable round of frenetic self-definition to create a cohesive working image for the event. It is a useful watershed for the period, marking the passing of a time of modest but fruitful cultural definition across the country, and an increasing international profile for its culture. While its focus is Sydney, it presents an opportunity to review Australian architecture at the new millennium, and the consolidation of the cultural re-definition of the 1980s and '90s.

chapter six

The Neoliberal Environment, 2000–

The year 2000 was less a watershed in Australian architecture than a stocktaking. Firms that had emerged in the previous two decades were gaining traction in both recognition and commissions. Internationally the Sydney Olympics drew predictable attention to the city, its relative lack of cynicism for the event garnering widespread admiration from administrators and athletes alike. This was no surprise to Sydney inhabitants themselves, in a city and a nation that respected sport as a model, workable if not flawless, of a meritocracy. The site chosen was a remediated industrial peninsula on the upper reaches of the harbour, with water frontage and remnant mangroves. A spur rail was built off the main western line, and ferry services were initiated to the northern tip. The opportunities afforded by the site were vast. As with many of the city's waterside peninsulas, it was free of through traffic and invisible to most inhabitants who passed its southern boundaries. The area was redeveloped as a complex of sporting venues, new parklands, housing and exhibition grounds for the Royal Easter Show, an annual agricultural showpiece supplemented with an amusement park that had previously been held on an inner-city site since 1881.

Even with these additions, the Olympic site still appears as a series of architectural set pieces in a landscape. The main stadium was designed by Bligh Lobb Sports Architecture, an association between local firm Bligh Voller Nield and international stadium specialists Lobb Architects, together with HOK Sport. It was the largest Olympic stadium ever built and the design was driven by player and spectator comfort. With more than 110,000 spectators for Olympic events, massive steel bow trusses supported the roofs over the eastern and western tiers, while cantilevered and raked seating to the north and south expanded capacity for more hardy patrons. These were later removed to reduce capacity but increase covered seating, as the stadium shifted to hosting recurrent sporting events.[1]

The pragmatic side of the country was very much on display for the event. There was little satisfaction for those fascinated by grotesque budget overruns and key deadlines unmet: the construction schedule proceeded according to plan, and after the Olympics the venues all continued to host events. Steel was the predominant building material for

Bligh Lobb with HOK Sport, Sydney Olympic Stadium, 1996–9.

Durbach Block Architects, Olympic Amenities Buildings, Sydney, 2000.

venue superstructures, its relative lightness and speed of construction, coupled with off-site fabrication, aiding the tight scheduling. The buildings that drew the most architectural attention were the smaller ones, where scale allowed a more considered implementation of ideas. The glowing forms of the amenities buildings by Durbach Block, made with translucent fabric skins over non-identical swelling steel frames, provided a needed contrast to the generally utilitarian tenor of the games buildings. The archery centre by Stutchbury & Pape also subverted the repetitive logic of steel construction with a twisting roof profile, showcasing the potential of framed and sheeted construction when approached with imagination.

The housing for the athletes was walking distance to the event stadia and halls, as much a result of building for their convenience as for using the village as a catalyst for new housing development in the area. The design was undertaken as a summary of urbanist thinking rather than as formal invention, an approach showing the prevailing tendency to look to historical models to inform density, street layouts and degrees of privacy. There were two components to the village: a section predicated on new urbanist thinking directed by a consortium headed by Cox Architecture, PTW Architects and HPA, and a linear complex by Bruce Eeles and Associates with HPA and Vote Associates that looked to the models of high modernism such as the Deutscher Werkbund's Weissenhof Estate, rendered as market-driven apartments.

The latter was sited on a ridge overlooking the newly laid-out parklands and remnant natural habitat, and was a reminder of the picturesque aspect of high modernism when placed within contrasting landscaping. It evoked

Stutchbury & Pape, Sydney Olympic Park Archery Centre, 1999.

Bruce Eeles and Associates with HPA Architects and Vote Associates, Newington Apartments, Sydney, 1997–2000.

the old trope of the reconciliation of contemporary dwelling with nature, using the latter as a corrective to modern life. The adjoining village took the new urbanist approach of trying to make the act of dwelling more organic, with servicing and waste minimized as part of a wider desire to live more frugally. Both views would inform urban thinking in the coming decades, with a revived modernism useful in promoting densification through apartments, and the new urbanist logic transforming tract housing by reducing lot sizes and providing communal facilities on the village model.

The Architecture of Uncertainty

The sense of a coming of age for practitioners like Durbach Block, Peter Stutchbury and Bruce Eeles belied their previous achievements in smaller scale work. It was simply that the Olympics gave an unprecedented audience to their work. In another location, the following year also gained wide exposure for Ashton Raggatt McDougall through their National Museum of Australia (with Robert Peck von Hartel Trethowan). This was a different proposition in terms of identity, which emerged unselfconsciously in the Olympic site through local architects expediently using

Sydney's construction industry. In the National Museum of Australia the demand for historical judgement was always explicit, and in the hands of a firm devoted to the toolbox of meanings opened in the wake of modernism's decline the project exuded possibilities.

Following on from Peter Corrigan's recurrent observations on the incomplete nativity of modern Australians, the building itself sets out to be a trenchant comment on fragmented identity.[2] It avoids any unified attempt to summarize history, and presents as a collection of architectural references, copies and ideas that pointedly stand unreconciled, but not without a linking sentiment. It is, in John Macarthur's inimitable phrase, an architecture of 'ecstatic pessimism'.[3] Few buildings so comprehensively display the demise of earlier certainties: in progress, in rationalism and in the colonial project. The fragments of famous buildings reproduced in the museum would be familiar to architects, but not always to the general public. The most recognizable among these are the sections of glazing to the Main Hall modelled on the Sydney Opera House glass walls, and a copy of part of Le Corbusier's 'Villa Savoye' rendered in black, with some distortion of scale. This cannibalizing of architectural history is not unique, given the worldwide proliferation of buildings inspired by Mies van der Rohe, for example. Here, however, the highly distinctive forms and patterns

HPA Architects, Cox Richardson, Peddle Thorp & Walker, Virginia Kerridge, Tonkin Zulaikha, Howard Tanner, Order Architects, Grose Bradley and Gordon & Valich, Sydney Olympic Village, 1997–2000.

ARM and Robert Peck von Hartel Trethowan, National Museum of Australia, Canberra, 1997–2001.

are provocative in their recall, inviting the viewer to fill in for themselves the meaning of these reproductions, rendered more crudely than the original.

The disquiet the building engenders with its walkway roof as a ribbon to nowhere, and the anti-prettiness of its composition, is bolstered by a central courtyard titled the Garden of Australian Dreams. The garden space inscribes a map of Australian ideology with both irony and bitterness. As an experience of contemporary Australia there is little comfort given to ideas of curatorship, or collective successes, but rather a chronicle of differences is intended with an indeterminate redemption hinted at. As Howard Raggatt wrote, 'we hoped to make something projective, a sign of our longing'.[4]

The year 2000 also saw the opening of the Melbourne Museum by Denton Corker Marshall. In contrast to their commercial work, which often contained major spaces hidden deep within the building mass, this work gave the architects the opportunity to create a public building of civic scale and significance. Directed by a curatorial ambition to make the building popular, and to break down the distinction between artefacts of academic and popular significance, the complex provides exhibition spaces in an arrangement that deliberately fragments the story of the city. It has this quality in common with the Museum of Australia, but architecturally the Melbourne Museum presents a far more polished image for its intentions. This renders its contents and design at odds. While seeking to undermine history as written by the powerful, the architects use the openness of the structure and its monumental raked wings, as well as the prominent ordering grid, to convey that the building 'is to be confident and mature, elegant and visionary; a key Melbourne building for the next 100 years'.[5]

How differently this reads from the poetic hedging of significance that the architects of the Canberra Museum offer. Ashton Raggatt McDougall have made a building of lesser elegance than the Melbourne Museum,

Denton Corker Marshall, Melbourne Museum, 1994–2000.

but their outlook is in sympathy with a curatorial philosophy founded on doubt about the validity of post-war certainties. Denton Corker Marshall subsume these doubts into an ordering grid, itself a cipher for rationalist constructs. The Melbourne Museum reasserts the validity of architecture by directing it according to larger urban determinants, using historical ordering devices like the city grid. Indeed the museum is described by the architects as a building composed of buildings, as the complex reproduces a city fragment within a single institution.[6]

If anything, this reveals the rise of city structure and history as the repository of certainty, at a time when architecture itself succumbed to radical doubt. To describe a building as a city in miniature was to use it to invoke the syntax that made the city legible: streets, lanes, pathways, grids, gardens. Along with these came a new sort of soft egalitarianism, as the public realm of streets and lanes penetrated indoors to the new museums, as well as into the new internalized shopping centres that proliferated.

In a sense this reprised Seidler's vision of public realm on private land, except Seidler worked in an era of greater social idealism and had less regard for the preservation of historical forms and structures. The shift to respecting the urban grid, and its historical mission, was not only a reaction to cities becoming less legible, as large developments consolidated sites together. It was also a consequence of the growth of neoliberalism, which invoked history to counter any radical potential that might lie in an unconstrained remaking of the city. The popularity of new urbanist ideas in planning, with their conservative ecologies, added a further critique to notions of progress.

Neoliberal Renovation

By 2001 there remained few places where the social idealism of the 1980s, and before, could hold out. The gutting of government architects' offices at both state and federal level continued, and public design was largely undertaken through tender processes, with very few design competitions held to elicit architectural quality. Over the same period urban planning and design began to favour firm city boundaries, with new development taking place in areas converted from industrial uses, or in suburbs of low density. This happened first and quickest in Sydney. By the 1990s the old financial arrangement of existing ratepayers funding new infrastructure was superseded by one where the costs of access and services were shifted onto new homeowners.[7] This increased the price of new building blocks and made local authorities reluctant to approve them without the means or the desire to pay for roads and pipes. Development at the city fringe slowed down markedly, aided by the growing demonization of suburbs as profligate and socially isolating. New apartment buildings in old suburbs became the preferred form of development, and from the turn of the century the number of apartments built in Sydney exceeded the number of houses.[8] This was a significant change in a country where most of the population aspired to detached houses.[9]

The shift provided increasing work for architectural practices at a time when they were diverging in size. Consolidation of practices and overseas work, particularly in Asia, saw the rise of the mega-firm, at least by Australian standards. At the same time the formation of small firms with low overheads continued, living off a handful of residential or commercial projects.[10] The demise of government architectural offices catalysed a redefinition of architectural ambitions, since there were fewer outlets for unalloyed idealism. Programmatically buildings converged around private or commercial concerns, and even the suburban churches or new factories that leavened practice loads in the 1970s ceased to be built. The values by which architecture came to be judged within the profession also narrowed, as efficiency of construction or ambition of social programme faded from interest. Drawing on its English roots, architecture in Australia turned to craft to assert its cultural value.

Given the exposure it now enjoyed internationally, the profession raised its standard in craft and formal skill through new models absorbed via travel and the international press. The appeal of Australian regionalism declined as its message became anaesthetized through repetition, and the simple construction of framed and sheeted buildings fell short of the level of craft demanded for international exposure. In almost cyclical fashion attention turned again to the Mediterranean, this time to the strength of Spanish and Portuguese architecture as it flourished in the years after the end of their dictatorships.

Initially the appeal of masonry and concrete construction manifested in a minimalism, where rational and tightly repetitive design could be read as a style in the Australian tradition of utilitarian good sense. Altair Apartments in Sydney, by Tina Engelen and Ian Moore, sat above one of the city's major inner traffic arteries. Located in the nightlife centre, now gentrifying, Altair exuded an air of urban sophistication through its clean surfaces and city views. This version of urban chic would have a brief flowering, its appeal limited to the novelty of the inner city as a site for reinventing personal identity. Minimalism emerged as the aesthetic of a polished urbanity, as it shed the sentimentality of the suburban origins of most young inner-city inhabitants. As the novelty of this urban anonymity wore off, the aesthetic was supplanted by blocks of dwelling units that sought to copy the screened balconies of Spanish apartments, with Coderch's 'La Barceloneta' (1951) as a popular model.

ALTAIR

The quality of apartments varied greatly, depending on the location and final profit margin. The redevelopment of a large city-fringe precinct in Sydney, Victoria Park, produced a collection of superior designs by a number of firms working to a masterplan. Conceived and executed as a showpiece development, it reflected the kind of urbanity imagined for the city as it moved from low to high density.[11] The form is loosely European, with continuous podiums to street alignment surmounted by residential towers. Among the best of these is Form (2005) by a consortium of Turner with Bolles+Wilson and Nation Associates. Working through traditional studio design sessions in Peter Wilson's office in Münster, Germany, the group pushed hard to exploit a development format that remains popular in Australia, despite its evident limitations. The shortcomings derive mainly from a naive urbanity that continues to inform urban design: the assumption that apartment blocks will provide the necessary density for lively streets as a matter of arithmetic. The ahistorical nature of this view has often made for areas of barely animated streets and little genuine urban texture, a monoculture that reflects the awkward mix of rationalized detailing, high rents and poor connections to existing shopping areas that characterizes most new medium- and high-density development. The redeveloped suburb of Rhodes in Sydney, for example, has been carefully planned and ambitious standards have been applied to both buildings and landscaping, yet despite extensive water frontage, it has little evident public activity in its streets.

Where apartment buildings sit in the prevailing street grid, they are free of the demand to create a new urban condition. Candalepas Associates have cultivated a reputation for ambitious architecture in apartments that emulate the amenity of houses. Pindari (2005) looks to the upper end of the market and brings the architectural techniques of regionalism – clerestory windows for views into the tree canopy, broad oversailing roofs and timber screens – into apartment design. The intention is to incorporate architectural spaces honed through the design of individual houses into multi-unit complexes, a model that counteracts the lowest-common-denominator logic of most apartment developments. However the distinction remains, as the expense of Candalepas's high-quality concrete work and complementary timber detailing confines the model to areas with high property values.

Nonetheless it shows that the renovation of suburbs to greater density can take various forms. Alex Popov had long sought to inject the sophistication of Jørn Utzon, his father-in-law for a period, into houses and townhouse complexes. His complex of terraces and units known as Canopy, overlooking a gully in Northbridge, also aimed to bring some of the appeal of modernist space, now solidly in its historicist reincarnation, to common-wall living.

Engelen Moore, Altair Apartments, Sydney, 2001.

Most new apartment buildings were met with some misgiving in their suburbs. All councils in Sydney since the turn of the century have been under intense state government pressure to provide additional dwellings by increasing building heights and densities, a move resisted by existing residents who fear diminished amenity. In wealthier suburbs the resistance has been fierce and costly in legal fees.[12] Where they have been encouraged, like those in the vicinity of the Olympic Stadium, new developments have allowed a comprehensive vision of a denser Sydney to arise. On the fringe of the city the new urbanism has been particularly influential and has had occasional successes, despite its conservative leanings. The new Rouse Hill Town Centre (2008), an exercise in private place-making, has overtones of post-war suburb-making in the placement of a library at its heart. While this is not unusual, the development is noteworthy for what is essentially a large shopping centre configured as a town centre around a planned crossroads, with shops fronting lanes and roads rather than internalized pedestrian malls.

The model had some success in the warm weather of Queensland, but the cooler weather of western Sydney has not precluded its successful implementation.[13] Its success is due to being primarily retail, with a small residential component. Its animated streets rely on the underground car

Candalepas Associates, Pindari Apartments, Sydney, 2005.

Rice Daubney, Allen Jack+Cottier and Group GSA with Civitas Urban Design, Rouse Hill Town Centre, Sydney, 2008. Shopping centre as urban fragment.

park and the many visitors who come to it as a shopping mall, but the astute judgement of scale on the part of the designers, architects Rice Daubney, Allen Jack+Cottier and Group GSA with Civitas Urban Design and Planning, makes it a convincing fragment of a vision imperfectly taking shape in all Australian cities. In Melbourne the South Bank area has seen an almost complete transformation, with apartment buildings now making up a large proportion of the city skyline, as is the case with Brisbane.

Vestiges of Idealism

Despite the plethora of apartment building in Melbourne, its state government, through the Victorian Office of Housing, still sponsored building projects of some idealism that ran counter to market forces. In 2007 the practice of DesignInc completed the K2 apartment complex in inner-city Windsor. In its intentions the building reads as a corrective to prevailing development, having public and private gardens to encourage resident interaction, as well as north-oriented living rooms and systems to aid the heating and cooling of units without gas or electricity.

The most striking attribute of the building, though, was the architectural effort expended on it in an age of frugal cooperative or public housing provision. The buildings have a high degree of physical articulation, with facade projections of windows and balconies creating the impression of individuality in unit design, despite the strong underlying rationalism of the planning. The persistence of some degree of idealism in Victorian apartments was anomalous. New South Wales had moved almost entirely to housing provision that relied on market solutions, even when tailored to public tenants. There was little appetite for architecturally distinguished public or state-assisted housing.

K2, as a project, not only rode on its intentions to provide a building that encouraged social interaction: it also set ambitious goals for performance in servicing. Using rainwater capture, recycled water, solar water heating and roof-mounted photovoltaic cells, the complex claims to have halved its usage of reticulated gas, electricity and water over conventional developments. Its proximity to the city and to public transport reduces occupants' reliance on private cars.[14]

The building could serve as an exemplary conjunction of the older, modernist concerns of providing adequate housing for all and the post-modern environmentalist critique of market solutions. The former was committed to accommodating those too poor to compete in the rental market, where apartments are built to return average yields. These earlier housing blocks, built by the Victorian Housing Commission in the 1960s, brood more visibly over inner Melbourne than any other Australian city. The economics of the original public housing schemes were viable because the land value gradient of the time, which fell away from city centres before recovering in more desirable suburbs, made city-fringe sites far cheaper than at present. For cash-poor governments of the 2000s their inner-city holdings yielded low returns compared to the cash windfalls from outright sale, and making new purchases in good locations was beyond their reach. Instead arrangements were sought with developers whereby additional floor-space bonuses would be swapped for cash or land contributions for building public facilities.

Buildings like K2 made the confluence of modernist social concerns and environmental ones appear inevitable. In the early years of the welfare state prevailing social analysis had ascribed a role in capitalism to reserve populations of workers, or renters, who kept wages low and rents high through a desperation born of exclusion. An unconstrained housing market had no social obligation to house everyone: indeed it used the unhoused to demonstrate that rental thresholds were market driven and

DesignInc, K2 Apartments, Melbourne, 2007.

unsentimental. Thus the provision of public housing, like unemployment benefits, mitigated the excesses of capitalism, which seemed to exist as structural necessities. Neoliberalism discredited these analyses as ideology, while maintaining them as social realities. State housing provision had a greater rollback than most other government-funded areas, but its function as perhaps the largest moral imperative in modernist architecture has left a historical imprint on the profession.

In its wake the matching moral imperative of early post-modernism was to preserve the city and to reverse the post-war diminution of its role as a place for the exchange of ideas – and money. The cult of the pedestrian, prefigured in the anti-car movement of the 1970s, was born. Walking meant human contact, fewer exhaust emissions, better health and animated streets. It also meant the vilification of the suburb as the antithesis of the walking city.

Concerns about rising atmospheric carbon dioxide levels as a general consequence of industrial modernity were also absorbed into this critique. The historical city was idealized as an artefact of pre-modernity, as if within

the traces of its street grids lay a formula, long ignored, of a frugal urbanity that nonetheless enabled the city to do its social work. Leon Krier's seductive medievalist drawings laid the basis for this view in both urban design and architecture in the 1970s. Regionalist sentiments in adapting to climatic conditions gave it a technical overlay.[15]

K2 was a project that aimed to address all of the above. Within the architectural profession it seemed that the old social concerns of modernism could be addressed through an invigorated and humanized urbanity, relatively blind to class. At the same time the technical concerns of reducing carbon dioxide emissions across the full life cycle of a building became more ingrained into architectural thinking. A complementary project to K2, also by DesignInc, was Council House 2, a purpose-built office block for the City of Melbourne. The building has low-energy environmental control and humanized workspaces as its driving design principles. Air is purged at night, using Melbourne's nocturnal temperature drop to cool the interior. Thermal inertia keeps the building cool in the morning, after which evaporative cooling and, later, conventional air conditioning take over. Passive systems using rising hot air also drive interior air changes twice an hour.[16]

With its exterior planting, balconies and roof-mounted exhaust turbines, the building conveys a cheerful vision of the simple expedient of improving morale through more comfortable interiors, and through the idea of working in a building designed to be environmentally responsible. The complex cooling and venting systems have their justification in the notion of building as organism, which mimics an autonomic regulation of temperature and air quality. The moving sunshades, made of recycled timber, add to this effect. Despite the didactic properties of the building, its countercultural sentiments of folk and organic sympathies, in practice if not in form, have limited its appeal for the corporate sector at large.

The more abstract possibilities inherent in emulating natural form had already been mined by Ashton Raggatt McDougall in Storey Hall. This trend continued in the large development in central Melbourne known as Federation Square, built over a large tract of rail lines. The result of an international 1997 competition won by the partnership of Peter Davidson and Donald Bates (LAB), in association with Bates, Smart, the complex has become a central focus for the city's recreation and civic events.

The scale of building is enormous and takes in retail spaces, galleries and a television studio, in a configuration that creates a large and open urban square. Bates had worked for Daniel Libeskind on the extension to the Jewish Museum, Berlin. The fragmented geometry of this work has found its way into the Melbourne complex, alongside systems of non-repetitive geometries that allude to the cladding of Storey Hall. In

DesignInc, Council House 2, Melbourne, 2006. Turbines on the roof drive vertical air circulation.

Federation Square these geometries manifest in various ways: as cladding patterns to building facades, and as structural and glazing systems for the atrium. As a public building, or collection of buildings, the complex has a dual life. It has first created a civic square for the city, devoted to leisure and the arts, but which can accommodate public gatherings and protests. This it achieves through the recovery of lost urban space by building a deck over the rail lines, and it fulfils a need by virtue of this simple urban addition. As urban design the buildings shape the open space, and allow numerous points of entry that emulate Melbourne's distinctive laneways. Its second life is that of a representative architectural work that projects discipline-specific concerns. The use of computers in generating and documenting the building geometries shows a faith in technology to represent its own potential, confined at this stage to decoration. The projected promise is of something more substantial to come: that there are properties of function, or of thinking, that will emerge through the medium of computing itself, in ways opaque to prediction.

This idea of the buildings representing the potential, not fully realized, that is inherent in the process of their making is part of the hedged optimism of the project. It underpins the 'excessiveness of the design strategy', in Gevork Hartoonian's words, while remaining puzzling to the public at large.[17] This, too, serves a purpose in asserting the independence of architecture from civic populism. While the message may be indeterminate, it is consistently so. As John Macarthur observed, commonly held expectations are negated to 'stand against understanding culture as the simple-minded affirmation of the world as it is'.[18]

The space, and the buildings, are intensively used, and the generosity of the state of Victoria in funding Federation Square made it unusual in twenty-first-century developments for not being an adjunct to a large commercial redevelopment. Over time it has assumed a central role in the life of the city, and the challenge posed by its architecture has grown less potent with greater familiarity. The liberating potential of the technology used in its design has yet to be realized, but its decorative value has been widely assimilated in the city. Indeed, despite clear international antecedents, the architecture of Federation Square has most succeeded within a cultural regionalism.

Other cities also added to their stock of museums and galleries, as they strove to maintain cultural relevance. The new galleries were generally built to extend core collections held both federally and in individual states. The cultural complex on Brisbane's South Bank added a Gallery of Modern Art (GOMA) by Architectus, led by Lindsay and Kerry Clare. The building houses galleries of various sizes for significant but temporary exhibitions, complementing the permanent collection of the neighbouring State

Gallery by Robin Gibson. It is of a different ilk to the earlier building, with the Clares' climatic consciousness in evidence with the large oversailing roof sheltering a collection of volumes that house galleries and lecture theatres. This theme of the primacy of the roof had long been in evidence in Queensland, but here it is elevated to civic scale, in effect creating a sheltering micro-climate within a subtropical site. The gallery spaces are arranged about a broad cruciform passage that itself can hold exhibits, serving both sealed spaces and glazed viewing boxes looking back to the city. The building volumes are clad in a range of materials, from zinc to timber battens, but these distinguish individual facades that read as secondary to the plane and protection of the roof.

This transposing of principles and forms honed at smaller scale reversed the city's growing pre-occupation with surface and texture as championed by Donovan Hill, visible in the adjoining State Library of Queensland

LAB Architecture Studio with Bates Smart, Federation Square, Melbourne, 1997–2002.

Lindsay and Kerry Clare (Architectus), Gallery of Modern Art, Brisbane, 2002–6.

(with Peddle Thorp). Here the array of finishes, printed and textured, cast and fixed, takes Gibson's work as a starting point, but with the concrete shell carved and adorned. The textural efflorescence has a different intent from that of the Clares, though equally contextual. Donovan Hill reference the modernist tradition of Brisbane as well as the uneven timberwork of Andresen O'Gorman, with climatic control achieved through filtered light and broad internal volumes. It is a technique less precise than that of the GOMA, with cultural allusion interwoven with shading, evoking a popular view of Queensland as a state as one of heightened, exotic colouring.

The building of galleries continued through subsequent years, with Johnson Pilton Walker's National Portrait Gallery in Canberra opening in 2009. Joining the group of the High Court and National Gallery of the 1980s, the Portrait Gallery is a more modest endeavour, aiming for an intimacy of experience that contrasts with the more monumental spaces of the National Gallery, where the artwork is dissociated from everyday life. The Portrait Gallery displays the craft of building in its making, again a sign of its anti-monumentality, with its five extruded pavilions revealing their sectional layers as they front Parkes Place. The interior of the pavilions make extensive wall lengths available for display, with serendipitous circulation lightly choreographed.

The most unconventional of the galleries built in the period is the Museum of Old and New Art (MONA) in the Hobart suburb of Berriedale. Designed by Melbourne firm Fender Katsalidis, it is conceived as windowless, sunken box of considerable sophistication that leads visitors down to encounter the art below. Built with private money – the owner, David Walsh, funded both collection and building – it differs from public collections in curatorship and brief. For Walsh the collection is based on 'sex and death', and his indulgence in a collection that ranges broadly about these themes has elicited a building that still maintains an avant-garde intention to shock or discomfort.[19] Fender Katsalidis are too adept not to offset this with sculptural invention and a strong sense of material ambience, but the singular vision behind the museum has conflated the collection and its housing.

Donovan Hill with Peddle Thorp, State Library of Queensland, Brisbane, 2004–6.

The result is a series of powerful spaces marked by coffered structural ceilings and a circulation path that is purposefully obscure. The iconography is loosely post-industrial, supporting a collection shaped to provoke, but with a curatorial reluctance to give historical context to this intent. This is exacerbated by the generally veiled nature of Australian philanthropy, where private money is given quietly but with strong preferences. The intent at MONA is to revive something of the countercultural mission of art and to strengthen Hobart's cultural credentials. It has proven hugely popular with locals and visitors alike, but the vague discomfort of hidden circulation and curatorial nihilism reinforce that this is an institution of private will intended as public utility.

Sydney added a new gallery devoted to contemporary art in 2012, as an extension to the institution that had been operating since 1991 in a converted government building fronting the city's waterside centrepiece of Circular Quay. The extension, by Sam Marshall of Architect Marshall, drew its cues from the textures of the surrounding urban collage of

Johnson Pilton Walker, National Portrait Gallery, Canberra, 2006–8.

Fender Katsalidis, MONA, Hobart, 2011. Serendipitous circulation marks the building.

expressway, stone-clad structures and the Harbour Bridge itself. The building used the language of abstract, geometric modernism to accommodate exhibitions and educative events, in a composition that symbolizes the socially progressive rather than radically subversive programme that now attaches to contemporary art.[20]

One senses in these new public or semi-public galleries – Brisbane's GOMA, the National Portrait Gallery and Sydney's MCA – a profound shift in the exhibition and reception of art. There is no abetting of the mystification of art, as the National Gallery achieves in its more dimly lit galleries with highlighted individual works. All three newer buildings aim for a more accessible display of work, with views to the outside and natural light, where possible, combined with clear entrances and circulation paths. Art, and contemporary art in particular, has been democratized as a well

Sam Marshall with NSW Government Architect's Office, Museum of Contemporary Art extension, Sydney, 2010–12.

for culture at large, as the progressive programme of the early millennium devolves its concerns to individual consciences and tastes.

Contexts Large and Small

The large project that filled the gap created by the demise of class politics was the environmental one. It had the distinction of being agnostic to class, with both working-class suburbs and corporate operations and buildings coming under criticism. The new suburbs had accommodated the domestic life of all classes in the post-war period, although the old urban cores of Australian capital cities had not experienced the abandonment suffered by many American counterparts. Nonetheless throughout the 1950s and '60s working-class communities were decanted to new housing tracts, where space allowed a version of detached-house suburbia for most working families. While some lacked amenities and had little tree cover, they provided a degree of control over tenure and space use that is historically unusual for working-class families. The environmentalist critique of suburbia – its inefficient use of space, the reliance on cars and the extent of infrastructure needed to service it – generally overlooks the relative autonomy it engenders for each household. This point was made explicit by planner Patrick Troy in 1996, but the shift to higher densities is now an article of faith in all jurisdictions.[21]

The environmentalist critique also extends to city offices, as evident in the brief and design for 'Council House 2'. Indeed, the building serves as a summary of those concerns and as one version of how they might be addressed. It is a distinctive feature of environmentalism that it can easily be allied to old social critiques that view capitalism as blindly growth driven, and exploitative, but it can also be folded into corporate capitalism itself. In other words it is not, at its core, founded on class concerns but on a broader disquiet with modernity itself. Thus it can serve as a universal critique of contemporary life and can manifest in many ways.

The corporate sector has moved to embrace this view slowly but relentlessly. The model of 'Council House 2' was too fragmented for the tastes of a refined corporate sector, which aimed for a seamless object that conveyed a sense of compressed value in its form and details. Renzo Piano's Aurora Place in Sydney, completed in 2000, had demonstrated one version of a soft corporatism. The Italian practice has long had a reputation for technical sophistication and for developing facade details and glazing systems for individual projects. The Sydney complex comprises an office tower and a lower set of apartments facing the Botanic Gardens. The building is distinguished by a curved, glazed eastern facade that extends beyond the floor plates in an implied wrapping, with chamfered edges that reference the curves and counter-curves of the Opera House. The refinement of the practice shows best in the several cladding systems visible at lower levels. The terracotta finish had been tested on earlier projects, and its remarkably precise tolerances convey both durability and precision.[22] The louvres to the apartment balconies are set within a structural system made of glass, whose transparency hints at an architecture for climatic control both sophisticated and dematerialized.

The appeal of these systems would exert an influence on subsequent Sydney architecture. Richard Francis-Jones, for one, had worked with Romaldo Giurgola since 1989 in the firm of Mitchell/Giurgola & Thorp, established for the design of the new Parliament House. The office was subsequently divided into Sydney and Canberra branches, with Sydney transforming into fjmt, a practice led by Francis-Jones, Jeff Morehen and Richard Thorp. As a designer Francis-Jones has aimed for reconciling the organic, understood as climatically responsive building systems or quasi-organic forms and materials, with the corporate imperative of seamlessness.

His design for the new centrepiece of the University of New South Wales in 1999, the Scientia Building, combines two stone-clad masses on either side of a glazed canopy sitting astride the path of the main university axis. The canopy structure is a set of steel and timber columns surmounted by fanning struts in a stylized row of trees, a theme taken up in the major hall with its timber-lined and fretted ceiling panels, arranged in a bowed structure onto timber posts with exaggerated entasis.

This theme of architectural integration is extended to encompass some of the oldest and most prized Georgian-era structures in the country, in the firm's addition to the heritage government precinct of Macquarie Street, Sydney. Treading carefully at the rear of the colonnaded row, the 2004 building, known as The Mint, is the headquarters of Sydney Living Museums. Devoted to operating and preserving historic buildings bequeathed to government, the complex reuses the remains of the old minting factory and creates a series of boxes interspersed among remnant shells of Georgian buildings. The clear distinction between old and new masks the variety created within the new, where transparency is moderated by timber louvres arranged in banks that tilt fully open. It can also accommodate small social functions in the entry pavilions and theatrette. The whole, designed with heritage specialists Clive Lucas, Stapleton & Partners, is conducted at an intimate scale that transposes set modernist pieces among heritage items. This easy conflation of periods is achieved within the historical Sydney taste for proportion and minimal decoration, and the complex can be read as an affirmation of that taste.

By the late 2000s the sharp distinctions between Sydney, Melbourne and Brisbane had diminished. The strident geometric schemes that marked Storey Hall and Federation Square had seen their initial promise extended by firms like Lyons. The firm, founded in 1996 by brothers Corbett, Cameron and Carey Lyons, has pursued an agenda indebted to Melbourne culture as delineated by Ashton Raggatt McDougall. Lyons's work displays a strong interest in ideas, understood as abstract generators of form through mediated processes. These reflect contemporary concerns of signification and the economy of the computer, which can direct production of building parts individually and thus achieve an efficiency previously reserved for mass production.

Renzo Piano Building Workshop with Innovarchi Architects and Lend Lease Design Group, Aurora Place, Sydney, 1997–2000. The complex comprises an office tower with a lower apartment block (foreground).

This has imbued their work with a geometric restlessness, both formal and decorative, that affirms a faith in history as an engine of innovation with all the promise, and threats, that entails. This is, in itself, a provocation when held against the clarity of purpose and building structure pursued by firms such as fjmt, and their grounding in an ethic of reconciliation of parts. The John Curtin School of Medical Research, completed by Lyons in 2006 for The Australian National University, presents an entry

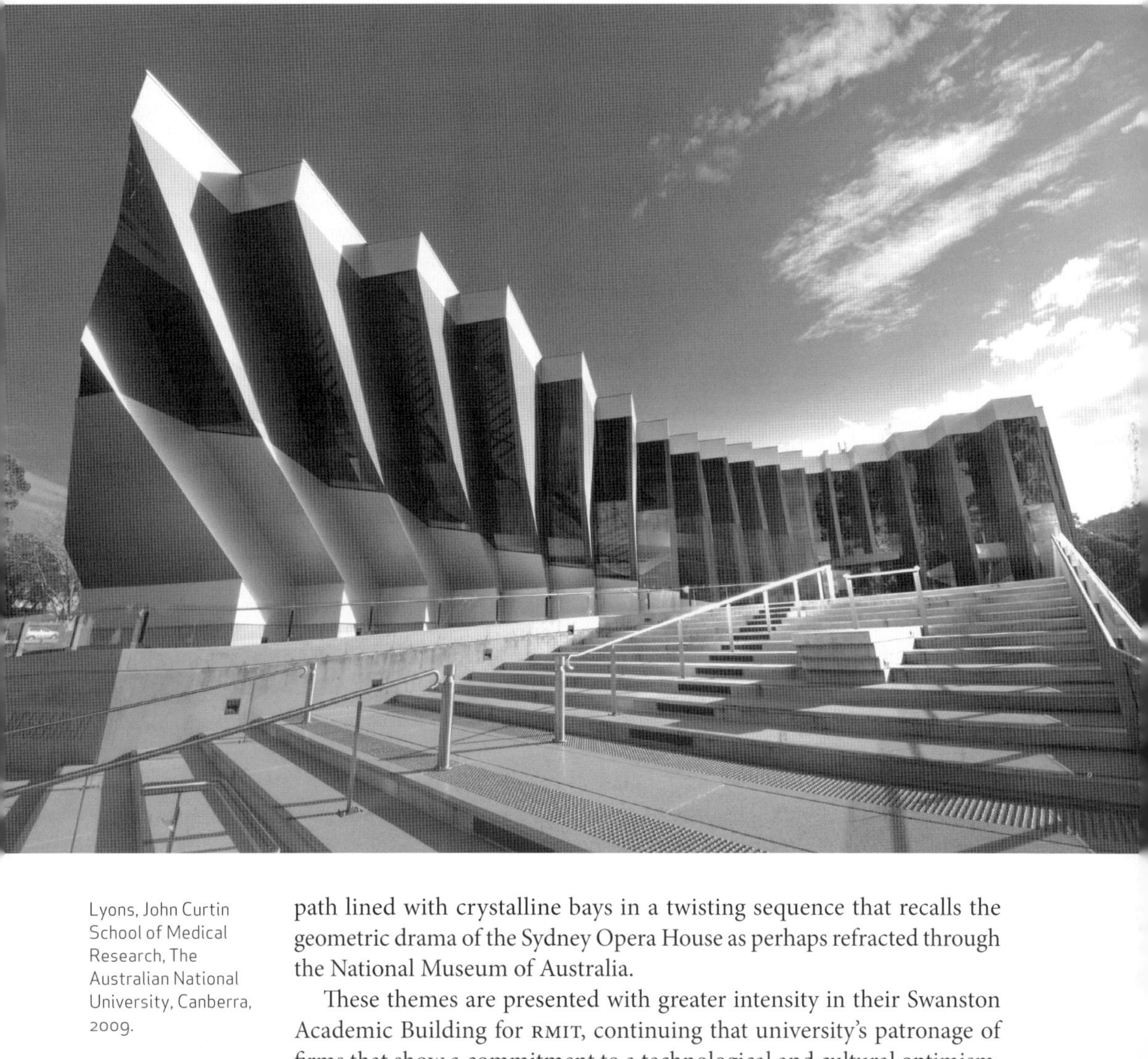

Lyons, John Curtin School of Medical Research, The Australian National University, Canberra, 2009.

Mitchell Giurgola Thorp, Scientia Building, The University of New South Wales, Sydney, 2000.

path lined with crystalline bays in a twisting sequence that recalls the geometric drama of the Sydney Opera House as perhaps refracted through the National Museum of Australia.

These themes are presented with greater intensity in their Swanston Academic Building for RMIT, continuing that university's patronage of firms that show a commitment to a technological and cultural optimism, also projected in the university's image. The Swanston Building does this in three dimensions, with a sinuous exterior wrapped in sharply triangulated glazing shaded by fields of projecting fins. The volume is punctured by openings generated as extruded complex shapes, mimicking the intersections of extrusions that arises easily in computer-aided design. There is a virtuosity in simply holding these geometries together, and the building affirms the role of computers in aiding the conception, and execution, of the design. The interior occasionally invokes the Hibernian green, in various shades, of Storey Hall, as a nod to the Melbourne tactic of cultural dissonance.

The impact and future of the computer in architecture has played a profound role in the work of firms like Lyons and Elenberg Fraser, to name just two. Its uptake was more visible in Melbourne because of a pre-existing fondness in the profession for dominant ideas as elucidated by Boyd and expanded by subsequent practitioners. The cultural influence of computers hinges on how technology is viewed historically, and their emerging role in a period of disenchantment with capitalism as a transforming force. Douglas Spencer has argued that computer-aided bio-mimicry in architecture is an expression of neoliberalism, expressing the belief that the market provides emergent solutions and products in the same way as evolution provides organic solutions through myriad iterations of generations.[23] Thus the idea of emergent design, achieved by running iterative computing design scripts through sets of parameters that transform each iteration to more closely conform to the parameters, is analogous to evolution. Its key distinction in architecture is that the process leapfrogs rationalist design, which proceeds from an abstract analysis of requirements and then aims for the simplest form that accommodates those requirements. Rationalism is reductive in its drive and in its economy, and it is assessed on those terms. By contrast, emergent design does not impose a particular economy, but tolerates excess as a necessary condition to allow a solution to emerge.

The promise of efficiency in emergence relies on the parameters that shape it. In evolution this acts through reproductive advantage, which in turn relies on efficient feeding within an ecological niche. In emergent design by computer the framing of the parameters is a cultural act, not one of blind survival. Computer-aided design has struggled with this, as the parameters become more challenging than simply solving technical issues, like the most efficient way of cutting patterns from specific sheet sizes. Following Spencer, we might say that emergent design has achieved only partial technical success, which has been outstripped by its success as representation in architecture.

Thus the Swanston Academic Building is a powerful, and indeed seductive, symbol of a technological future, one where buildings might display emergent solutions to climatic control with flair and colour, but it remains a promise. Nonetheless it points to one possible resolution of the longed-for reconciliation between technology and nature: that of the one folded into the other as technology becomes increasingly responsive to aiding building performance.

The alternate view, one that still subscribes to the economy of rationalism, continues to inform work into the new millennium. It has been

Lyons, Swanston Academic Building, Royal Melbourne Institute of Technology (RMIT), 2010–12.

reinvigorated in Melbourne through the work of Sean Godsell and Kerstin Thompson, among others. While all contemporary architects practise in a milieu where modernism has come to be understood as an aesthetic as much as an economy, despite its early claims to have transcended style, its historical affinity with industrialized building still has some currency. This problem, the transforming of efficient construction and planning into something of cultural potency, was addressed in a compelling way by Murcutt. In Australia the challenge of designing within the modernist economy has retained its appeal and its immediacy. The potential liberated by the high modernists within this mode of working – the allure of dematerialization, for example, or powerful spaces achieved through structural repetition or austere poetics – has fostered work like that of Godsell, who works to achieve a consistent skin condition or envelope as a generator of form and space. In his own house in Kew (1997) this took

Sean Godsell with Peddle Thorp, RMIT Design Hub, Melbourne, 2007–12.

the form of an oxidized rectangular steel frame glazed and sheeted, and protected on the north and west by operable fine louvred shutters. These have the same appearance as the frame, and the exterior appears as a uniform refined enclosure that modulates sun penetration, interior light and glass protection.

This calculated faith in the exterior condition is underlined by its application to whole facades. In a more sophisticated reiteration of this belief, Godsell combined with Peddle Thorp Architects to produce the Design Hub for RMIT (2012), who continued to add to their portfolio of noteworthy buildings. The Design Hub is entirely sheathed in circular glass cells, again creating a uniform condition but one that allows cells to pivot to follow the sun, and to be upgraded over time. The idea of a constant material condition persists in the lining of interior spaces, and is most compelling in the long stair that drops to subterranean studios and galleries. These achieve a poetic austerity that marks the rationalism of their conception and testify to Godsell's ambition of transcendence. As Juliana Engberg has noted, there are overtones of Dante in the central stair, and references to Giuseppe Terragni's unbuilt Danteum come to mind.[24]

Sean Godsell, Godsell House, Melbourne, 1996–7.

Kerstin Thompson has also developed a mode of practice that mines a modernist economy for the moments where it can be subverted. By tamping down the register of expression through simple forms and clean details, she effects subtle distortions in what appear to be rationally driven works. In her 'House at Big Hill' (2011), a holiday home on the southern coast of Victoria, she takes a plan of Le Corbusian efficiency and configures it to provide both shelter and outlook for the coastal views and changeable weather. The simple plan belies a precise use of space, and a small distortion in the roof plane injects a discrete level of dynamism between wall and roof. The restrained palette of concrete block, offset with timber

Durbach Block Jaggers, Holman House, Sydney, 2004, cliffside view.

fixtures and window reveals, make for interiors that are robust in the tradition of the modest post-war holiday house.

The appeal of the house lies in this reversal of the opulence of its age. With the decline of public works, particularly in housing, the generation of architects who matured before the millennium, often through modest projects, found themselves building for wealthy private clients. Through these commissions came many of the most memorable buildings since 2000, but they often present elaborations of positions, and ambitions, that preceded large budgets. The 'House at Big Hill' garnered state awards and a national commendation, but its modesty was the exception rather than the rule.

The elaborate residence was more on display in New South Wales than in Victoria or Queensland. Perhaps due to the exceptional sites available around Sydney, a string of spectacularly placed houses dominated state awards.[25] Although not necessarily large, these houses exhibited a level of detailing and architectural ambition intended to maximize the amenity afforded by their sites. Among the most spectacular was the Holman House in Sydney's coastal Eastern Suburbs, winner of the state's Wilkinson Award in 2005. The house perches on the cliff edge, a place of geological instability when measured over millennia. Designed by Durbach Block Architects, it projects living areas in a shallow arc above the cliff, presenting vistas of uninterrupted sea and horizon. To the side of the arc a coved courtyard provides a sheltered reprieve from the wind, and a set of terraces with an inset pool drop to the cliff edge.

Durbach Block had achieved some prominence through their Olympic amenity blocks and the Droga Apartment, but the Holman House extended their knowing take on modernist architectural history through evocation of Corbusian geometries, the bent plans of Coderch and Adalberto Libera's 'Casa Malaparte' on Capri. If this was to come to fruition anywhere it would be in Sydney's east, with its unique mix of urban beachside culture, access to the city and architecturally receptive clientele. Durbach Block's position as partly immigrant was akin to that of Popov, with a connection to the modernist tradition that was overt and less concerned with remaking that tradition to a local mould. The issue of authenticity, for them, is less than that of a learned reworking of modernism as it seeks fulfilment through site-specific refinement. Architecture's liberatory potential, in their work, lies in its evocation of modernism's free space, where aesthetics supplanted sentiment in volumes of light-led invention.

This can be contrasted with the 2012 Wilkinson Award winner, the 'Cliff Face House' by Fergus Scott with Peter Stutchbury. Located on the winding road serving the northern Pittwater peninsula, the house and its grounds drop to the sheltered side overlooking the bay of Pittwater itself.

Technique distinguished this house, from its polycarbonate-clad lantern rooms under protective fly roofs, to the immaculate teasing out of durability and craft in the stairs and walls. The echo of early Brutalist houses remains in the unadorned presentation of materials, but with the time and effort added to raise these to an uncommon degree of jointing and finish. The house evokes Japanese influences in the way each component displays the refined logic of its fixing and finishing.

Looking Outwards

In Sydney this polarization between a local architecture, founded on regional ideas of authenticity, and one based on a universal architectural culture made locally explicit, has diminished since the turn of the century. International interest in Australian work has seen these rival claims converge, as each is held to the expectations, and standards, of an international publishing industry in architecture. This has raised the refinement of all work with serious ambition, and the pride that drives local invention has been tempered by the inevitable desire to make the work accessible to international viewers.

On the eastern seaboard there has been a turning back to the aspirations of an economy of means, as the charms of high modernism are revisited. Firms such as Neeson Murcutt, formed in 2004 by Rachel Neeson and Nick Murcutt, comfortably work within a historically informed mode resting heavily on Iberian precedents like Coderch or Álvaro Siza, while still subscribing to the site-specific ethos that Sydney inculcates. The practice, which survived the untimely passing of Murcutt in 2011, is representative of a new generation of practitioners working easily between both the nativist tradition and one with an eye towards international precedents and accessibility. Their Prince Alfred Park Pool (2013, with the landscape architect Sue Barnsley) blends lessons from Spanish urban design, visible in the levity and visual patterns of the yellow umbrellas, with a highly urbane green public space. The mounding and planting that surmount the changing facilities create the oscillating landscape/building perception pioneered by Gustav Peichl, but rendered here in the refined modernist palette tested under Spanish skies. The location of the pool, alongside Sydney's main rail corridor to the south and west, has ensured that the project is cognizant of the history of the site as a neglected fragment on the city's edge. The nature here is neat artifice, in the same way as Le Corbusier's urban greenery was always to be tame.

A similar trend can be discerned in the reworking of a disused underground water reservoir in Sydney's pre-eminent Victorian suburb of Paddington. Architects Tonkin Zulaikha Greer have prised open sections of the reservoir to create a sunken garden interspersed with conservation set-pieces. Entry is via a new ramp and stairs surmounted by metal-leaved vaults reprising the vaulting of the original chamber. What is significant here is the valorization of history, and the care with which it has been curated.

These projects speak to a new internationalism as Australian architects grow increasingly confident of the validity of their work. Mass travel has lessened the impact of distance. In 2016 Australian residents made 9.9 million visits abroad, in a population of 24 million. This was double the number of visits a decade earlier. It is a well-travelled nation now, and familiarity with events, and buildings, internationally is as strong as ever.[26]

In terms of the models of practice that inform professional judgements, the European traditions continue to be highly influential. The English value of craft in architecture, achieved though comprehensive and detailed documentation of projects, remains strong and is well represented in awards. The skill of Spanish and Portuguese work over the past decades has also left a firm imprint, rendered all the more attractive as Australian cities move

Neeson Murcutt, Prince Alfred Park Pool, Sydney, 2013.

towards European densities. The formal qualities of these precedents, and their suitability for the Australian light, have been noted and emulated. Collectively these influences have diluted the strident nationalism of the 1970s and '80s, and with it the fixation on authenticity.

In part this can be attributed to the internationalism of the environmental movement, with its emphasis on local action to address global issues. This has had the effect of reshaping regionalist approaches to architecture that originally sought to create works that performed well climatically by absorbing local models and features. In the new environmental internationalism, every act of accommodation to climate that reduces energy use is seen as having relevance, regardless of where it comes from. There have been concerted efforts to develop prototypes at every scale for buildings to minimize energy use, using different principles. While 'Council House 2' presented one version reliant on mass and shading, in Sydney a collaboration between Architectus and German practice Ingenhoven produced 1 Bligh Street, a 28-storey office building in the financial precinct. With ambitious performance goals, the tower uses a glazed double-skin facade with enclosed louvres to reduce heat gain into the building interior. The double facade also allows trapped air to rise and discharge through exterior vents, drawing in cooler air at the base of the floors.

Given the building's realization as a rationalist project, devoted to achieving a set of measurable innovations in energy and water usage, it comfortably draws on the modernist ambition of dematerialization sketched out in Mies van der Rohe's early tower studies. The architects set out to control heat gain while admitting as much natural light as possible, leading to full-height glazing for each floor and a concerted effort to maintain transparency across the building floor plates. The eccentrically positioned atrium rises through the full building height, serving both to circulate air and as a modern version of the glazed halls of early modernity, such as the Crystal Palace and the late nineteenth-century shopping galleries, which too carried the ambition of captive idealized environments.

The compelling image of the building rests on its promise of technical solutions to the dilemmas of modernity, solutions which are also compatible with refined corporate environments. This technological optimism is a necessary antidote to the nihilism of more radical critiques of modern building and of the transformative powers of capitalism. It is a vision that has a parallel demonstration in the new precinct of Central Park, on a redeveloped brewery site close to Sydney's Central Railway Station. The most prominent component is the residential block designed by Ateliers Jean Nouvel, which demonstrates a set of judgements that depart from the prevailing norms, enshrined in legislation as well as practice, of apartment

Tonkin Zulaikha Greer, Paddington Reservoir Gardens, Sydney, 2006–9.

Architectus with Ingenhoven Architects, 1 Bligh Street, Sydney, 2011.

design. The building is noteworthy for the hanging vegetation that adorns its facades, conceived by Patrick Blanc. While this is a common contemporary proposal, its execution in One Central Park was unique in Sydney for its sheer size and its sophisticated implementation. The second distinctive innovation is two large fields of mirrors, one in sun and one in shade, that combine to reflect light into a central recreation area and a retail mall below. This exuberant manipulation of sunlight to overcome a problem of overshadowing is a further demonstration of technological optimism in the service of creating an idealized, dense city form.

Urbanity, rather than amenity, is the goal here. Taken as a whole, the project posits that the emerging city produces its own environmental norms, where convenience to city services and facilities offsets the windowless bedrooms that are the inevitable consequence of deep buildings. This has become the norm in new Victorian apartment blocks: in New South Wales there is still resistance to these studio apartments that comprise a good proportion of new developments.

In the design of individual city buildings it is still possible to see the quest for the reconciliation of modernity and nature, with nature conceived now in performance terms as a state of minimal human impact on natural systems. Other shades of this view are evident in buildings like fjmt's (Francis-Jones Morehen Thorp) EY Centre, an office building that builds on the firm's prior work in making overt use of natural materials. In the EY Centre a sealed double facade encloses timber louvres, and the floor plates rest on a core that is clad in Sydney sandstone, a material that conveys a generic sense of Sydney identity. The overall effect is of a public realm at the base lined in wood and stone, finely rendered, with a timber-hued tower above using the rounded forms of a new aerodynamic aesthetic that evokes not speed, but clean movement of air. The sandstone cladding, decorated with carvings by Judy Watson, serves as an apt summary of the building's critical regionalist credentials as outlined by Kenneth Frampton, one of Richard Francis-Jones's early mentors.[27]

A similar intent, but with more universal aspirations, can be seen in International House Sydney (2017) by Tzannes architects for the developer Lendlease. Built street-side in the city's new commercial precinct of Barangaroo, the structure consists of six levels of commercial office space constructed entirely from engineered timber, resting on a ground floor of conventional concrete framing. The long spans achieved with timber are expressed in the full-height glazing to each floor, emphasizing the commercial-grade flexibility and modernist transparency possible with the material. Implicit in this is the role of timber as a store for carbon, and the avoidance of the energy-intensive manufacturing of the cement required for concrete. The large timber members have local precedent in the

Francis-Jones Morehen Thorp, EY Centre, Sydney, 2016.

Ateliers Jean Nouvel with Foster & Partners and PTW Architects, One Central Park, Sydney, 2012–13.

hardwood framing of Sydney's voluminous historic finger wharfs, but the role of timber as a carbon sink encourages its use in quantity, giving the building structure a solidity borne of mass. This stands in contrast to the dematerializing intent evident in buildings such as 1 Bligh Street, which rely on sophisticated venting of their transparent double facades.

The demise of government architecture offices in the new millennium has shifted the design of public buildings almost entirely into private hands. Large commissions are often awarded through limited competitions and significant new buildings for education, research or medicine have been designed by architects collaborating to bring different perceived strengths

Tzannes, International House, Sydney, 2017.

to the project. In the best instances, works of originality provide strong identities for the commissioning institutions. The 2013 Translational Research Institute at the Princess Alexandra Hospital paired Brisbane firms Donovan Hill with Wilson Architects, who have deep expertise in research facilities. The resulting design creates a vast atrium behind a hanging tinted screen of glass panels, with a forest of planting set within a street-level composition of small architectural set pieces. It is a space of enormous seductive appeal in a warm climate, in contrast to the starkly institutional adjoining hospital. The plastic skills of Donovan Hill are clearly on display, their small shifts in geometry shaping plan form and space along public routes as a counterpoint to the necessary regimentation of the research floors.

This refinement in creating public space has been widely mastered by firms entering into institutional design. John Wardle has honed it over two decades, and his collaboration with the U.S.-based NADAAA in the new Melbourne School of Design at the University of Melbourne shows his refined geometries imbued with a syncopated sense of excess, visible in the interiors. The skilfully composed exterior yields to an enclosed atrium that presents dramatically angled skylights and a suspended studio within its volume. Mesh balustrading on sculpted steel balusters adds a gritty reference to the post-modern practice of valorizing cheap materials.

An exception to this deliberate and careful geometric play – a denatured de-construction – is the work of Kerry Hill, a Perth-based architect with extensive built work in Asia. Hill resisted absorbing the critical formalism of the past decades in Australian architecture, preferring to pursue a poetic approach that seeks opulence in refinement. Unlike the technological version of this, evident in work like 1 Bligh Street, Hill used crafted materials to pursue a classicist architecture of legibility and proportion. The State Theatre Centre in Perth (2010) has elements of Hill's Asian experience, with slender hanging anodized tubes lining the ascending stair to the main theatre. The theatre itself is sheathed in Tasmanian blackwood, a striated timber that emphasizes the grain and texture of the walls and ceiling. This sits in sharp contrast to the light steel frame of the building's long elevation, reprised in the austere central court. Hill here continued the tradition, extending through Leplastrier and Peter Muller, of locating Australian identity in a generic classicism, ideally one of transcendence, that seeks common elements from European and Asian precedents. It was a fusion championed by Geoffrey Bawa in Sri Lanka, but in Australia it can be traced as far back as Hardy Wilson.

Donovan Hill with Wilson Architects, Translational Research Institute at Princess Alexandra Hospital, Brisbane, 2012, view of semi-enclosed atrium.

The selection processes for architectural services in the new millennium have had the effect of distancing form from content in larger projects. Clients are generally cognisant of different strengths among practices and select accordingly. Those that specialize in hospital design, for example, may not have exceptional skills in crafting building image as it inheres in facade design and public spaces. Collaborations are increasingly common, and some of the very large firms with staff numbering in the hundreds have the capacity to deal with all aspects of architectural design at a consistently high level.[28] However, with the Australian economy increasingly becoming a service one, the range of building types undertaken by architects has become confined to housing, health, education, art and offices, with a scattering of other briefs.

Contemporary practice has little latitude for radical programmes, since funding sources rarely have an interest in deep social critique. Instead environmentalism has become the default critique within practice, but its very breadth has divorced it from the class-based concerns of modernism. Its

John Wardle with NADAAA, Melbourne School of Design, The University of Melbourne, 2009–14.

Kerry Hill Architects, State Theatre Centre of Western Australia, Perth, 2011.

concerns are diffuse and open to contradiction, as modernity turns on itself. The proposed solutions can vary from an anti-modernity to a technological idealism, both with long histories, but also carrying the risk of being confined to building systems that do not necessarily yield architectural interest.

Elusive Reconciliation

For commercial works and large housing developments there is generally little latitude to make statements of gravity. As Sandra Kaji-O'Grady has observed, the provocative image of William Barak inscribed in the facade of Swanston Square has little connection to the building's small apartments aimed at international investors and urban first-homeowners.[29] Barak was a leading elder of the Wurundjeri tribe, who inhabited the site on which Melbourne was established. A mounted trooper in the colonial police, he served as advocate and negotiator for his clan and won wide respect. His portrait serves as a reminder of the unfinished project of reconciliation between aboriginal and colonial Australia, and their descendent institutions

and populations. His portrait reads as opportunistic activism, seized as part of a commercial development by architects ARM (Ashton Raggatt McDougall), and eventually gaining the consent of the developer.

At a finer scale the collision of aboriginal inhabitation and colonial modernity has continued to manifest in the incompleteness of native adaptation to modern Australia, a complement to the incomplete nativism of Australians of exotic origins. Spearheaded by indigenous art, which found contemporary expression with the aid of modern acrylic paint from the 1960s onwards, the cultural life of remote communities has become visible through artworks sold or exhibited in major centres.[30] Martumili Artists, a collective based in the Western Australian town of Newman, commenced design for the East Pilbara Arts Centre in 2011 with assistance from the local council and transnational mining company BHP Billiton. The limited competition was won by the Perth practice Officer Woods Architects, who avoided facile readings of indigenous iconography to address the brief through a time-honoured Australian expedient, the big shed. Within this shed, barcoded in orange and red to reference *Learning from Las Vegas*,[31] the specific facilities called for in the brief are housed in a free-standing composition of smaller defined rooms. The shed solution provided considerably more sheltered area than expected, and the retracting panels allow free movement from inside to out. It is a solution of some grace and economy, aided by the sheer value of industrial space over solutions based on image.[32]

Other remote architectural works have taken a similar approach. Also based in Perth, Iredale Pedersen Hook have built projects that include transitional housing for indigenous families to assist them in owning their homes, and a prison (with TAG Architects) that aims to relieve the alarming levels of distress affecting indigenous inmates. The Walumba Elders Centre shows Iredale Pedersen Hook's considered language as it evolved in response to tight budgets, hot and dry climates, and cultural sensitivities and customs that are often opaque to architects. As in their earlier work, the firm relies on building volume to mitigate the climate, and lightweight cladding on steel frames allows for speedy erection and cheap enclosure. While budget constraints demand that a sense of economy prevail, the buildings are cranked and faceted to achieve broad-stroke compositions at large scale, using a locally derived palette of colours.

The planning deals with requirements for gender and clan separation, natural light and breeze capture. The key to these successful newer buildings in remote communities is the reassertion of the economy of modernism in the service of thoughtfully articulated goals. These projects all have the virtue of clear need, met without bending the materials or logic of mass-produced buildings to the service of formal, rather than programmatic, solutions.

ARM, Swanston Square facade inscribed with portrait of William Barak, Melbourne, 2015.

This virtue has highlighted the dilemmas of Australian architecture in an age of partial services, with architects serving as one among many consultants and managers, and in a time when institutional and private clients seek cultural validation. This has not necessarily been to the detriment of architecture as craft, or spatial skill, as contemporary magazines can attest. The standard of corporate and institutional architecture is high, and the best work has a skilled playfulness that is the equal of buildings anywhere. Rather the dilemmas arise from the anodyne nature of clients, and the receding sense of imperative that fuelled the best of post-war work. Neoliberalism has diminished the notion of the public realm, in its eyes an adjunct to private interests.

This loss can be sensed in a renewed interest in affordable housing in the face of rising house and apartment prices. But the finance underwritten by the state no longer exists, and North American models of cooperative ownership are quietly gaining traction.[33] For a generation schooled in the formal luxuries of high-end housing and institutional image-making, the modest opportunities in these buildings may yet prove a challenge. The dearth of opportunities for small practices, apart from housing, has made for a deskilled profession. The shift to a service economy has made for more homogenous cities and less varied building types. While it is

Officer Woods Architects, East Pilbara Arts Centre, Newman (Western Australia), 2016.

Iredale Pedersen Hook, Walumba Elders Centre, Warmun (Western Australia), 2014.

possible to discern a restlessness in this, a desire for more variety in spaces and programmes to challenge architectural ingenuity, it may persist for some time. Universities are adding to their portfolios, but the procurement process is difficult for emerging firms. Hospitals require a track record in the area. New churches are rare, mosques less so, and factories are almost absent.[34] A few brave architectural competitions for large new works would not go astray.

accenture
accenture

Epilogue

The rate of change in the Australian building industry over the past two decades has been constant, if not dramatic. This in turn has masked the cumulative effect of the change, which has been profound. It seems useful to separate these out into larger issues that may impinge on architecture in years to come, and the response of architectural design itself to these issues.

As a mature economy in the western orbit, Australia has become a service one, supported by a large mining and agricultural sector that nonetheless employs few people. There is some manufacturing and a building industry, but Australia makes little that is exported. In short the country is largely urbanized and people overwhelmingly work in shops and offices, wards and classrooms. There is a steady flow of immigrants to the country, as there has been since the 1950s, among whom is a fraction that are wealthy and are looking for somewhere pleasant to live. The large immigration programme in recent decades has seen the proportion of Australians born overseas rising to nearly 30 per cent, its highest level in more than a century.[1]

While this rise has been achieved with little real social tension, it has again forced a consideration of what may be perceived as authentic in Australian culture, even as nationalism remains problematic for its insular focus. In architecture this has been accommodated by an evolving view of its role in delineating national and transnational imperatives. Many Australian firms now work overseas, in the Middle East and Asia, from a practice base developed locally. In so doing they have exported some aspect of their identity, either in aesthetic preference or organizational culture. That they have found considerable success is testament to the attractiveness of both in commercial terms.

Architecture has always benefited from requiring no translation, and international trends as disseminated through various media have only become more visible with the rise of the internet. Australian schools of architecture teach a large number of overseas students, with many intending to stay, but many also return to practise in China, India, Singapore and Malaysia. These students have forced teaching to be less concerned with the

Rogers Stirk Harbour + Partners, International Towers, Sydney, 2010–16.

local, and to find a mode of design that has relevance to those from abroad. Academics, too, move between institutions, which mitigates against localism in teaching and in practice. Old university reputations, here for technical excellence, there for liberal speculations, have less and less relevance.

Collectively these developments work against traditions or sentiments taking root, and regional differences have probably diminished across the country. Conclusions about state-by-state inflections or techniques that were apt in the 1960s, for example, may no longer have any currency. The broad differences can still be discerned, if one allows for some subjective vision. Melbourne values the idea, and the good fight, as ever. Sydney retains a classicist sensibility and eschews radicalism for good taste. Brisbane builds on its climatic credentials, and Perth remains connected to its vast hinterland. Hobart is elemental, and almost unconcerned with reputations, and Adelaide is cautious. Capital cities come to represent states, often imperfectly (as any Queenslander will point out), because that is where the wealth and the architects cluster.

Little has changed in the limited role architects play in the building industry at large. Almost all houses are built without architects. Large buildings happen with greater involvement. There is some comfort for free-marketeers here. Except for apartment blocks in New South Wales, there is no legal requirement to employ an architect for any building. This situation is unusual in developed countries, but it means the profession exists in Australia as a cultural and organizational imperative, not a legal one. The title of architect is protected by law – the work they do not so. The fact that so many people still want to be architects, and that there is still an active profession with offices ranging in size from one to hundreds of architects, can be seen as a great, and successful, experiment in their relevance and appeal.

There remains great pleasure in the work itself. With a willing client, institutional or private, the act of shaping a building and crafting its spaces is as absorbing as any. But the vast numbers of formulaic apartment blocks now under construction do not always provide this experience, and the partial services now common means the architect is employed for the look and the plan, and the execution is overseen by construction managers.[2] This has diminished the level of control of architects compared to their traditional role, where buildings were fully designed and documented before construction commenced, and builders were held to the original documents on which they had tendered.

Excellent work still occurs, and the appeal of designing houses on challenging sites for enthusiastic clients remains because they can be shaped with great control. With the small range of building types being built, though, reinvention of recurrent building types occupies an inordinate amount of effort. It seems hard to imagine that this will change in coming years: a society of service industries, and one that is increasingly secular, has a limited number of building design opportunities.

The withdrawal of governments from architectural design has also taken the institutions they built out of non-market hands. The focused idealism of the high decades of these buildings – the 1960s and '70s – may not come again for a generation or more. There are strong pressures on the welfare state, brought about by an ageing population, that demand that money be directed to recurrent spending on pensions and medicine. There are large hospitals being built in growing areas, and housing for the aged is expanding, but these are conservative domains without the breakneck pace demanded by post-war optimism.

Even the old sectarian divides no longer hold as they did. The Labor Party, long a bastion of Catholic working-class interests, was revived as a national force by Gough Whitlam, a Presbyterian by upbringing. Bob Hawke, who set Labor on a popular course, was from a Congregationalist household. The Federal Liberal Party, Labor's main political opponent in the post-war years, was dominated under Prime Minister Tony Abbott by alumni of Sydney's elite Catholic schools. Even class distinctions within parties have faded as working-class voters, who were encouraged to become small contractors in the 1980s, moved towards the Liberals, while the growing urban intelligentsia has become integral to Labor's electoral success.

This makes political definitions of architectural objectives, or ideals, tricky. As noted, the polymorphous nature of environmentalist politics has allowed it to move to the fore, but its totalizing critique ironically has made it amenable to all forms of class politics. Given the imperatives of its mission, any money spent on reducing energy consumption is seen as desirable in the long run, with only sporadic assessment of whether that money is well spent. The vision of each household or building generating its own energy, and harvesting its own water, is highly compatible with a neoliberal view that emphasizes individual agency and devalues the great collective effort of centralized and reticulated services that marked the ascent of modernity. Over time this strategy runs the risk of having public utilities only for those that cannot afford to install their own, with a subsequent degrading of supply.

Australian architecture, and public life, has been at its best when it is collectively minded. The great achievements of the nation-state since Federation have been in the building of an excellent public realm, founded on intolerance for any great divide in means. It is not, by most measures, a particularly equal society, but it is one where most people lived the same kind of life at the end of the twentieth century. The building programmes of 1950–80 no doubt contributed to this.

Room 11 Architects, Glenorchy Art and Sculpture Park, Hobart, 2013.

The prevailing vision for Australian cities is now consistent across the country and provides the matrix in which building will take place. The shift to apartment living has been underway in Sydney for three decades and has transformed many of its suburbs into dense precincts that have strained existing infrastructure. The same processes are underway, with some time lag, in all other cities. The results have been patchy, with areas like Brisbane's Fortitude Valley being transformed beyond recognition, its distinctive urban form and scale all but effaced. In other locations like Melbourne's Docklands the results are anodyne: apartment blocks built to street alignments, with little of the promised street life that supposedly follows density, and full of apartments hostile to family life.

These developments have given a curious smoothness to architectural practice in Australia, with many practices mastering the required balance between yield and image, nominal sustainability and the preservation of comfort, architectural interest and formulaic repetition. Architecture is widely visible, but excellence is rare. Analytic abilities of architects are rarely stretched, and ideas constitute a spatial lexicon rather than programmatic or social insights. International practices are also increasingly designing buildings in the country: witness Grimshaw's Spencer Street Station in Melbourne, Gehry's Dr Chau Chak Wing building for the University of Technology, Sydney, and the massive towers by Rogers Stirk Harbour + Partners for Sydney's waterside Barangaroo redevelopment. These add Australia to the story of contemporary architecture globally surveyed, but only occasionally do they say something about the specific experience, intellectual as well as physical, of living in cities such as Sydney or Melbourne.

The capacity to trade on a regional identity, which served Australia well from 1970, has been diluted by this two-way flow, import and export, of architectural services. Murcutt encapsulated something already passing at the moment of its articulation. His work on the Pritzker jury has increased his personal quest to transcend a regionalist identity, but the modesty of many of the best works now being undertaken precludes their international exposure. Smaller works of visual strength, like Room 11's Glenorchy Art and Sculpture Park, or Durbach Block Jaggers' North Bondi Surf Life Saving Club, seem to be where something distinctive still resides, aided undoubtedly by physical context. Remoteness can also be a virtue. Hobart is undergoing something of a renaissance, its compact form and island isolation attracting tourists and new inhabitants seeking some respite from the growing pains of the mainland cities. Its waterfront has immense charm and is now bookended by two confident buildings that utilize the extruded form of waterside sheds, but with finely modelled ends: the hotel Macquarie Wharf 01, by Circa Morris-Nunn Architects (2017),

Durbach Block Jaggers with Peter Colquhoun, North Bondi Surf Life Saving Club, Sydney, 2013.

John Wardle with Terroir, Institute for Marine and Antarctic Studies, Hobart, 2014.

and the Institute for Marine and Antarctic Studies (2014) by John Wardle Architects in association with Terroir.

Because of its lack of legal coercion, architecture in Australia is still practised by many small firms in the spirit of the amateur, in the sense of the work taking precedence over remuneration. This is a difficult path to follow in a profession that remains labour-intensive and resistant to automation. The promises of computers have only partially come to pass. The parametric generation of buildings, where the rules are written and the design emerges, has remained problematic as the rules prove elusive and the results have to be shaped to aesthetic predilections. The computer-controlled cutting of individualized components has only been demonstrated in small projects, and has not yet achieved economic leverage by making this building method noticeably cheaper.

The one area that has seen advances is the controlling and documenting of complex shapes in architecture, and these are evident in most large contemporary buildings. The resulting geometries are seductive and lend considerable interest to form. John Wardle has developed great skill in this, and buildings like the South Australian Health and Medical Research Institute by Woods Bagot, adjoining the Royal Adelaide Hospital, have used these techniques to produce a convincing dissolution of the architectural object when viewed against its modernist predecessors. But this is only a fraction of the capabilities of computing. How they might interact in coming years with a building industry that still uses hand-erected formwork for concrete is still unclear.

The structure of the profession, too, reflects wider issues of professional practice. Males and females enter university courses in equal numbers, but in the profession women formally register at lower rates than men and earn less over a career.[3] There appear to be deep structural reasons for this. Architectural services are often forced to compete on design grounds and the temptation exists to work long hours. With projects taking years to reach fruition, the profession is unkind to those who work part-time, or who take time off. Changes to the building industry have seen more women on large building sites, which could be outright hostile places three decades ago. But advancement in the profession still requires a single-minded commitment and a sometimes exhausting attention to detail. Through these things the identity of the profession is shaped.

There remains a curious atavism in architecture in Australia. Its cultural relevance has deep roots in its preservation of craft, and the Arts and Crafts movement found wide acceptance at the end of the nineteenth century. This remains a central tenet in the profession, the accommodation with industrialized production notwithstanding. It accounts for the large role that free-standing houses have played in its modern history, since they were ideal incubators of the sort of localized detailing that corroded or resisted the reductive tendencies of industrial building. Left to its own devices, the building industry produces few places of desire.

Woods Bagot, the South Australian Health and Medical Research Institute, Adelaide, 2013.

There is still enough building work at small scale to provide opportunities for small practice, which seems critical to the process of architectural renewal. National legislation mandating the use of architects for large buildings would direct more fees their way, but its overall effect would be unclear. The results have been mixed where architects' participation is mandated, and many buildings still only just conform to professional standards. Universities too are changing, and the training programmes have ceded autonomy to academic criteria that rarely favour the intensive studio-based training that has been the norm. Architectural cultures now survive largely within the profession and their transmission, or disappearance, will be one of the more interesting dynamics of coming years.

In the end, the architect remains a citizen, their concerns derived from broader life. The agency and effectiveness of architecture to initiate social change no longer holds the imaginative power it enjoyed under modernism. Buildings often signal social critique while simultaneously embodying the status quo, since there remains so little latitude for anything else. The difficulty lies in identifying and affecting those things that architecture can claim responsibility for, if we aim to be useful. But when buildings are viewed collectively we can discern bigger things at play, and architecture draws our attention to these in its symbolic struggles, despite its inability often to make a real difference.

Being constrained in action does not negate the value of architecture. One could argue that believing otherwise, that buildings could change things, was an affectation of modernism. The profession is too old, its history too variegated, to be reduced to issues of efficacy. Even uncovering its role as ideology does not eliminate spatial affect or haptic pleasure. These many aspects of architecture render it continuously fascinating, in Australia no less than anywhere else.

References

Introduction

1 Geoffrey Blainey, *The Tyranny of Distance: How Distance Shaped Australia's History* (Melbourne, 1966).

2 Australian Electoral Commission, '1999 Referendums Reports and Statistics', www.aec.gov.au, accessed 26 September 2018.

3 Ray Gilliland, *The Nullarbor Kid: Stories from my Trucking Life* (Crows Nest, NSW, 2012).

4 Manfredo Tafuri, *Architecture and Utopia: Design and Capitalist Development*, trans. Barbara Luigia La Penta (Cambridge, MA, 1976).

5 Australian Bureau of Statistics, Catalogue Number 3105.0.65.001, 18 September 2014, www.abs.gov.au.

chapter one From Federation to Metropolis, 1901–29

1 Vance Palmer, *The Legend of the Nineties* (Melbourne, 1954), p. 32.

2 John Manning Ward, *The State and the People: Australian Federation and Nation-making, 1870–1901* (Leichhardt, NSW, 2001), p. 14.

3 Geoffrey Blainey, *A Shorter History of Australia* (Melbourne, 1994), p. 76.

4 Edward Bellamy, *Looking Backward: 2000–1887* (Cambridge, MA, 1967).

5 Blainey, *A Shorter History*, p. 121.

6 Mark Stiles, 'Reading Ruskin: Architecture and Social Reform in Australia, 1889–1908', PhD thesis, University of NSW, 2010, p. 97.

7 John Phillips, 'John Sulman and the Question of an Australian Style', *Fabrications*, VIII/1 (1997), p. 93.

8 Ibid., p. 96.

9 John Ruskin, *The Seven Lamps of Architecture*, 6th edn (Orpington, 1889), p. 56.

10 Ibid., p. 41.

11 J. M. Freeland, *Architect Extraordinary: The Life and Times of John Horbury Hunt, 1838–1904* (Melbourne, 1970). See also Peter Reynolds, Lesley Muir and Joy Hughes, *John Horbury Hunt: Radical Architect, 1838–1904* (Sydney, 2002).

12 Cited in Hugh Fraser, *The Federation House: Australia's Own Style* (Sydney, 1986), p. 20.

13 Ibid., p. 54.

14 Ibid., p. 60.

15 Stiles, 'Reading Ruskin', p. 100.

16 Harriet Edquist, *Harold Desbrowe-Annear, 1865–1933: A Life in Architecture* (Carlton, VIC, 2004) pp. 47–8.

17 Harriet Edquist, *Pioneers of Modernism: The Arts and Crafts Movement in Australia* (Carlton, VIC, 2008), p. XIII.

18 Ibid., p. 62.

19 Noni Boyd, 'No Sacrifice in Sunshine: Walter Liberty Vernon, Architect, 1846–1914', PhD thesis, RMIT, 2010.

20 James Weirick, 'Spirituality and Symbolism in the Work of the Griffins', in *Beyond Architecture:*

Marion Mahony and Walter Burley Griffin, America, Australia, India, ed. Anne Watson (Haymarket, NSW, 1998), p. 63.

21 Jeff Turnbull and Peter Navaretti, eds, *The Griffins in Australia and India: The Complete Works and Projects of Walter Burley Griffin and Marion Mahoney Griffin* (Melbourne, 1998), p. 49.

22 Weirick, 'Spirituality and Symbolism', p. 59.

23 Turnbull and Navaretti, *The Griffins*, p. 23.

24 William Hardy Wilson, *Old Colonial Architecture in New South Wales and Tasmania* (Sydney, 1924).

25 Immanuel Kant, *Critique of Judgement*, trans. Werner S. Pluhar (Indianapolis, IN, 1987), p. 65.

26 Enzo Traverso, *The End of Jewish Modernity*, trans. David Fernbach (London, 2016).

27 Blainey, *A Shorter History*, p. 135.

28 Zeny Edwards, *William Hardy Wilson: Artist, Architect, Orientalist, Visionary* (Surry Hills, NSW, 2001), p. 109.

29 Leslie Wilkinson, 'Domestic Architecture', in *Domestic Architecture in Australia*, ed. Sydney Ure Smith, Bertram Stevens with W. Hardy Wilson (Sydney, 1919), p. 3 [special number of *Art in Australia*].

30 W. H. Bagot, 'A Plea for Tradition', ibid., p. 27.

31 R. S. Dods, 'The Architect and the Future', ibid., p. 33.

32 'Fenton – Edgecliffe, Sydney: The Residence of Mr R. S. Dods', *The Home* (February 1920), p. 21.

33 Dods, 'The Architect and the Future', p. 31.

34 H. Desbrowe-Annear, 'The Recognition of Architecture', in *Domestic Architecture*, ed. Smith, Stevens and Wilson, p. 22.

35 Wilkinson, 'Domestic Architecture', p. 8.

36 Commonwealth Bureau of Census and Statistics, *Oversea Trade. Bulletin No. 25* (Canberra, 1929). Figures extracted from Table II: Class VI, pp. 70–71, and summary in Table IX, p. 664. The largest import categories are textiles, metals and machinery.

37 Frank Bingham and Australian Department of Foreign Affairs and Trade, *Australia's Trade since Federation*, June 2016, https://dfat.gov.au.

38 Edward Shann, *An Economic History of Australia* (Cambridge, 1948), p. 395.

39 Commonwealth Bureau of Census and Statistics, *Census of the Commonwealth of Australia*, 1921, Catalogue Number 2111.0, www.abs.gov.au.

40 Cited in Edquist, *Desbrowe-Annear*, p. 91.

41 W. Hardy Wilson, 'Building "Purulia"', in *Domestic Architecture*, ed. Smith, Stevens and Wilson, p. 15.

42 Meredith Walker, 'The Development at Castlecrag', in *The Griffins in Australia and India*, ed. Turnbull and Navaretti, pp. 74–85.

43 Weirick, 'Spirituality and Symbolism', p. 82.

44 Robert Freestone, 'Introduction', in *Town Planning for Australia*, ed. George A. Taylor (Abingdon, 2015), p. viii.

45 George A. Taylor, *Town Planning Association: Why It Is Necessary* (Sydney, 1913), p. 13.

46 See, for example, Florence Taylor's denunciation of 'communistic seething hot beds of men with warped minds', in 'Sydney's Domain', *Building* (12 March 1934), p. 36c.

47 'Development by Private Enterprise: New York's Aerial Way Proposed for Sydney', *Building* (12 February 1924), p. 60.

48 Florence Taylor, 'The Commonwealth Bank Head Office, Sydney', *Building* (12 September 1916), p. 60.

49 Graham Jahn, *Sydney Architecture* (Balmain, NSW, 1997), p. 98.

50 'Commonwealth Bank Building, Brisbane', *Building* (12 August 1929), p. 54.

51 Florence Taylor, 'Modern Architectural Development: Tradition or Vision', *Building* (12 July 1928), pp. 46–52.

52 'Freak House Design: Futurism in Germany', *Building* (12 July 1928), p. 54.

chapter two Harsh Lessons and their Effects, 1930–45

1 Florence Taylor, 'Slum Areas: How They Can Be Abolished', *Building* (12 July 1933), pp. 29–31.

2 John Sulman, 'Address to the Town Planning Association of New South Wales', *Architecture* (15 May 1921), pp. 154–5.

3 Derek Sawer, *Australians in Company: The Broken Hill Proprietary Company Limited in its One Hundredth Year* (Melbourne, 1985), p. 147.

4 R. W. Connell and T. H. Irving, *Class Structure in Australian History: Documents, Narrative and Argument* (Melbourne, 1980), p. 271.

5 K. S. Inglis, *Sacred Places: War Memorials in the Australian Landscape* (Carlton South, VIC, 1998), p. 199.

6 Ibid., pp. 299–301.

7 Ibid., p. 305.

8 Ian Stapleton and Maisy Stapleton, 'C. Bruce Dellit and Emil Sodersten', in *Architects of Australia*, ed. Howard Tanner (Melbourne, 1981), p. 122.

9 Paul Sheehan, 'Peace Offering that Shocked the Church', *Sydney Morning Herald*, 19 April 2004.

10 Inglis, *Sacred Places*, p. 307.

11 Ibid., p. 321.

12 Geoffrey Serle, 'Monash, Sir John (1865–1931)', *Australian Dictionary of Biography*, http://adb.anu.edu.au, accessed 4 February 2019.

13 Inglis, *Sacred Places*, pp. 315–23.

14 See Roy Lumby, 'Art Deco Architecture in Australia', in *A Spirit of Progress: Art Deco Architecture in Australia*, ed. Patrick Van Daele and Roy Lumby (North Ryde, NSW, 1997), p. 14.

15 Cited ibid., pp. 21–2.

16 David Dean, *Architecture of the 1930s* (New York, 1983), p. 14.

17 'Commercial Architecture: Its Development in Australia', *Building* (13 May 1929), p. 71.

18 See cover graphic by Hera Roberts and Adrian Feint, *The Home: The Australian Journal of Quality*, IX/10 (1 October 1928).

19 Lumby, 'Art Deco', p. 22.

20 A. C. Gray, *Life Insurance in Australia* (Melbourne, 1977), p. 140.

21 'A.C.A. Building, Sydney: A Record in Building Speed', *Construction and Real Estate Journal*, 1432 (11 September 1935), p. 7.

22 'New Head Office: Mutual Life and Citizen's Assurance Co. Ltd, Sydney', *Architecture* (1 February 1937), p. 26.

23 R. H. McConnell, 'Modern Architecture and Architectural Ornament: What Are Their Tendencies', *Building* (12 April 1928), p. 39.

24 Hugh Denison, 'New York – The Modern Babylon', *Building* (11 August 1928).

25 Leighton Irwin, 'The Trend of Design as Shown by Modern Architecture', *Building* (12 June 1930), pp. 83–6.

26 D. L. Johnson, *Australian Architecture, 1901–51: Sources of Modernism* (Sydney, 1980), p. 99.

27 'The Changing Face of Sydney', *Building* (12 February 1934), p. 16.

28 'Mitchell House, Melbourne, Victoria: A Striking Design', *Building* (24 July 1937), p. 37.

29 'Railway Building, Wynyard, Sydney: A Modern and Colourful Facade', *Building* (12 June 1936), p. 21.

30 Ibid.

31 Manfredo Tafuri, *Architecture and Utopia: Design and Capitalist Development* (Cambridge, MA, 1976), p. 48.

32 G. Sydney Jones, 'Australia and Civic Art: A Factor in National Life', *Architecture* (October 1917), p. 87.

33 Florence Taylor, review of 'Towards a New Architecture', *Building* (12 December 1928), pp. 91–4.

34 Florence Taylor, 'The Spanish-American Influence in Australia: Will the Colourful Style be Transitory', *Building* (12 October 1928), p. 57.

35 C. A. Jeffries, 'Architects, Bolsheviks, and the I.W.W.', *Architecture* (20 July 1918), pp. 8–10.

36 F. G. Costello, 'Town Planning and its Effect on the Liberty of the Individual', *Architecture* (1 April 1933), p. 100.

37 Frank G. Costello, 'First Steps in the Town Plan of Sydney', *Architecture* (1 April 1938), pp. 91–4.

38 Henry Pynor, 'An Architectural Foreign Specialist in Russia', in *Modernism and Australia: Documents in Art, Design and Architecture, 1917–1967*, ed. Ann Stephen, Andrew McNamara and Philip Goad (Carlton, VIC, 2006), p. 334.

39 Julie Willis, 'Conscious Design: The Melbourne University Architectural Atelier, 1919–1947', *Fabrications*, XIII/2 (May 2004), pp. 43–62.

40 David Walker, 'Monumental Modernist', *RIBA Journal*, 98 (August 1991), pp. 20–25.

41 James Stephens, 'The Cairo: Romance and the Minimum Flat', *Assemble Papers*, 18 June 2012, https://assemblepapers.com.au.

42 Table in *Building* (24 January 1938), p. 69, and 'Australia is Prosperous: Encouraging Statistics', *Building* (24 January 1939), p. 16.

43 'Hastings Deering Building, Sydney', *Architecture* (1 August 1938), pp. 184–8.

44 Barbara Chapman and Duncan Richards, *Marshall Clifton: Architect and Artist* (Fremantle, WA, 1989), p. 40.

45 R. J. Ferguson, *Crawley Campus: The Planning and Architecture of the University of Western Australia* (Nedlands, WA, 1993), p. 25.

46 Sydney Ancher, 'The Evolution of Modern Architecture', *Architecture* (1 December 1939), p. 247.

47 Richard E. Apperley and Peter Reynolds, 'Ancher, Sydney Edward Cambrian (1904–1979)', *Australian Dictionary of Biography*, http://adb.anu.edu.au, accessed 4 February 2019.

48 John Shaw, *Sir Arthur Stephenson: Australian Architect* (Sydney, 1987), p. 6.

49 Bernard Smith, review of 'Architecture in Australia', *Historical Studies* (October 1969), p. 89.

50 Rebecca Hawcroft, ed., *The Other Moderns: Sydney's Forgotten European Design Legacy* (Sydney, 2017).

chapter three Post-war Optimism: Everyone Becomes a Modernist, 1946–61

1 Patrick Troy, *Accommodating Australians: Commonwealth Government Involvement in Housing* (Sydney, 2012), pp. 47–66.

2 J. M. Freeland, *Architecture in Australia: A History* (Ringwood, VIC, 1968).

3 Walter Bunning, *Homes in the Sun: The Past, Present and Future of Australian Housing* (Sydney, 1945); John D. Moore, *Home Again: Domestic Architecture for the Normal Australian* (Sydney, 1944).

4 Australian Bureau of Statistics, Catalogue Number 3412.0, 'Migration, Australia' accessed 13 September 2018.

5 Geoffrey Blainey, *A Shorter History of Australia* (Melbourne, 1994), pp. 189–90.

6 Commonwealth of Australia, 'Architecture of Australia's Tax and Transfer System: Historical Trends in Tax', https://taxreview.treasury.gov.au, accessed 13 September 2018.

7 Sydney Ancher served as a sapper and engineer in the early war years, Arthur Baldwinson designed factories for aircraft production and John D. Moore designed camouflage alongside photographer Max Dupian and artist Frank Hinder. See *Australian Dictionary of Biography*, http://adb.anu.edu.au, accessed 13 September 2018.

8 Michael Bogle, 'Arthur Baldwinson: Regional Modernism in Sydney, 1937–1969', PhD thesis, Royal Melbourne Institute of Technology, 2008, pp. 160–81.

9 Connie Boese, 'Ancher, Sydney', in *The Encyclopedia of Australian Architecture*, ed. Philip Goad and Julie Willis (Port Melbourne, VIC, 2012), pp. 17–19; Philip Drew, 'Architect Sydney Ancher – Experiences and Recollections', interview with Sydney Ancher, University of Newcastle Recording Archives, https://soundcloud.com, accessed 17 September 2018.

10 Andrew Metcalf, *Architecture in Transition: The Sulman Award, 1932–1996* (Sydney, 1997), pp. 76, 77.

11 See, for example, Sydney's Kindersley House by McConnel, Smith & Johnson, 1960.

12 Bunning & Madden, *The Work of Bunning & Madden: Architects and Town Planners* (Sydney, 1970), p. 30.

13 Harry Margalit, interview with Kevin John Smith, 7 April 1993, in Harry Margalit, 'Reasoning to Believe: Aspects of Modernity in Sydney Architecture and Planning, 1900–1960', PhD thesis, University of Sydney, 1997.
14 See Colonial Mutual Life, Melbourne, by Stephenson and Turner, 1963.
15 Philip Goad, 'Moderate Modernism 1945-77', in *Bates Smart: 150 Years of Australian Architecture*, ed. Philip Goad (Fisherman's Bend, VIC, 2004), p. 162.
16 Colin St John Wilson, *The Other Tradition of Modern Architecture: The Uncompleted Project* (London, 2007).
17 Philip Goad, ed., *Melbourne Architecture* (Sydney, 1999), p. 158.
18 Robin Boyd, *Victorian Modern: One Hundred and Eleven Years of Modern Architecture in Victoria, Australia* (Melbourne, 1947).
19 For example his article in *Country Life Stock and Station Journal* (12 January 1945), p. 14.
20 Robin Boyd, *Australia's Home: Its Origins, Builders and Occupiers* (Carlton, VIC, 1987), p. 139.
21 Conrad Hamann, 'Roy Grounds 1905–, Frederick Romberg 1913– and Robin Boyd 1919–1971', in *Architects of Australia*, ed. Howard Tanner (South Melbourne, VIC, 1981), p. 137.
22 Robin Boyd, *The Australian Ugliness* (Melbourne, 1960), p. 9.
23 Ibid., p. 55.
24 Richard Black, 'Living Patterns: The 1950s Housing of Neil Clerehan', in *The Architecture of Neil Clerehan*, ed. Harriet Edquist and Richard Black (Melbourne, 2005), pp. 63–94.
25 Morton Herman, *The Early Australian Architects and Their Work* (Sydney, 1954).
26 Kenneth Frampton and Philip Drew, *Harry Seidler: Four Decades of Architecture* (London, 1992).
27 Harry Seidler, *Houses, Interiors and Projects* (Sydney, 1954), p. xii.
28 Robin Boyd, *The Great Great Australian Dream* (Rushcutters Bay, NSW, 1972).
29 Neville Gruzman and Philip Goad, *Gruzman: An Architect and his City* (Fisherman's Bend, VIC, 2006).
30 Jennifer Taylor, *An Australian Identity: Houses for Sydney, 1953–63* (Sydney, 1972).
31 See Peter Muller, 'Forward' [*sic*], in *Adrian Snodgrass and the Wonders of his Secret Architectural Designs*, 2016, at au.blurb.com, accessed 18 September 2018.
32 Karen McCartney, 'The Jack House/Russell Jack', *50/60/70 Iconic Australian Houses: Three Decades of Domestic Architecture* (Crows Nest, NSW, 2014), p. 81.
33 See, for example, the small internal court in Pierre Koenig, Case Study House #21 (1958).
34 Kenneth Frampton, the chapter 'Regionalism: Modern Architecture and Cultural Identity', in *Modern Architecture: A Critical History* (London, 1985), pp. 313–27.
35 Conrad Hamann, *Cities of Hope: Australian Architecture and Design by Edmond and Corrigan, 1962–1992* (Melbourne, 1993), p. 18.
36 Robin Boyd, *Kenzo Tange* (New York, 1962).
37 Cited in Goad, *Melbourne Architecture*, p. 169.
38 E.J.A. Weller, ed., *Buildings of Queensland* (Brisbane, 1959).
39 Andrew Wilson and Angela Reilly, 'Reflections on an Enduring Partnership', in *Hayes & Scott: Post-war Houses*, ed. Andrew Wilson (St Lucia, QLD, 2005), p. 10.
40 Elizabeth Musgrave, 'The Plywood Exhibition House: An Investigation of Local Idiom', *Proceedings of the 19th Conference of the Society of Architectural Historians, Australia and New Zealand: Brisbane, 2002.*
41 Karl Langer, *Sub-tropical Housing* (Brisbane, 1944).
42 James Birrell in conversation with John Macarthur, https://architectureau.com, 1 March 2005.
43 Michael Markham, 'White Gothic', in *Summerhayes: Architectural Projects*, ed. Michael Markham and Meghan Nordeck (Crawley, WA, 1993), p. 4.
44 Jorge Otero-Pailos, 'Eucharistic Architecture: Jean Labatut and the Search for Pure Sensation', in *Architecture's Historical Turn: Phenomenology and the Rise of the Postmodern* (Minneapolis, MN, 2010), pp. 25–99.

chapter four The Very Good Times, 1962–80

1 For a selection, see Philip Goad, 'An Appeal for Modernism: Sigfried Giedion and the Sydney Opera House', *Fabrications*, VIII (July 1997), p. 143, and below. This list is far from exhaustive, with a notable addition in Philip Drew, *The Masterpiece: Jorn Utzon, A Secret Life* (South Yarra, VIC, 2001).
2 Robin Boyd, *Australia's Home: Its Origins, Builders and Occupiers* (Carlton, VIC, 1987), p. 125.
3 'Dane's Controversial Design Wins Opera House Contest', *Sydney Morning Herald*, 30 January 1957, p. 1.
4 Peter Murray, *The Saga of Sydney Opera House: The Dramatic Story of the Design and Construction of the Icon of Modern Australia* (London, 2004), p. 6. See also David Salter, 'The Conservatorium Director and the Witch', 'Good Weekend' supplement to *Sydney Morning Herald*, 3 July 1999.
5 Murray, *Sydney Opera House*, pp. 10–11.
6 Françoise Fromonot, *Jorn Utzon: The Sydney Opera House* (Corte Madera, CA, 1998), p. 84.
7 'Protest Meeting Rallies to Utzon', *Sydney Morning Herald*, 15 March 1966, p. 4.
8 Murray, *Sydney Opera House*, p. 144.
9 L. Peter Kollar, 'Four Lectures', *Architecture in Australia* (October–December 1958), p. 83.
10 'Flats at Ham Common by Stirling and Gowan', *Architectural Review*, 124 (October 1958), pp. 218–25, available at www.architectural-review.com, accessed 6 February 2019.
11 Philip Goad, 'Bringing It All Home: Robin Boyd and Australia's Embrace of Brutalism, 1955–71', *Fabrications*, XXV/2 (June 2015), p. 189.
12 Thomas Piketty, *Capital in the Twenty First Century*, trans. Arthur Goldhammer (Cambridge, MA, 2014).
13 Ann Curthoys, *Freedom Ride: A Freedom Rider Remembers* (Sydney, 2002).
14 Clive James, 'Renegade at the Lectern: Australia's National Philosopher John Anderson', *The Monthly*, July 2005, www.themonthly.com.au, accessed 6 February 2019.
15 Clive James, *Unreliable Memoirs* (London, 1980), p. 168.
16 Michael Bogle, 'Arthur Baldwinson: Regional Modernism in Sydney, 1937–1969', PhD thesis, Royal Melbourne Institute of Technology, 2008, pp. 160–81.
17 Robyn Holmes, 'Dream Library Takes Shape: Sir Robert Menzies and the Building of the National Library of Australia', www.nla.gov.au, 29 March 2016.
18 Barbara Chapman and Duncan Richards, *Marshall Clifton: Architect and Artist* (Fremantle, WA, 1989).
19 Joseph Buch, 'Architecture Building: You May Seek Him in The Building, interview with Vin Davies', *The Architect* (WA), XXXV/1 (1995), pp. 26–31.
20 Hannah Lewi and Stephen Neille, 'Drawing In and Fading Out: The Case of the Commonwealth Games Housing Village, Western Australia', *Journal of Architectural Education*, LXI/2 (2007), pp. 15–24.
21 Brit Andresen, 'J. D. Story Building, Brisbane', in *Tall Buildings: Australian Business Going Up, 1945–1970*, ed. Jennifer Taylor (St Leonards, NSW, 2001), pp. 208–21.
22 Michael Page, *Sculptors in Space: South Australian Architects, 1836–1986* (Adelaide, 1986), p. 226.
23 See Russell Rodrigo, 'The "Gold and Marble Palace": The Reserve Bank of Australia', in *Sydney's Martin Place: A Cultural and Design History*, ed. Judith O'Callaghan, Paul Hogben and Robert Freestone (Crows Nest, NSW, 2016), pp. 105–21.
24 Lindie Clark, *Finding a Common Interest: The Story of Dick Dusseldorp and Lend Lease* (Port Melbourne, VIC, 2002), pp. 83–4.
25 Paola Favaro and Harry Margalit, 'A Central Player: The Corporate Presence of the MLC', in *Sydney's Martin Place*, ed. O'Callaghan, Hogben and Freestone, p. 132.
26 Maryam Gusheh, 'Action Architecture: The Pedestrianisation of Martin Place, 1968–79', in *Sydney's Martin Place*, ed. O'Callaghan, Hogben and Freestone, pp. 173–89.
27 Aided by publications such as Morton Herman, *The Early Australian Architects and Their Work* (Sydney, 1954). The National Trusts were established in Australia from 1945 onwards in each state and territory to promote conservation broadly.

28 Paola Favaro, 'Architectural Education in 1950s Milan Polytechnic', in *The Contribution of Enrico Taglietti to Canberra's Architecture*, ed. Ken Charlton, Bronwen Jones and Paola Favaro (Canberra, 2007), p. 105.
29 Gerard Reinmuth, 'The Young House Then and Now', *Architectural Review Australia*, 61 (1997), p. 80.
30 Jennifer Taylor and John Andrews, *John Andrews: Architecture, A Performing Art* (Melbourne, 1982), pp. 20–29.
31 Paul Walker and Anthony Moulis, 'Finding Brutalism in the Architecture of John Andrews', *Fabrications*, XXV/2 (June 2015), pp. 215–33.
32 Taylor and Andrews, *John Andrews*, pp. 137–53.
33 For example Jennifer Taylor's observation that by the end of the 1950s 'the Melbourne school became stylized and often trite'. Jennifer Taylor, *Australian Architecture since 1960* (North Ryde, NSW, 1986), p. 14.
34 Giorgio Marfella, 'Inside the Square Box: Skyscrapers and Techno-economic Developments in Melbourne Central Business District, 1955–1995', PhD thesis, University of Melbourne, 2017.
35 Philip Goad, 'BHP House, Melbourne', in *Tall Buildings*, ed. Taylor, p. 261.
36 Ibid., pp. 278–80.
37 Conrad Hamann, *Cities of Hope: Australian Architecture and Design by Edmond and Corrigan, 1962–1992* (Melbourne, 1993), p. 18.
38 Jane Lawrence, 'McConnell Residence: Hassell McConnell and Partners', in *The Forever House: Time-honoured Australian Homes*, ed. Cameron Bruhn and Katelin Butler (Port Melbourne, VIC, 2014), pp. 98–109.

chapter five The Fragmentation of Identity, 1981–99

1 Malcolm Fraser, 'Preface', in *Malcolm Fraser on Australia*, ed. D. M. White and D. A. Kemp (Melbourne, 1986), pp. xvii–xviii.
2 Barry McNeill and Leigh Woolley, *Architecture from the Edge* (North Hobart, TAS, 2002), p. 30.
3 Ross Gittens, 'Economic Reforms that Transformed Australia', *Sydney Morning Herald*, 6 February 2014, www.smh.com.au.
4 See, for example, Aldo Rossi's collection of single family homes (1977) built in Mozzo, on the outskirts of Bergamo, Italy.
5 Leon Krier, 'The Idea of Reconstruction', in *Leon Krier: Houses, Palaces, Cities*, ed. Demetri Porphyrios (London, 1984), pp. 38–9.
6 Haig Beck, ed., *Parliament House, Canberra: A Building for the Nation* (Sydney, 1996).
7 For an extensive critique, see James Weirick, 'Don't You Believe It: Critical Response to the New Parliament House', *Transition*, 27/28 (Summer/Autumn 1989), pp. 7–66.
8 These included (in films) Bruce Beresford, Peter Weir, George Miller and the bands INXS, AC/DC, Men At Work, Midnight Oil and Crowded House.
9 Peter Fish, 'Jackson Pollock's Blue Poles Now Worth $350m', *Australian Financial Review*, 28 September 2016, www.afr.com.
10 Australian Treasury, 'Australia's Century since Federation at a Glance', www.treasury.gov.au, p. 58.
11 Jean Baudrillard, *For a Critique of the Political Economy of the Sign* (St Louis, MO, 1981).
12 Conrad Hamann, *Cities of Hope: Australian Architecture and Design by Edmond and Corrigan, 1962–1992* (Melbourne, 1993), pp. 9 and 102.
13 See Jorge Otero-Pailos, 'LSDesign: Charles W. Moore and the Delirious Interior', in *Architecture's Historical Turn: Phenomenology and the Rise of the Postmodern* (Minneapolis, MN, 2010), p. 114.
14 Hamann, *Cities of Hope*, p. vii.
15 Ibid., p. 47.
16 Ibid., p. 74.
17 Ibid., p. 137.

18 Cited in Royal Australian Institute of Architects (now Australian Institute of Architects), 'RAIA Gold Medalist 2004 Gregory Burgess: Jury Citation', *Architecture Australia*, 1 March 2004, https://architectureau.com.

19 Ian McDougall and Howard Raggatt, 'Asking the Big Questions: Ian McDougall and Howard Raggatt Reflect on the Work of ARM Architecture', *Architecture Australia*, 28 June 2017, https://architectureau.com.

20 ARM, 'RMIT Storey Hall and Green Brain', http://armarchitecture.com.au, accessed 23 September 2018.

21 S. Lang, 'The Principles of the Gothic Revival in England', *Journal of the Society of Architectural Historians*, XXV/4 (December 1966), pp. 240–67.

22 Anna Johnson, 'Green Brain', *Architecture Australia*, 15 December 2011, https://architectureau.com.

23 McDougall and Raggatt, 'Asking the Big Questions'.

24 Colin St John Wilson, *The Other Tradition of Modern Architecture: The Uncompleted Project* (London, 2007).

25 Glenn Murcutt, 'Details, Components and Drawing the Building', in *Glenn Murcutt: A Singular Architectural Practice*, ed. Haig Beck and Jackie Cooper (Mulgrave, VIC, 2002), p. 19.

26 Peter Spearritt, *Sydney's Century: A History* (Kensington, NSW, 2000), p. 66.

27 Beck and Cooper, *Glenn Murcutt*, p. 182.

28 RAIA, 'Architecture and Place', *Architecture Australia*, 1 January 1999, https://architectureau.com.

29 Peter Tonkin, 'Domestic Ideal', *Architecture Australia*, 1 May 1999, https://architectureau.com.

30 Sydney Living Museums, *The Moolomba House: Andresen O'Gorman*, www.youtube.com, 13 March 2017, accessed 8 February 2019.

31 Kenneth Frampton, 'Regionalism: Modern Architecture and Cultural Identity', in *Modern Architecture: A Critical History* (London, 1985), pp. 313–27.

32 David Bridgman, 'The Anglo-Asian Bungalow: Housing the Commonwealth Officer in the Northern Tropics of Australia', PhD thesis, Royal Melbourne Institute of Technology, 2006.

33 Belinda Willis, 'Top Architects Enjoy Win Worth Going Troppo Over', *The Advertiser* (Adelaide), 21 March 2014, p. 11.

34 Philip Goad and Patrick Bingham-Hall, *Troppo Architects* (Sydney, 2000).

35 For a review of these sources, see Philip Drew, 'Continuity' and 'The Glass Pavilion, 1970–73', in *Leaves of Iron: Glenn Murcutt, Pioneer of an Australian Architectural Form* (North Ryde, NSW, 1985), pp. 16–38.

36 Philip Drew, 'The Migration of an Idea', in *Harry Seidler: Four Decades of Architecture*, ed. Kenneth Frampton and Philip Drew (London, 1992), p. 30.

chapter six The Neoliberal Environment, 2000–

1 Harry Margalit, 'Stadium Australia', in *Olympic Architecture: Building Sydney 2000*, ed. Patrick Bingham-Hall (Balmain, NSW, 1999).

2 Peter Corrigan, 'Parts Unknown', in *New Directions in Australian Architecture*, ed. Patrick Bingham-Hall (Balmain, NSW, 2001), p. 9.

3 John Macarthur, 'Australian Baroque: Geometry and Meaning at the National Museum of Australia', *Architecture Australia*, 1 March 2001, https://architectureau.com.

4 Howard Raggatt, 'Architect's Statement', *Architecture Australia*, 1 March 2001, https://architectureau.com.

5 Denton Corker Marshall, 'Architect's Statement', *Architecture Australia*, 1 January 2001, https://architectureau.com.

6 Ibid.

7 Patrick N. Troy, *The Perils of Urban Consolidation: A Discussion of Australian Housing and Urban Development Policies* (Sydney, 1996), p. 71.

8 Australian Bureau of Statistics, Catalogue Number 8731.0, www.abs.gov.au, accessed 26 September 2018.

9 Jane-Frances Kelly, *The Housing We'd Choose* (Melbourne, 2011), available at https://grattan.edu.au, accessed 9 February 2019.
10 Architects Accreditation Council of Australia, 'The Business of Architecture', in *Industry Profile: The Profession of Architecture in Australia*, February 2018, www.aaca.org.au.
11 See Greater Sydney Commission, 'Greater Sydney's Changing Urban Form: 1996–2016–2036', *A Metropolis of Three Cities*, www.greater.sydney, accessed 26 September 2016.
12 Declan Byrne, 'North Shore Councils Willoughby, Ku-ring-gai and Lane Cove Stump Up More than $2 million for Legal Advice in the 2016–17 Financial Year', *North Shore Times* (Sydney), 5 June 2017, www.dailytelegraph.com.au.
13 Westfield North Lakes in Brisbane, opened in 2003, uses an open lane model.
14 DesignInc, 'K2 Apartments', www.designinc.com.au, accessed 26 September 2018.
15 Harry Margalit, *Energy, Cities and Sustainability: An Historical Approach* (Abingdon, 2016), pp. 11–133.
16 DesignInc, 'Council House 2', www.designinc.com.au, accessed 26 September 2018.
17 Gevork Hartoonian, 'Urbanity and Federation', *Architecture Australia*, March 2003, https://architectureau.com.
18 John Macarthur, 'The Aesthetics of Public Space', *Architecture Australia*, March 2003, https://architectureau.com.
19 Rachel Hurst, 'The Architecture Critic', *Architecture Australia*, 30 September 2011, https://architectureau.com.
20 Harry Margalit, 'Composing in Public: Sam Marshall at Sydney's Museum of Contemporary Art', in *Architecture By Hand and Mind*, ed. Xing Ruan and Ainslie Murray (Sydney, 2019), pp. 17–31.
21 Troy, *The Perils of Urban Consolidation*.
22 Notably Rue de Meaux Housing, Paris, 1991.
23 Douglas Spencer, *The Architecture of Neoliberalism: How Contemporary Architecture Became an Instrument of Control and Compliance* (New York, 2016).
24 Juliana Engberg, 'RMIT Design Hub', *Architecture Australia*, 21 May 2013, https://architectureau.com.
25 These include NSW Wilkinson Award winners Archer House (Craig Rosevear, 2001), Holman House (Durbach Block Architects, 2005), Whale Beach House (Neeson Murcutt Architects, 2009), Light House (Peter Stutchbury Architecture, 2015) and Tamarama House (Durbach Block Jaggers Architects, 2017).
26 Australian Bureau of Statistics, Catalogue Number 3401.0, www.abs.gov.au, accessed 26 September 2018.
27 Kenneth Frampton, 'Regionalism: Modern Architecture and Cultural Identity', in *Modern Architecture: A Critical History* (London, 1985), pp. 313–27.
28 Architects Accreditation Council, 'The Business of Architecture'.
29 Sandra Kaji-O'Grady, 'Swanston Square', *Architecture Australia* (September/October 2015), p. 31.
30 National Museum of Australia, 'Warakurna: Western Desert Art', www.nma.gov.au, accessed 26 September 2018.
31 Robert Venturi, Denise Scott Brown and Steven Izenour, *Learning from Las Vegas: The Forgotten Symbolism of Architectural Form* (Cambridge, MA, 1972).
32 Andrew Lilleyman, 'East Pilbara Arts Centre', *Architecture Australia* (January/February 2017), pp. 16–23.
33 Michael Zanardo, 'The Rise of the Not-for-profits', *Architecture Bulletin* (NSW) (Winter 2017), pp. 22–3.
34 The 2013 rebuilding of St Barnabas Anglican Church in Sydney after it was destroyed by fire was the first new church in the city in 48 years. Philip Drew, 'St Barnabas Anglican Church', *Architecture Australia* (4 October 2013), https://architectureau.com. Two significant mosques have been built in recent years – in Newport, Victoria, by Glenn Murcutt with Hakan Elevli, and Sydney's Punchbowl Mosque by Candalepas Associates. Factories feature in architectural publications only as they are converted to other uses.

Epilogue

1 Australian Bureau of Statistics, Catalogue Number 3412.0, 30 March 2016, www.abs.gov.au.

2 Australian Institute of Architects, 'Partial Core Services', 8 November 2011, https://acumen.architecture.com.au.

3 Gill Matthewson and The Association of Consulting Architects Australia, 2018 Salary Survey Findings, 17 August 2018, https://aca.org.au.

Bibliography

Architects Accreditation Council of Australia, *Industry Profile: The Profession of Architecture in Australia*, February 2018, www.aaca.org.au

Arrow, Michelle, *Friday on our Minds: Popular Culture in Australia since 1945* (Sydney, 2009)

Balmforth, Scott, Gerard Reinmuth, Richard Blythe, J. E. Malpas and Marcelo Stamm, *Terroir: Cosmopolitan Ground* (Sydney, 2007)

Baudrillard, Jean, *For a Critique of the Political Economy of the Sign* (St Louis, MO, 1981)

Beck, Haig, ed., *Parliament House, Canberra: A Building for the Nation* (Sydney, 1996)

—, and Jackie Cooper, *Denton Corker Marshall: Rule Playing and the Ratbag Element* (Basel, 2000)

—, and —, eds, *Glenn Murcutt: A Singular Architectural Practice* (Mulgrave, VIC, 2002)

Bellamy, Edward, *Looking Backward: 2000–1887* (Cambridge, MA, 1967)

Belogolovsky, Vladimir, *Harry Seidler: Lifework* (New York, 2014)

Bingham-Hall, Patrick, ed., *New Directions in Australian Architecture* (Balmain, NSW, 2001)

—, ed., *Olympic Architecture: Building Sydney 2000* (Balmain, NSW, 1999)

Blainey, Geoffrey, *A Shorter History of Australia* (Melbourne, 1994)

Bogle, Michael, 'Arthur Baldwinson: Regional Modernism in Sydney, 1937–1969', PhD thesis, Royal Melbourne Institute of Technology, 2008

Boyd, Noni, 'No Sacrifice in Sunshine: Walter Liberty Vernon, Architect, 1846–1914', PhD thesis, Royal Melbourne Institute of Technology, 2010

Boyd, Robin, *Australia's Home: Its Origins, Builders and Occupiers* (Carlton, VIC, 1987)

—, *The Australian Ugliness* (Melbourne, 1960)

—, *The Great Great Australian Dream* (Rushcutters Bay, NSW, 1972)

—, *Kenzo Tange* (New York, 1962)

—, *Victorian Modern: One Hundred and Eleven Years of Modern Architecture in Victoria, Australia* (Melbourne, 1947)

Bradley, Anthony, and Terry Smith, *Australian Art and Architecture: Essays Presented to Bernard Smith* (Melbourne, 1980)

Brew, Peter, and Michael Markham, eds, *Architectural Projects: Jeffrey Howlett* (Crawley, WA, 1992)

Bridgman, David, 'The Anglo-Asian Bungalow: Housing the Commonwealth Officer in the Northern Tropics of Australia', PhD thesis, Royal Melbourne Institute of Technology, 2006

Bruhn, Cameron, and Katelin Butler, eds, *The Forever House: Time-honoured Australian Homes* (Port Melbourne, VIC, 2014), pp. 98–109

Bunning & Madden, *The Work of Bunning & Madden: Architects and Town Planners* (Sydney, 1970)

Bunning, Walter, *Homes in the Sun: The Past, Present and Future of Australian Housing* (Sydney, 1945)

Callister, Winsome, 'Dealing with the "Sydney School": Perspectives on Australian Architecture in the 1950s and 1960s', *Transition*, 21 (September 1987), pp. 6–12

—, 'The Dialectic of Desire and Disappointment: Robin Boyd and Australian Architecture', *Transition*, 38 (1990), pp. 71–85 [special issue on Robin Boyd]

—, 'The Response to the City: Melbourne Regionalism of the 1950s and 1960s', *Transition*, 29 (Winter 1989), pp. 33–48

Chapman, Barbara, and Duncan Richards, *Marshall Clifton: Architect and Artist* (Fremantle, WA, 1989)

Charlton, Ken, Bronwen Jones and Paola Favaro, *The Contribution of Enrico Taglietti to Canberra's Architecture* (Canberra, 2007)

Clark, Lindie, *Finding a Common Interest: The Story of Dick Dusseldorp and Lend Lease* (Port Melbourne, VIC, 2002)
Commonwealth Bureau of Census and Statistics, *Oversea Trade Bulletin No. 25* (Canberra, 1929)
Connell, R. W., and T. H. Irving, *Class Structure in Australian History: Documents, Narrative and Argument* (Melbourne, 1980)
Cox, Philip, and John Maxwell Freeland, *Rude Timber Buildings in Australia* (London, 1969)
—, and David Moore, *The Australian Functional Tradition* (Fitzroy, VIC, 1988)
Curthoys, Ann, *Freedom Ride: A Freedom Rider Remembers* (Sydney, 2002)
Davison, Graeme, A. E. Dingle and Seamus O'Hanlon, *The Cream Brick Frontier: Histories of Australian Suburbia* (Clayton, VIC, 1995)
Dobney, Stephen, ed., *Ken Woolley and Ancher, Mortlock & Woolley: Selected and Current Work* (Mulgrave, VIC, 1999)
—, *The Masterpiece: Jorn Utzon: A Secret Life* (South Yarra, VIC, 2001)
Drew, Philip, *The Coast Dwellers: Australians Living on the Edge* (Ringwood, VIC, 1994)
—, *Leaves of Iron: Glenn Murcutt, Pioneer of an Australian Architectural Form* (North Ryde, NSW, 1985)
—, *Peter Stutchbury – Of People and Places: Between the Bush and the Beach* (Balmain, NSW, 2000)
Edquist, Harriet, *The Architecture of Neil Clerehan* (Melbourne, 2005)
—, *Harold Desbrowe-Annear, 1865–1933: A Life in Architecture* (Carlton, VIC, 2004)
—, and Richard Black, eds, *Pioneers of Modernism: The Arts and Crafts Movement in Australia* (Carlton, VIC, 2008)
Edwards, Zeny, *A Life of Purpose: A Biography of John Sulman* (Longueville, NSW, 2017)
—, *William Hardy Wilson: Artist, Architect, Orientalist, Visionary* (Surry Hills, NSW, 2001)
Evans, Doug, 'The Changing of the Guard: The Social and Cultural Reflections of Community in 1970s Melbourne Architecture', *Fabrications*, XV/1 (July 2005), pp. 39–53
Farrelly, E. M., *Three Houses: Glenn Murcutt* (London, 1993)
Ferguson, R. J., *Crawley Campus: The Planning and Architecture of the University of Western Australia* (Nedlands, WA, 1993)
Frampton, Kenneth, *Modern Architecture: A Critical History* (London, 1985)
—, and Philip Drew, *Harry Seidler: Four Decades of Architecture* (London, 1992)
Fraser, Hugh, *The Federation House: Australia's Own Style* (Sydney, 1986)
Fraser, Malcolm, *Malcolm Fraser on Australia*, ed. D. M. White and D. A. Kemp (Melbourne, 1986)
Freeland, John Maxwell, *Architect Extraordinary: The Life and Times of John Horbury Hunt, 1838–1904* (Melbourne, 1970)
—, *Architecture in Australia: A History* (Ringwood, VIC, 1968)
—, *Australia's Planning Heritage* (Collingwood, VIC, 2010)
—, *The Making of a Profession: The History, Growth and Work of the Architectural Institutes in Australia* (Sydney, 1971)
Fromonot, Françoise, *Glenn Murcutt: Buildings and Projects, 1962–2003* (London, 2003)
—, *Jorn Utzon: The Sydney Opera House* (Corte Madera, CA, 1998)
Gascoigne, John, *The Enlightenment and the Origins of European Australia* (Port Melbourne, VIC, 2002)
Goad, Philip, 'An Appeal for Modernism: Sigfried Giedion and the Sydney Opera House', *Fabrications*, VIII (July 1997), pp. 129–45
—, 'Bringing It All Home: Robin Boyd and Australia's Embrace of Brutalism, 1955–71', *Fabrications*, XXV/2 (June 2015), pp. 176–213
—, 'The Modern House in Melbourne, 1945–1975', PhD thesis, University of Melbourne, 1992
—, ed., *Bates Smart: 150 Years of Australian Architecture* (Fisherman's Bend, VIC, 2004)
—, *Melbourne Architecture* (Sydney, 1999)
—, and Patrick Bingham-Hall, *Troppo Architects* (Sydney, 2000)
—, Julie Willis, eds, *The Encyclopedia of Australian Architecture* (Port Melbourne, VIC, 2012)
—, Julie Willis and Rowan Wilken, *Australian Modern: The Architecture of Stephenson and Turner* (Carlton, VIC, 2004)

Gray, A. C., *Life Insurance in Australia* (Melbourne, 1977)

Gruzman, Neville, and Philip Goad, *Gruzman: An Architect and his City* (Fisherman's Bend, VIC, 2006)

Gusheh, Maryam, Tom Heneghan, Catherine Lassen and Shoko Seyama, *The Architecture of Glenn Murcutt* (Tokyo, 2008)

Hamann, Conrad, *Cities of Hope: Australian Architecture and Design by Edmond and Corrigan, 1962–1992* (Melbourne, 1993)

—, 'Modern Architecture in Melbourne: The Architecture of Grounds, Romberg and Boyd, 1927–1971', PhD thesis, Monash University, 1979

—, 'Nationalism and Reform in Australian Architecture, 1880–1920', *Historical Studies*, XVIII/ 72 (1979), pp. 393–411

—, and Chris Hamann, 'Anger and the New Order: Some Aspects of Robin Boyd's Career', *Transition*, 38 (1990), pp. 17–42 [special issue on Robin Boyd]

Hartoonian, Gevork, 'Harry Seidler: Revisiting Modernism', *Fabrications*, XX/1 (2011), pp. 30–53

Hawcroft, Rebecca, ed., *The Other Moderns: Sydney's Forgotten European Design Legacy* (Sydney, 2017)

Herman, Morton, *The Early Australian Architects and Their Work* (Sydney, 1954)

Howells, Trevor, and Michael Nicholson, *Towards the Dawn: Federation Architecture in Australia, 1890–1915* (Sydney, 1989)

Hyatt, Peter, *Local Heroes: Architects of Australia's Sunshine Coast* (North Ryde, NSW, 2000)

Inglis, K. S., *Sacred Places: War Memorials in the Australian Landscape* (Carlton South, VIC, 1998)

Jackson, Davina, and Chris Johnson, *Australian Architecture Now* (London, 2000)

—, Philip Drew and Peter Hyatt, *The Games Show: Australia 2000* (Parkville, VIC, 2000)

Jahn, Graham, *Sydney Architecture* (Balmain, NSW, 1997)

—, and Scott Frances, *Contemporary Australian Architecture* (Basel, 1994)

James, Clive, *Unreliable Memoirs* (London, 1980)

Johnson, Donald Leslie, *Australian Architecture, 1901–51: Sources of Modernism* (Sydney, 1980)

Kelly, Jane-Frances, *The Housing We'd Choose* (Melbourne, 2011), https://grattan.edu.au

Kollar, L. Peter, *On the Architectural Idea* (Sydney, 1983)

Langer, Karl, *Sub-tropical Housing* (Brisbane, 1944)

Leach, Andrew, Antony Moulis and Nicole Sully, *Shifting Views: Selected Essays on the Architectural History of Australia and New Zealand* (St Lucia, QLD, 2008)

Lewi, Hannah, and Stephen Neille, 'Drawing In and Fading Out: The Case of the Commonwealth Games Housing Village, Western Australia', *Journal of Architectural Education*, LXI/2 (2007), pp. 15–24

London, Geoffrey, *A Short History of Perth Architecture* (Balmain, NSW, 2002)

—, and Patrick Bingham-Hall, *Tonkin Zulaikha Greer* (Balmain, NSW, 2005)

London, Geoffrey, Philip Goad and Conrad Hamann, *150: An Unfinished Experiment in Living* (Crawley, WA, 2017)

Luscombe, Desley, 'Identical Dilemmas: The Problem of the Antipodes', *Transition*, 22/23 (Summer 1987), pp. 8–14

Lyons, *More: The Architecture of Lyons, 1996–2011* (Fisherman's Bend, VIC, 2012)

Macarthur, John, and Andrew C. Wilson, *Birrell: Work from the Office of James Birrell* (Melbourne, 1997)

—, Deborah Van der Plaat, Janina Gosseye and Andrew Wilson, eds, *Hot Modernism: Queensland Architecture, 1945–1975* (London, 2015)

McCartney, Karen, *50/60/70 Iconic Australian Houses: Three Decades of Domestic Architecture* (Crows Nest, NSW, 2014)

McCaughey, Patrick, and Daryl Jackson, *Evolutionary Modernism: Daryl Jackson 65/05* (Carlton, VIC, 2006)

McGillick, Paul, and Patrick Bingham-Hall, *Sydney Architecture* (Balmain, NSW, 2005)

Mackay, Ian, *Living and Partly Living: Housing in Australia* (Melbourne, 1971)

MacMahon, Bill, *The Architecture of East Australia: An Architectural History in 423 Individual Presentations* (Stuttgart, 2001)

McNeill, Barry, and Leigh Woolley, *Architecture from the Edge* (North Hobart, TAS, 2002)
Marfella, Giorgio, 'Inside the Square Box: Skyscrapers and Techno-economic Developments in Melbourne Central Business District, 1955-1995', PhD thesis, University of Melbourne, 2017
Margalit, Harry, *Energy, Cities and Sustainability: An Historical Approach* (Abingdon, 2016)
—, 'Reasoning to Believe: Aspects of Modernity in Sydney Architecture and Planning 1900–1960', PhD thesis, University of Sydney, 1997
—, and Philip Goad, *Durbach Block: The Luminous Space of Abstraction* (Balmain, NSW, 1999)
Markham, Michael, and Meghan Nordeck, eds, *Summerhayes: Architectural Projects* (Crawley, WA, 1993)
Memmott, Paul, *Gunyah Gondie + Wurley: The Aboriginal Architecture of Australia* (St Lucia, QLD, 2007)
Metcalf, Andrew, *Architecture in Transition: The Sulman Award, 1932–1996* (Sydney, 1997)
Mikami, Yuzo, and Osamu Murai, *Utzon's Sphere: Sydney Opera House: How It Was Designed and Built* (Tokyo, 2001)
Moore, John D., *Home Again: Domestic Architecture for the Normal Australian* (Sydney, 1944)
Murray, Peter, *The Saga of Sydney Opera House: The Dramatic Story of the Design and Construction of the Icon of Modern Australia* (London, 2004)
Musgrave, Elizabeth, '"Hot" and "Cool": Perceptions of Subtropical Modernism in Post-war Queensland', *Fabrications*, XXVII/2 (May 2017), pp. 200–230
—, 'The Plywood Exhibition House: An Investigation of Local Idiom', *Proceedings of the 19th Conference of the Society of Architectural Historians, Australia and New Zealand: Brisbane, 2002*
Nobis, Philip, 'Utzon's Interiors for the Sydney Opera House: The Design Development of the Major and Minor Hall, 1958–1966', BArch thesis, University of Technology, Sydney, 1994
O'Callaghan, Judith, and Charles Pickett, *Designer Suburbs: Architects and Affordable Homes in Australia* (Sydney, 2012)
—, Paul Hogben and Robert Freestone, eds, *Sydney's Martin Place: A Cultural and Design History* (Crows Nest, NSW, 2016)
Otero-Pailos, Jorge, *Architecture's Historical Turn: Phenomenology and the Rise of the Postmodern* (Minneapolis, MN, 2010)
Page, Michael, *Sculptors in Space: South Australian Architects, 1836–1986* (Adelaide, 1986)
Palmer, Vance, *The Legend of the Nineties* (Melbourne, 1954)
Phillips, John, 'In Search of a Modern Idiom for Australian Architecture: The Flat-roofed Houses of George Sydney Jones', *Fabrications*, I (December 1989), pp. 57–76
—, 'John Sulman and the Question of an Australian Style', *Fabrications*, VIII/1 (1997), pp. 87–116
Porphyrios, Demetri, ed., *Leon Krier: Houses, Palaces, Cities* (London, 1984)
Quarry, Neville, *Award Winning Australian Architecture* (Sydney, 1997)
Raggatt, Mark, and Maitiú Ward, *Mongrel Rapture: The Architecture of Ashton, Raggatt McDougall* (Melbourne, 2015)
Reynolds, Peter, Lesley Muir and Joy Hughes, *John Horbury Hunt: Radical Architect, 1838–1904* (Sydney, 2002)
Riddel, Robert, *Robin Dods, 1868–1920: Selected Works* (Melbourne, 2012)
Rodrigo, Russell, 'Banking on Modernism: Dr H. C. (Nugget) Coombs and the Institutional Architecture of the Reserve Bank of Australia', *Fabrications*, XXVI/1 (February 2016), pp. 73–101
Royal Australian Institute of Architects, ACT Chapter, *Canberra: An Architectural Guide to Australia's Capital* (Canberra, 1982)
Royal Australian Institute of Architects, WA Chapter, *Perth Fremantle: An Architectural Guide* (Perth, 1985)
Ruan, Xing, and Ainslie Murray, eds, *Architecture by Hand and Mind* (Sydney, 2019)
Ruskin, John, *The Seven Lamps of Architecture*, 6th edn (Orpington, 1889)

Saunders, David, and Catherine Burke, *Ancher Mortlock Murray Woolley: Sydney Architects, 1946–1976* (Sydney, 1976)
Schoffel, Sarah, 'Women in Architecture in Victoria from 1939–1960', *Architectural Theory Review*, I/1 (April 1996), pp. 104–11
Seidler, Harry, *Houses, Buildings and Projects: 1955/63* (Sydney, 1963)
—, *Houses and Interiors* (Mulgrave, VIC, 2003)
—, *Houses, Interiors and Projects* (Sydney, 1954)
Serle, Geoffrey, *From Deserts the Prophets Come: The Creative Spirit in Australia, 1788–1972* (Clayton, VIC, 2014)
—, *John Monash: A Biography* (Carlton, VIC, 1998)
—, *Robin Boyd: A Life* (Carlton, VIC, 1995)
Shann, Edward, *An Economic History of Australia* (Cambridge, 1948)
Shaw, John, *Sir Arthur Stephenson: Australian Architect* (Sydney, 1987)
Sowden, Harry, *Towards an Australian Architecture* (London, 1970)
Spearritt, Peter, 'The Concept of Regionalism Today', *Transition*, IV/3 (July 1985), pp. 3–17
—, *Sydney's Century: A History* (Kensington, NSW, 2000)
Spencer, Douglas, *The Architecture of Neoliberalism: How Contemporary Architecture Became an Instrument of Control and Compliance* (New York, 2016)
Stephen, Ann, Andrew McNamara and Philip Goad, *Modern Times: The Untold Story of Modernism in Australia* (Carlton, VIC, 2006)
—, eds, *Modernism and Australia: Documents in Art, Design and Architecture 1917–1967* (Carlton, VIC, 2008)
Stiles, Mark, 'Reading Ruskin: Architecture and Social Reform in Australia, 1889–1908', PhD thesis, University of NSW, 2010
Tafuri, Manfredo, *Architecture and Utopia: Design and Capitalist Developmen*t, trans. Barbara Luigia La Penta (Cambridge, MA, 1976)
Tanner, Howard, *Australian Housing in the Seventies* (Sydney, 1976)
—, ed., *Architects of Australia* (South Melbourne, VIC, 1981)
Taylor, George A., *Town Planning Association: Why It Is Necessary* (Sydney, 1913)
—, *Town Planning for Australia* (1914) (Abingdon, 2015)
Taylor, Jennifer, *Australian Architecture since 1960* (North Ryde, NSW, 1986)
—, *An Australian Identity: Houses for Sydney, 1953–63* (Sydney, 1972)
—, ed., *Tall Buildings: Australian Business Going Up, 1945–1970* (St Leonards, NSW, 2001)
—, and John Andrews, *John Andrews: Architecture, A Performing Art* (Melbourne, 1982)
Thalis, Philip, and Peter John Cantrill, *Public Sydney: Drawing the City* (Sydney, 2013)
Thorne, Ross, *Picture Palace Architecture in Australia* (South Melbourne, VIC, 1976)
Towndrow, Jennifer, *Philip Cox: Portrait of an Australian Architect* (Ringwood, VIC, 1991)
Troy, Patrick, *Accommodating Australians: Commonwealth Government Involvement in Housing* (Sydney, 2012)
—, *The Perils of Urban Consolidation: A Discussion of Australian Housing and Urban Development Policies* (Sydney, 1996)
Turnbull, Jeff, and Peter Navaretti, eds, *The Griffins in Australia and India: The Complete Works and Projects of Walter Burley Griffin and Marion Mahoney Griffin* (Melbourne, 1998)
Ure Smith, Sydney, Bertram Stevens with W. Hardy Wilson, eds, *Domestic Architecture in Australia* (Sydney, 1919) [special issue of *Art In Australia*]
Urford, Jacqueline, *Peter Muller: The Complete Works* (Cammeray, NSW, 2008)
Van Acker, Wouter, 'Peter Corrigan, the Bodgie Wolf, and Other Larrikin Tygers of Wrath', *Fabrications*, XXVIII/1 (2018), pp. 3–24
Van Daele, Patrick, and Roy Lumby, *A Spirit of Progress: Art Deco Architecture in Australia* (North Ryde, NSW, 1997)
Van Schaik, Leon, *Sean Godsell: Works and Projects* (Milan, 2005)
—, *Volume: John Wardle Architects* (Fisherman's Bend, VIC, 2008)
—, ed., *Non-fictional Narratives: Denton Corker Marshall* (Basel, 2008)
Vulker, Judy, *Studying Australian Architecture* (Red Hill, ACT, 1990)

Walker, Paul, and Karen Burns, 'Constructing Australian Architecture for International Audiences: Regionalism, Postmodernism, and the Design Arts Board, 1980–1988', *Fabrications*, XXVIII/1 (January 2018), pp. 25–46

—, and Anthony Moulis, 'Finding Brutalism in the Architecture of John Andrews', *Fabrications*, XXV/2 (May 2015), pp. 214–33

Ward, John Manning, *The State and the People: Australian Federation and Nation-making, 1870–1901* (Leichhardt, NSW, 2001)

Watson, Anne, ed., *Beyond Architecture: Marion Mahony and Walter Burley Griffin, America, Australia, India* (Haymarket, NSW, 1998)

—, *Building a Masterpiece: The Sydney Opera House* (Aldershot, 2006)

Weirick, James, 'Don't You Believe It: Critical Response to the New Parliament House', *Transition*, 27/28 (Summer/Autumn 1989), pp. 7–66

Weller, E.J.A., ed., *Buildings of Queensland* (Brisbane, 1959)

Weston, Richard, *Utzon* (Hellerup, 2002)

Willis, Julie, 'Conscious Design: The Melbourne University Architectural Atelier, 1919–1947', *Fabrications*, XIII/2 (May 2004), pp. 43–62

—, and Bronwyn J. Hanna, *Women Architects in Australia, 1900–1950* (Red Hill, ACT, 2001)

Wilson, Andrew, ed., *Hayes & Scott: Post-war Houses* (St Lucia, QLD, 2005)

Wilson, Colin St John, *The Other Tradition of Modern Architecture: The Uncompleted Project* (London, 2007)

Wilson, William Hardy, *Old Colonial Architecture in New South Wales and Tasmania* (Sydney, 1924)

Ziegler, Oswald Leopold, Max Dupian and Arthur Boothroyd, *Sydney Builds an Opera House* (Sydney, 1973)

Acknowledgements

In putting this book together, my greatest debt, by some margin, is to Eric Sierins. Eric supplied the bulk of the photos from his collection, and photographed many more buildings specifically for the book. He is also custodian of the Max Dupain and Associates archive, and he supplied quality scans and information about copyright holders for the Dupain images we have included. The photographing trips we took together were among the most memorable of the project, one that would have been harder and less enjoyable without Eric's participation.

Rhodri Windsor-Liscombe commented closely on an early draft of the text, and his comments were insightful, useful and encouraging. Alan Peters and Maryam Gusheh also provided valuable impressions on the early text. My colleague Paul Hogben has been ever generous with assistance from his broad knowledge of Australian architectural history. I also owe Gevork Hartoonian my gratitude for his constant encouragement, and personal example as a working architectural historian. My home institution, the University of New South Wales, supported the book through a book publication subsidy, and a programme of teaching relief during which the first draft was completed.

This book is the accretion of impressions and memories from many years of looking at buildings in Australia. Different guides conveyed the uniqueness of their cities when I visited over the years: Stephen Neille and Xing Ruan in Perth, Peter Brew and Andrea Mina in Melbourne, Gaetano Palmese in Hobart, and the tours run in conjunction with the annual conference of the Society of Architectural Historians, Australia and New Zealand (SAHANZ), held in various locations.

In collecting the photos for the book, the individual photographers I approached invariably supplied images under the most generous of terms, and I thank them. They include Peter Bennetts, Vanessa Couzins, Robert Frith, Brett Boardman and Michael Wee. I would also like to thank the staff at the various institutions who assisted in locating photographs and providing copyright permission. At the State Library of Western Australia Helen Ouf went beyond the call of duty in trying to locate obscure historic images. My gratitude, also, to Ted Quinton for redrawing plans for publication.

At Reaktion Books, my thanks to editor Vivian Constantinopoulos for leading me gently and expertly through the writing process, and to Amy Salter for doing the same in production.

And finally to my wife Anne, who has now seen a couple of my books reach fruition, and has displayed remarkable equanimity throughout in the face of my more unreasonable characteristics.

Photo Acknowledgements

The author and the publishers wish to express their thanks to the below sources of illustrative material and/or permission to reproduce it. Every effort has been made to contact copyright holders; should there be any we have been unable to reach or to whom inaccurate acknowledgements have been made please contact the publishers, and full adjustments will be made to any subsequent printings.

Peter Bennetts: pp. 165, 188, 327 (courtesy Iredale Pederson Hook); Brett Boardman: pp. 310 (courtesy Durbach Block Jaggers), 313 (courtesy Neeson Murcutt); Harold Cazneaux, from *Domestic Architecture in Australia*, ed. Ure Smith et al. (Sydney, 1919): p. 48 (top); Vanessa Couzens: p. 175; courtesy Sue Dalton and State Library of Queensland, South Brisbane: p. 213; Max Dupain: pp. 104, 114, 119, 120 (courtesy Evelyn Smith), 124 (courtesy O'Brien Glass), 141 (courtesy Peter Muller), 144 (courtesy Conrad Gargett), 145 (courtesy Conrad Gargett), 146 (courtesy Peter Muller), 150 (courtesy Evelyn Smith), 151 (courtesy Evelyn Smith), 176 (courtesy Cox Architecture), 178 (courtesy Adam Guy Madigan), 180 (courtesy Cement, Concrete & Aggregates Australia), 181 (courtesy UNSW), 196, 204 (courtesy Enrico Taglietti), 209 (courtesy Cement, Concrete & Aggregates Australia), 220 (courtesy Pettit and Sevitt), 226 (courtesy Adam Guy Madigan), 231, 233 (courtesy Cox Architecture), 234 (courtesy Cox Architecture), 249, 258 (courtesy Glenn Murcutt), 260 (courtesy Glenn Murcutt), 261 (courtesy Glenn Murcutt); Jim Fenwick, courtesy Newspix: p. 161; Robert Frith: pp. 323 (courtesy Kerry Hill Architects), 326 (courtesy Officer Woods); Fryer Library, University of Queensland, Brisbane, Hayes and Scott Collection (UQFL278): pp. 156, 157; Sam Hood, courtesy State Library of NSW, Sydney: p. 82; Fritz Kos, courtesy State Library of Western Australia, Perth: pp. 186, 187; Fritz Kos, courtesy Schmidt-Lademann family: p. 164; Harry Margalit: pp. 20, 23, 34, 47, 54, 65, 70, 105, 106, 148, 163, 172, 179, 183, 184, 185, 194, 205, 206, 224, 228, 266, 333 (top), 334; National Archives of Australia, Canberra: p. 30 (A710, 38); National Library of Australia: pp. 25 (A.G. Foster, nla.obj-142771518), 33 (MAP G8984.C3S1 Gri 1913), 44 (nla.obj-362409353); National Library of Australia Pictures Collection, Canberra, courtesy Katie Molnar: p. 6; Gervaise Purcell, Australian National Maritime Museum collection, reproduced courtesy of Leigh Purcell: p. 160; Ted Quinton: pp. 158, 223; © Penelope Seidler: 135 (photo Max Dupain, 1991), 198 (photo Max Dupain), 199, 200 (photo Max Dupain, 1967), 202 (photo Max Dupain, 1979), 239 (photo John Gollings, 1987); Eric Sierins: pp. 24, 26, 27, 36, 37, 48 (below), 51, 58, 63, 66, 67, 69, 72, 73, 76, 78, 79, 80, 83, 87, 88, 89, 94, 96, 98, 99, 100, 101 (left and right), 102, 103, 107, 108, 113, 122, 123, 136, 137, 139, 142, 143, 147, 149, 152, 154, 155, 166, 174, 177, 182, 190, 191, 192, 193, 197, 207, 210, 212, 214, 215, 219, 222, 229, 235, 236, 237, 238, 240, 243, 244, 246, 252, 253, 254, 257, 262, 268, 272, 274, 276, 278, 279, 280, 281, 282, 283, 286, 288, 289, 291, 292, 295, 296, 297, 298, 299, 300, 303, 304, 305, 307, 308, 309, 314, 317, 318, 319, 320, 321, 322, 324, 328, 333 (below), 335; State Library of Victoria, Melbourne: pp. 35 (Lyle Fowler, Harold Paynting Collection), 45 (H2004.65/186), 84 (WG Alma Collection), 97 (H2003.101/247); 131 (Leslie H Runting, H2004.65/8); State Library of Victoria Pictures Collection, Wolfgang Sievers: pp. 110, 126, 127, 216, 218, 221; State Library of Victoria Pictures Collection, Mark Strizic: pp. 128, 132; Troppo, courtesy Phil Harris: p. 271; Michael Wee: pp. 265 (courtesy David Walker and Karen McCartney), 267 (courtesy Karen McCartney).

Index

Page numbers in *italics* indicate illustrations